THE GALBRAITHIAN VISION:

The Cultural Criticism of John Kenneth Galbraith

C. Lynn Munro

University Press of America™

ACKNOWLEDGEMENTS

Almost from its inception, this book has developed
and asserted a momentum of its own. It has taken
me places I had never intended to go and returned
me to areas of study long neglected. The journey,
though sometimes taxing, has, on the whole, been a
pleasurable one.

A large part of that pleasure has been in the
collaboration with my fellow travelers as it were.
Dr. Alexander C. Kern has been constant and invalu-
able as a director of this project. The breadth of
his knowledge and the incisiveness of his vision
have been a continual spur to further study and revision. He has had, on occasion, to put up with
ideas some of which were only partially thought
through and others of which were ill conceived. Yet,
through it all, he has treated me with patience and
offered encouragement.

My thanks go also to Drs. Carol Whitehurst and
Gerald Nordquist who have read and challenged the
ideas presented herein. With their assistance I have
been able to refine and sharpen the analysis and to
expand the scope of this study to include counter
arguments which might otherwise have been ignored.
Whatever limitations remain in this treatment are,
however, solely my responsibility.

Thanks also to Drs. Edward Lawler and William
Fox and the myriad mentors, colleagues and friends
who stood by me throughout my graduate career and,
at times, goaded me to continue when I might otherwise have succumbed to the frustrations and pressures
inherent in this type of apprenticeship. And to
those who buoyed my spirits and kept me from despair
during my period of structural unemployment following
the completion of my doctorate. Especially to Char
Hawks who has been of immeasurable assistance with
this revision.

Special thanks to my husband, Ralph J. Nollen-
berger, who, while not always eager to wade through
another revision, has helped me clarify and articulate
inchoate ideas and theses. And, finally, to John
Kenneth Galbraith, without whom this study would have
been impossible.

PREFACE

John Kenneth Galbraith, by his very reputation, has
secured a place in the history of the twentieth century. This study, born of a longstanding respect for
his willingness, in fact his insistence, to challenge
conventional wisdom as it is reflected in socioeconomic theory and practice, attempts to assess his contribution to the genre of social criticism.

The methodology employed is a variant of the
sociology of knowledge. I have attempted to capsu-
late his perspective as it relates to economics, society, the place and responsibility of the individual
within society, and social reform. I have been primarily interested in understanding the cultural and
intellectual forces which have shaped his vision and
the transition through which his various ideas have
gone. Special emphasis is awarded those events and
experiences which seem to have had the most profound
impact.

The introduction sets forth the broad outlines
of the critical perspective. It attempts to demonstrate the indispensibility of cultural criticism and
to differentiate the role of the critic and that of
the scholar. The claim is not that scholarship,
bounded by perspectival limitations, is unimportant
but, rather, that it is incapable of challenging
accepted world views. From a sociological point of
view, criticism offers an alternative definition of
the common sense reality.

Galbraith's role as a social critic is herein
described as an outgrowth of a populist background.
Like Veblen, Galbraith was raised in a relatively
endogenous community which emphasized hard work and
pragmatic action; the cleavage between the English
and Scotch engendered a suspicion of cant and privilege among the latter. These influences, conjoined
with the experiences of the Depression, his work in
agricultural economics, his exposure to Berkeley
radicals, his early involvement with the Keynesian
revolution and the New Deal all moved Galbraith
toward the holistic perspective which informs his
writing.

His primary concern is with uneven development and social inequalities which he sees as systemic. Technology and the corporation must, in his view, be transformed in order to align them with the public purpose. Economic goals must become secondary; growth must become subordinate to social balance and must be restrained when it conflicts with environmental preservation or personal well-being.

Perhaps overly optimistic about the possibility of transforming American society and socializing both the large corporation and the public services, Galbraith has a vision which is entirely democratic. He writes from deep within the progressive, Jeffersonian tradition which seeks to expand the options available to the individual and to divest powerful interest groups of their ability to dictate national policies and goals. To advance these ends he unleashes a broad angled program of social reform which, while lacking in specifics, seems to grasp the general contours which must be followed in order to elicit change.

Since the publication of __American Capitalism__ in 1952, Galbraith has aimed his writing toward the general public rather than confining it to those within the economics profession. Through his books, no less than his articles and lectures, he has attempted to shake the hold of the conventional wisdom and spur people to question the priorities and goals of American society. With the release of __The Age of Uncertainty__, designed in conjunction with the BBC, there is reason to believe that his views will get an even larger hearing. In order to understand the debate which is likely to surround many of his interpretations, it is necessary to gain some appreciation of the perspective from which he speaks.

TABLE OF CONTENTS

INTRODUCTION: THE CRITICAL CHALLENGE

One of the most significant, albeit elusive, problems
confronting modern societies is the establishment of
a sound socio-economic policy. Regardless of the
specific issue at hand, a spate of "authoritative"
opinion is forthcoming. Recent events, however, have
done much to discredit the espousals of libertarians
and statists alike.

Despite assurances dating back to Adam Smith,
David Ricardo and Thomas Malthus that the market is,
and should be, the final arbiter, the pressing problems of the elderly, the chronically ill and the
unemployed, no less than the realities of metropolitan decay, environmental blight and the risk of
nuclear destruction persist. Yet, in spite of these
aberrations, economic advisors in the vein of Alan
Greenspan and William Simon have continued to endorse
increased productive efficiency and private consumption as the key yardsticks by which to measure
the progress and vitality of the American economy.

In contrast to the cumulative technological and
social changes, the shifts in loyalties among the
population and the protests by those outside the
mainstream, there has been little transformation of
our social or political orientations. Instead, we
have continued to respond to slogans and proposals
rooted in nineteenth century social thought. Andrew
Jackson's "monster bank" seems to have been replaced
by the "sprawling Washington bureaucracy" as the
rallying point of would-be reformers.

A review of the dominant rhetoric of the 1976
Presidential campaign reveals a certain ideological
schizophrenia on the part of many contenders. Although a thorough discussion of this development is
beyond the scope of this book, it should be observed
that the "anti-Establishment" sentiments espoused by
candidates of every persuasion are somewhat antithetical to the economic and social problems which
each would presume to remedy were he elected. What
emerged from the political debate (if it can be
called such) was not a programatic response but what
Marvin Meyers has labeled a persuasion--"a broad
judgment of public affairs informed by common

sentiments and beliefs about the good life in America."[1]

This arcadia, as it is portrayed by prominent spokesmen of both parties, would be more secure and more efficient than contemporary American society. America would retain her technological superiority within a new institutional context which would be less centralized and less bureaucratically obtuse. In order to maintain a balanced budget--one of the central tenets of neoclassical economics--social services would either be cut back or would revert to state administrations. Such schemes lend credibility to Frederick Duttons's observation: "America should now be far more capable of thoughtfully meeting a national testing of turmoil and change than was the poorer, less educated, more constrained society of the Depression. Yet there is strong sentiment of late to hold to ways of thinking and governing rooted almost entirely in the last four decades, or to turn still further back to many of the WASPish views and values of a still earlier time."[2]

The mandate for social services, no less than the emergence of the multinational corporation, belies the claim that it remains possible to revert to earlier, less complex, forms of social organization. For better or worse, the twentieth century is keynoted by technological and social imperatives which simultaneously expand and limit available options. To attempt the restoration of values applicable to the agrarian democracy of the nineteenth century, would involve the denial of rights and opportunities to all those who remain unprepared to compete in a technologically sophisticated society. While such a course is plausible, it cannot but be assessed as wasteful and exceedingly undemocratic.

It is for this reason, that it becomes increasingly necessary to examine and question the quality of American life. At present, deficiencies in education, health care, social and cultural opportunities and regional development persist despite our high standard of living. While such inequities were both expected and sanctioned in feudal societies, they have never been in consonance with the American Dream. While not of a particularly egalitarian bent, the founding fathers espoused a set of principles and ideals which flamed the hearts of the lower strata and put into motion pressures for social as well as political and economic equality. The debate over power and privilege in an ostensibly democratic society has taken many forms and could easily fill volumes in the annals of American life. Yet, for our purposes, it is sufficient to note that since the turn of the century, the ongoing hope among humanistic social scientists has been that economic and technological development would generate a significant improvement in the human condition.

This faith has led economists to focus their attention upon unemployment and aggregate growth; they have been less interested in assessing the performance of specific sectors of the economy than in measuring macroeconomic developments. In consequence, the majority of economists have continued to propose monetary and fiscal measures to cure the economic ills and to hope that, in time, the glaring socio-economic problems would be ameliorated. Thus, rather than proposing redistribution of funds into the public sector, they have shied away from such qualititative judgments and condoned past policies.

Yet, if it is admitted that the problems we currently face are no longer strictly economic insofar as they involve choices as to the distribution and utilization of resources, it becomes necessary to consider moral and ethical questions. It is toward this end that John Kenneth Galbraith has directed his writing as well as his thinking; he has questioned the assumptions made by economists and politicians, as well as the implications of the policies which they are espousing and enacting. Further, he has cautioned and challenged them to shift their priorities in order to realize the possibilities afforded by the abundance of American resources. In his view, the time has come to shift attention from unemployment and growth to the "improvement of what may broadly be called the quality of life."[3]

The importance of his urgings becomes obvious when one considers the increasing reliance upon governmental intervention into the economy. No longer do we rely upon the "invisible hand," but on very visible hands whose actions are still conditioned by a philosophy of laissez faire economics rather than a philosophy which emphasizes social responsibility. The problem is that economists, in Sievers' words, "have not always seemed to be adequately aware of the need for reshaping their thinking to fit the continually changing reality."[4]

The root of the scholar's reluctance to deviate from the accepted paradigm of his/her discipline is suggested by Thomas Kuhn in his masterful analysis of the manner in which the scientific community is forced to reassess its understanding of the external world. Science, in this view, proceeds not by simple accumulation nor by minor modification, but by the "revolutionary" redefinition of the discipline.[5] Kuhn's point, although made in regard to the natural sciences, would seem equally applicable to economics; rather than holding fast to neoclassical wisdom, there is a need to restructure the gestalt which guides the research and action of both the academic and the policy maker.

In the absence of a new philosophy which emphasizes the political and social implications of economic measures, we cannot hope to come to terms with the disparities and inequities of the current situation. The point is well expressed by Robert Heilbroner who argues that volition is of increasing relevance in the domain of public policy. Among the salient questions which he identifies are: "Do we want a more equal distribution of income or a less equal distribution? Do we want big business or little business? Do we want free labor unions or circumscribed labor unions? Do we want inflation or deflation?"[6] These, and many other choices, must be faced if we are to create the kind of future we want. A thoroughgoing evaluation--a demystification, if you will--of economic assumptions and priorities is essential if we are to meet the challenges of our abundance and create a viable institutional structure which will better serve the goals of the people at large.[7]

Herein lies the importance of Galbraith's persistent efforts to revamp our economic and social moorings in order to bring them into congruence with existing conditions rather than conformity with intricate theoretical models. Moving beyond political economics, he has managed to incorporate both historical and cultural factors into his vision. It is, in this sense, that his work falls within the genre of social criticism and must be so viewed.

Recognizing the interaction between ideas and events, Galbraith sets forth in each of his books an intellectual history as well as a critique of the conventional wisdom, demonstrating how social conceptions have led to certain assumptions and certain ways of looking at both economic and social phenomena. Additionally, he provides a new way of perceiving the structure, function and interconnections of these phenomena. In this manner he offers the reader a means of altering his/her understanding of the common sense reality as well as a means of more fully appreciating the position of the individual within the larger institutional network.

The importance of this alternative point of view, although not quantifiable, can be understood within a sociological framework. Accordingly, insofar as each individual's behavior is influenced by the social as well as the physical environment, there emerges a common objectivity (set of symbols, meanings and associated objects) through which people mediate reality. Social institutions, be they religious or secular, are established in order to insure order and provide individuals with a felt-understanding of the external environment. Just as animism and magic once sanctified certain beliefs, rituals and taboos which engendered a certain sense of security among tribal groups, modern institutions provide individuals with explanations of the world and expectations as to what should and should not be done. Insofar as patternized behavior requires far less forethought and risk than does random human activity, it has the unquestionable advantage of seeming natural and hence correct. It is in this sense that Wheelis calls institutionalization "the quest for certainty." Because the institution channels human activity into acceptable and predictable patterns of expression, it effectively contains the uncertain dynamic of everyday relations and allows the individual to transcend his/her own vulnerability to circumstances. [8]

Although institutions emerge as embodiments of individual ideas and ideals, they come, in time, to have a life independent of their creators. It is in this sense that institutions not only objectify the status quo but also serve to legitimate it. As Veblen once remarked, "So soon as a given proclivity or a given point of view has won acceptance as an authoritative standard or norm of life it will react upon the

society which has accepted it as a norm."[9] It is,
then, institutionalized patterns of behavior which
allow members of a particular society and culture to
take everyday reality for granted and to rest assured
that their knowledge and/or understanding is self-
evident and unalterable.

At the same time, however, this shared world is
capable of being transformed by the addition or modification of knowledge and/or vantage point.[10] All
institutional patterns are arbitrary and subject to
transformation and/or replacement if an alternative
arrangement can demonstrably deal more effectively
with the needs of the various participants. It is
this mutability of the givenness of reality which
produces the dynamic interaction between the individual and society; each individual possesses the
ability to transform not only his/her own thinking,
but others' perceptions as well and, in some cases,
to direct the historical process.

In order for innovative ideas to have an impact
upon others' interpretations and shape subsequent
events, however, they must be both accessible and
comprehensible. Further, they must not only show the
inherent limitations of existing conceptions but also
provide constructive and manageable alternatives. It
is for this reason that cultural criticism, which
calls attention to existing disparities and proposes
alternative arrangements, is essential if a society is
to realize present possibilities, maintain a dynamic
process of social change and take advantage of the new
developments. In its absence, defenders of the status
quo will doubtless find it convenient to rely upon
past prescriptions and formulations.

III

Cultural criticism, rather than becoming less important as we become more industrialized and affluent,
assumes a new urgency. Insofar as technological
rationality which defines everything in terms of productivity and efficiency has become the subtle but
pervasive rationale employed by politicians, states-
men, engineers and educators, "people are led to find
in the productive apparatus the effective agent of
thought and action to which their personal thought and
action can and must be surrendered. And in this
transfer, the apparatus also assumes the role of a
moral agent. Conscience is absolved by reification,
by the general necessity of things."[11] It is in this

6

sense that technological rationality becomes the universal, omnipotent mode of thought constraining imagination and channeling behavior.

The point which must be stressed is that technological rationality is not, in itself, restrictive; it provides a means of ordering the world and preparing for the future. Given the current ordering of society, however, it has become destructive and will remain so until its creative powers are domesticated. Gibson Winter argues that the alienation associated with technology under existing social arrangements is an outgrowth of its domination of everything, including man, and of its propensity to reduce "everything to calculable quantitites in its programs." He continues, "The techno-society develops highly motivated engineers to program everyone's life, giving the elite prestige and power in return for selfless services."[12] It is for this reason that it rests with the critic to transcend the givenness of existing institutions and frames of reference, to question their legitimacy and implications and to evaluate possible alternatives.

In order to perform these functions, one cannot simply be a specialist; one must, in some ways, be a generalist who is familiar with several areas and cognizant of their interrelationships. One must be able to step outside the assumptions and methods of any given field and in this sense be an iconoclast who challenges the sacrosanct patterns and institutions. Additionally, one must be willing to look beyond theoretical formulations and to test them against concrete realities and changes which are either ignored or obscured by the accepted paradigms.

The critic must, then, to borrow Alan Gruchy's term, be a "cultural scientist" whose aim is to develop a broader, more realistic discipline which draws upon the contributions of economics and psychology, no less than sociology and anthropology.[13] Recognizing that "any period is characterized by a typical limitation of basic orientations and specific theories available in the culture as a whole,"[14] the critic must preserve his right to question the assumptions and conclusions as well as the standard methodology of his/her discipline.

The need for such scrutiny is especially pronounced in light of the recent reliance upon mathematical models that isolate only those factors which can be operationalized. The most important limitation of this methodology is that its supposed objectivity often disguises ideological and political biases. The denunciation of _Time on the Cross_[15] as distorted and misleading is perhaps the most widely known recent instance in which statistical data, far from clarifying an issue, has merely muddied it further. The debate surrounding this book calls to mind Marcuse's warning that the operationalized concept, despite its therapeutic value "becomes false to the extent to which it insulates and atomizes the facts, stabilizes them within the repressive whole, and accepts the terms of this whole as the terms of the analysis."[16]

Any model, in addition to providing a systematic arrangement of components, also makes certain background assumptions.[17] These assumptions incorporate qualitative judgments about how things are and/or how they will (should) be. They also constitute the framework of interpretation into which the individual inserts thoughts on specific issues and on the basis of which he/she draws conclusions. The applicability of these assumptions, however, is affected by temporal and social changes. Thus they must be constantly reevaluated to avoid making unwarranted decisions. This reexamination, however, is more often then not resisted by those who have been trained to employ a given model and view things in terms of an established perspective. Sievers explains: "A static mathematical model of the economy has the great advantage of specifying relationships exactly--and for those who understand their mathematics, the further advantages of greater clarity." "But," he cautions, "such a model resembles a machine more than an organism; it tends to be rigid, whereas an organism grows and changes internally. Thus model-building is more suited to the solar system than to an economic system."[18]

The result of overreliance upon mathematical models is that despite the dynamism of events, the model tends to remain static and thus becomes outmoded. Rather than employing accepted models one must, therefore, use one's discipline as a tool with which to assess society and measure its qualitative performance rather than as a means of sanctioning existing arrangements and measuring its quantitative accomplishments.

In short, the critic must assume the responsibility for evaluating the society. He/she must not only understand how various sectors are functioning, but also must evaluate these functions in terms of their implications for the quality of life which they are sustaining or producing. One must take not a functional, but what the Goodmans call a "neo-functional " approach--evaluating the worthiness of various functions and goals as well as the means of attaining them.[19] Criticism, then, provides a means of unpacking the conventional wisdom and demonstrating how traditional preconceptions are no longer applicable to the current situation. It also provides a means of assessing constancies and changes in terms of their implications for the quality of life in a particular society. Finally, it provides a vehicle with which to reorder social priorities and evoke additional social change. For these reasons, the critic's job is, as C. Wright Mills has noted, to take private woes and make them public worries--to force the society to become reflective and assess its goals and priorities.

Herein lies the essential distinction between the role of the critic and the scholar. Edward Shils, among others, defines the key responsibilities of the scholar as the cultivation of the works of a given field, the transmission of the body of material through interpretation and the creation of symbols of general significance.[20] All of these activities are ostensibly "neutral" and "objective." The scholar is instructed to remove himself from his work and conduct "value free" inquiries into social problems and propose solutions for them. What is not mentioned is that these so-called solutions, insofar as they are couched in the terms and confined within the boundaries of the status quo, serve the authorities (be they advertisers, industrial managers or the federal bureaucrats) in their efforts at pacification and containment of dissenters.

Based on his experience at Wisconsin, John R. Commons concluded that the scholar "can furnish only technical details and then only when he is wanted by politicians who really govern the state." He remembers having seen "individuals coming and going according to whether or not they furnish the President with what he wants."[21] In this sense, the work of the scholar is circumscribed by external pressures to produce research which is "useful" to those in positions of power. Identification of social problems and creation of tenable remedies is particularly meritorious and relieves the scholar of the burden of carefully scrutinizing his/her society. In the words of Sidney Willhelm, "To admit the existence of problems simultaneously sanctifies the correctness of any given system. In functionalist terminology, problem-oriented scholars declare boundary-maintaining principles; they conduct their inquiries in accordance with equilibrium concepts. Proceeding along these lines, the system itself never comes under scrutiny or challenge to its validity."[22]

The critic, as suggested above, assumes a more active stance. He/she considers alternative courses of action and challenges the fundamental assumptions of the status quo. He/she is, in the words of Malcolm Cowley, "open to ideas" and maintains that "society can be improved by finding the right ideas and putting them into practice."[23]

Daniel Bell advances a similar distinction between the intellectual (here the same as the social critic) and the scholar. "The differences between the intellectual and the scholar without being invidious, are important to understand. The scholar has a bounded field of knowledge, a tradition, and seeks to find his place in it, adding to the accumulated, tested knowledge of this part as to a mosaic. The scholar, qua scholar, is less involved with his "self." The intellectual begins with his experience, his individual perceptions of the world, his privileges and deprivations and judges the world by these sensibilities."[24] The key word which Bell, perhaps inadvertantly, deemphasizes is judges; the intellectual performs a critical and constructive function outside of the established parameters which channel and check the research of the scholar.

The critic, in Emerson's words, is "Man Thinking"--an individual with an active soul engaged in a daily encounter with his environment and skeptical of "established" truths. Such truths, according to Emerson, are the source of books written "by thinkers, not by Man Thinking; by men of talent, that is, who start wrong, who set out from accepted dogmas, not from their own sight of principles."[25] A similar belief leads Gouldner to conclude that critics are "therefore less vulnerable to the temptations and seductions of the present." He continues, "From the standpoint of their more conventional contemporaries, such men are often seen as flawed. Yet they are frequently flawed in a productive manner; for being less subject to the influences of the dominant surround, they are often critically sensitive to the limitations of the established intellectual paradigms and can work in a manner that is creatively at variance with them."[26] In essence, this is the same conclusion advanced by Thomas Kuhn and James Watson in their accounts of paradigm shifts in the scientific world.[27]

Rather than a rationalized non-accountability for one's research, then, the critic takes and defends a particular position and offers others a new way of seeing and unearthing previously inarticulate assumptions. He/she dares to question and grapple with anomalies which are not comprehensible within the current frame of reference. Finally, the critic is willing to examine the goals toward which the society is headed, to consider the disparities between the possibilities and actualities and to evaluate the quality of life produced by existing systems.

As evidenced by the frequent dismissals of academics who attempt to challenge the status quo or espouse unpopular beliefs, execution of these critical functions has always provoked a certain resentment and suspicion. Thus, the dismissal of Edward W. Bemis from Chicago in 1895 was not only justified by the administration, but, in fact, applauded by the local press. In the words of the Chicago Journal: "The duty of a professor who accepts the money of a university for his work is to teach the established truth, not to engage in the 'pursuit of truth.'"[28] A similar treatment, it should be noted, was accorded the early institutional economists elsewhere. Both John R. Commons and Richard T. Ely were repeatedly obliged to resign their positions as a result of their stances on contemporary social issues such as labor relations. Thorstein Veblen, easily the most unsparing critic of the Gilded Age, was constantly on the lam and anything but secure.[29] "Because his vocation is to be a critic of society," Christopher Lasch argues, "the intellectual's relation to the rest of society is never entirely comfortable."[30]

IV

Despite their rather marginal status, intellectuals have relentlessly preserved their distance and critical perspective. As defenders of the status quo applauded American progress, intellectuals raised questions about the consequent costs involved in this advancement as well as the direction American culture was headed. They questioned existing values and institutions, pointing to the need for change; they fought for a culture which was open-ended and dynamic rather than static and stable. In short, they have, until recently, maintained a dialogue with their society.

Although a comprehensive accounting of the critical tradition in America is beyond the scope of this discussion, mention should be made of what might be called their "progressive" philosophy.[31] By and large the philosophy is an outgrowth of Jeffersonian values and ideals, stressing the importance of individual action and fulfillment. Even as technological and social change have altered the specific application of these ideals, the critical effort to enlarge individual freedoms has been a recurrent aim of American critics.

Economists such as John R. Commons, Walter Hamilton, Wesley C. Mitchell and Thorstein Veblen refused to ignore their public responsibility. They saw conflicts of interests between business and the public and were led, accordingly, to argue "that market forces could reconcile some but not all of these conflicting interests of the modern world and that a complex industrial society continually created new conflicts whose equitable resolution required government action."[32] The challenge which the institutional economists presented to their more orthodox colleagues was not without effect. As Gruchy has indicated, the orthodox thinkers have found it increasingly difficult "to withstand the attacks of those who regard the current situation as a great opportunity in which to create a better social and economic order."[33]

Increasingly, it has become obvious that no one branch of the social sciences can offer a total explanation of a given phenomenon. Philosophically, the orderly, stable Newtonian universe has been forced to yield to the dynamic, evolving Darwinian universe. With the pragmatism of William James and Charles Pierce, augmented by John Dewey's instrumentalism, there has been a growing recognition of the need for experimentation and improvement within society.

Among the most outspoken critics was the ir-
reverant iconoclast, Thorstein Veblen, who relentlessly debunked national myths and conventional ideas,
analyzing all which he found insidious in the American
way and urging the replacement of outdated institutions. He probed the inner dynamics of business as
well as the irrationalities of the rich. He was,
as Heilbroner notes, a stranger who adapted to the
world "as a missionary might to a land of primitives,
refusing to go native, but preserving his integrity
at the cost of frightful solitude."[34] To have conducted more "objective" research simply to avoid re-
buke would have been alien to Veblen's sensibility--
he seldom minced words to curry favor from higher-
ups. His more conventional colleagues, most of whom
are now forgotten, clearly had more academic security.
And it may well have been this contrast which led to
the retreat from the critical challenge. The lesson
that "A safety is to be gained by donning the mantle
of neutral coloration for a presumed dedication to
bias-free research exempts the scholar from assumptions of unprofessional deportment,"[35] was perhaps
too well learned.

V

Although no exact date can be given for the shift in
orientation, it is significant that with the advent of
World War II, academics were granted a new status.
Research was seen as both necessary and praiseworthy;
new funds and positions were offered to the scholar
and (perhaps inadvertantly) the intellectual. Thus
the intellectuals were faced with the dilemma of ab-
dicating their new-found positions of power and influence or relinquishing their critical perspective.

Believing, perhaps, that real change was in the
offing, most opted for the latter alternative and became reconciled to American policies. Their assumptions became those of the mainstream; their methods
those of positivism and technological rationality and
their defense the advancement of knowledge. Their
choice is not hard to understand insofar as it is
"characteristic for a social group that finally arrives
following what it considers to have been a hard fought
engagement to come onto the scene...."[36] And this was
exactly the case with American intellectuals.

Shils' investigation into the position of the
intellectual in America suggests, in fact, that the
pre-World War II peripherality of the intellectual,

13

especially when contrasted to the status accorded
intellectuals in foreign countries, evoked a genuine
resentment. They came to believe that America was
culturally provincial and wished it were not so. As
a result, "They embraced with enthusiasm the escape
from peripherality in a province to centrality in a
metropolis."[37] This new position, however, had its
price; intellectuals were forced to justify their
change of mood not only to others but to themselves
as well. And so emerged the standard defense: America
has reached the "end of ideology." In a pluralistic
society, it was argued, the proper role of the
intellectual is "civil politics" rather than ideological criticism.[38]

This defense, however, is misleading insofar as
it oversimplifies the relationship between man and
society. Although class cleavages and family capitalism may be of diminishing importance, it does not
follow that the need for criticism has lessened.
Prosperity and rising standards of living need not
indicate that the social system is providing the
optimum amount of freedom or permitting responsive
change. What they may instead signify is that rights
and liberties (e.g. freedom of speech, freedom of
thought, right to political opposition) which were
once critical ideas have become institutionalized to
such an extent that they have been divested of both
their function and their significance. Gibson Winter
makes a similar point in his discussion of the trans-
valuation of basic freedoms in a technologically
integrated society. He notes that whereas individual
drive and initiative were once the keys to success,
access to external resources and services have become
virtually mandatory. Thus, if one is born into a
family or community which lacks full participatory
status, is perhaps unstable, or is deficient in educational facilities, proper medical care or access to
key facilities, one is effectively excluded from the
society from the outset.[39]

Similarly, tolerance of deviation and conflict,
rather than constituting a liberating pluralism may
well disguise a totalitarian repression. Significantly, Jameson notes that "toleration can be said to
be generally repressive in that it offers a means of
defusing the most dangerous and subversive ideas; not
censorship, but the transformation into a fad, is the
most effective way of destroying a potentially threat-
ening movement or revolutionary personality."[40]

Accordingly, although institutionalization and toleration have, in large measure, made old ideologies incapable of eliciting social change, the fact remains that the "advanced industrial culture is more ideological than its predecessors inasmuch as today the ideology is in the process of production itself."[41] It is, in fact, the very pervasiveness of the technological ideology which has enabled authorities to contain dissent and to channel thinking. Due to the ability of technological development to sate modern man's material desires and improve his standard of living, additional production seems to promise progressive improvements.

Because technological innovation and refinement conjoined with expansion of production are seen as the central means of securing a better future, we no longer consider alternative forms of organization or resource allocation to enhance the quality of life. Instead, we ask individuals to adjust to institutional requirements and to compensate themselves with increased consumption. It is in this manner that technological rationality has attained its hold upon the individual and become the omnipotent mode of thought and guide of action. "Every unit--whether man or thing--has to be reduced to a calculable quantity so that it can be brought within the logic of technology. The power of technology depends upon extending the horizon of calculability."[42]

It is because of this transformation of the very way we interpret the problem and envision the solutions, that the existence and practice of the critic is essential. Only through criticism can we transcend what Marcuse calls "one dimensional society," undermine its supportive network of "one dimensional thought" and propose viable alternatives. In this sense, it rests with the critic, as Commons expressed it, "to jerk up routine into the irritation of doubt"[43] in order to narrow the gap between what is possible and what currently exists.

It is time we realize that theoretical models demonstrating a highly functional system are not, in fact, reliable indicators of the way the real system is operating. They say nothing about those qualitative aspects which defy quantification--quality of education, health care services or housing, for example--and which belie announcements of our rising standard of living. Neither do they take into account

very real changes within the culture and society. As
a result, there is an ever widening gap between social
theory and social policy largely because social
scientists have failed to "submit this changing, developing age to close scrutiny, so that less-detached
people in the world of politics may have the full
benefit of whatever social science generalizations
may be worked out."[44] Thus the importance of the
social critic: "in a competitition to develop and
reveal the quality of our society, we must not rely
on the wisdom of the solemn men. They will tell us
this is no time for reform--that, as always, other
things are more urgent....They will fail to see that
our greatest achievements are those that depend on
our capacity for economic and social experiment and
change, and on the diversity and freedom of our
culture."[45]

VI

The preceeding emphasis upon economic questions and
issues is not accidental. In many ways, the economist
has become both priest and savior in the volatile
world of money and material ambition.[46] Peter Berger's
"sacred canopy"[47] has, as his most recent book makes
clear, lost much of its plausibility as modernity
has ushered in a cognitive style which emphasizes,
among other qualities, the componentiality of reality,
the separation of means and ends and the segregation
of the public and private spheres of life.[48] Whereas
the integration of pre-industrial societies was generally achieved by reliance upon religious definitions
of reality, the pluralization of life-worlds so
characteristic of modern societies has undermined this
unity and engendered what Berger, et al. identify as
"a deepening condition of homelessness."

These shifts in consciousness have left the individual dependent upon secular agencies to safeguard the
orderliness of daily life. The economist, for his part,
has been charged with keeping the wolves from the door.
He has, in this sense, been made keeper of the keys and
is expected to understand and control those factors
which influence the performance of the economy so as
to permit all individuals and families to plan their
futures with a relative degree of security in terms of
employment and/or an adequate income.

Thus it is that it falls upon secular institutions
to mediate, interpret and manage highly specialized
bodies of knowledge. Unlike the legal codes which tend
to be of only sporadic relevance to the life world of

16

the layman, economic concerns have a pervasiveness which enables them to impinge upon all other segments of life. And, given the primacy of economic institutions and policy in contemporary society, economic assumptions and preoccupations must be constantly reviewed to keep them attuned to the ever changing social process. There exists, however, a certain reluctance on the part of many economists to deviate from the accepted perspective.

It is for this reason that I have chosen to analyze the work of John Kenneth Galbraith. Galbraith has stepped outside the traditional economic perspective and has challenged a number of fundamental presuppositions made by conventional theorists. His work is important not only because of the issues he raises and the charges he levels against other economists, but also because of the widespread publicity which his ideas have received. In addition to being an academic economist, he is, so to speak, a popular economist who takes a holistic look at the society through the means of economic theory. As economist Charles Hession has noted, "In an allegedly one-dimensional society, he has been a multi-dimensional man with extraordinary influence on the thinking of his time."[49]

Galbraith has not confined his vision of America to economics any more than he has tailored his view of our industrial system to make it conform to the competitive model. Throughout his books, he asks the reader (and the society) to become reflective and to realistically assess the disparities between our potential and our actuality, to come to terms with public squalor amidst affluence and to realize the disproportionate power of big business, the inequalities in income and the victimization of the individual. He asks the people in general and economists in particular to shed their faith in an outmoded conventional wisdom, to free themselves and their thinking from the assumptions appropriate to an earlier stage of development, to reorder national priorities and to redefine goals in such a way as to enhance the quality of life rather than the efficiency of production.

With each book he demonstrates anew his active engagement, not only with his society, but with himself. Knowing the inherent limitations of rigid dogmatism, he constantly reassesses past assumptions and

conclusions. Some, such as the overly optimistic
notion of countervailing power, are later dismissed;
others, such as the need for reallocation of resources,
are subsequently reassessed and refined. Both the
initial formulations and the reformulations reveal an
attempt to come to terms with important issues and
provide viable alternatives to the one dimensional
thought mentioned above.

Because of both the primacy of economics in our
everyday life and the insightfulness of Galbraith's
critique, his work merits attention. Although some
have questioned the legitimacy, not to mention the
wisdom, of a student of American Studies rather than
economics undertaking such a task, I feel it is important to consider Galbraith's work from a cultural
rather than an economic perspective with emphasis
upon his role as a cultural critic. His economic
theories are not at issue here; these I leave to the
economists. What is at issue is his analysis and
criticism of the ideological underpinnings of the
American economic and social systems. I will focus
my attention on several major aspects of his work: his
intellectual orientation, his portrayal of American
society, the position of the individual within that
society, the distribution of power within America, the
major disparities in contemporary society and his
hopes for America's future. Using techniques
borrowed from the sociology of knowledge, I will
attempt to view each of these aspects contextually
giving attention to personal as well as social conditions which may have had an impact upon his thinking.

Before turning to the various ideas which he
presents, however, it is important to gain an understanding of the man. In order to facilitate this
goal, I will spend the next chapter outlining Galbraith's background, prior to 1952, in an attempt to
explicate some of the influences and motives which led
him away from the mainstream and induced him to assume
the mantle of a cultural critic.

Rejection of or serious challenge to the accepted world
view leaves one vulnerable to charges of impracti-
cality, delusion, and even madness. Or, in Veblenese,
"one cannot but be sensible of the fact that the innovator is a person with whom it is at least dis-
tasteful to be associated and from whose social contact one must shrink."[1] Unlike the designer of an
"improved" deodorant, who is applauded as an enter-
prising innovator, the designer of a new social order
is adjudged mad, or, at best, seriously misguided.
Yet, Bertrand Russell once remarked, "I would rather
be mad with truth than sane with lies." So it is with
rebel economist John Kenneth Galbraith.

There is little doubt that the more orthodox
economists deem Galbraith a good deal closer to madness than sanity; it is doubtful, however, that they
would identify possession of truth as the primary
cause. In fact, Heilbroner suggests that "to a substantial number of economists, particularly those of
the 'Chicago school,' his name is very nearly an anathema."[2] Perhaps the most serious charge which has been
leveled against Galbraith is that he has violated the
canons of his trade. As mentioned in the introduction,
social scientists have become increasingly method-
ology-minded in an attempt to discern the true patterns
and measurements of social phenomena. Accordingly, it
has been argued that economics can succeed as a discipline only insofar as it remains empirical and approaches the standards of the natural sciences. As a
result, there has arisen a methodology which "dictates
that the only questions to be entertained are those
which can be asked and answered with precision, prefer-
ably by means of econometrics, statistics or game
theory."[3]

Due to his disregard of this dictum, many have
suggested that economics "has passed Mr. Galbraith by
on the mathematical side."[4] Thus, while some have
granted that Galbraith's conclusions are tenable in
extreme and exceptional cases, most have remained convinced that the "only conclusion permitted...is that
Galbraith's notions are remarkably consistent in their
inability to find confirmation."[5]

Statistical studies have consistently "disproved"
Galbraith's conclusions just as they were thought to
have discredited C. Wright Mills' conclusions regarding
the power elite. Thus, especially to the mathematically oriented social scientists, Galbraith remains a
charlatan bent upon deluding the unwary.[6] His conclusions are viewed in a similar manner as ungrounded
and therefore unsupportable. Further, the issues
which he raises often seem to lie outside the established confines of economics. Jean Boddewyn, for example, rails at Galbraith for his "predilection for
social and moral issues" claiming that this choice
"presents us with the strange spectacle of a moralist
using economic concepts such as rationality and mar-
ginalism where moral ones would certainly appear
more appropriate."[7]

As an outgrowth of this rejection, economics continues to be taught and economic proposals and policies
continue to be made according to neo-classical assumptions about the economy which hold that in a competitive market, the consumer determines what is produced
and the corporation responds in kind.[8] Similarly,
G.N.P. continues to be the measure of our progress and
well-being. According to Galbraith, until recently,
this measurement went unquestioned: "a successful society was the one with the largest increase. Even now,
those who challenge this measure are thought to raise
an interesting question. They are not imagined to be
at all practical."[9]

Herein lies at least part of the reason for Galbraith's importance as well as the economists' negative
reception of his work. Significantly, Irving Kristol
argues that before the emergence of Galbraith, cultural
criticism posed less of a threat to the status quo because none of the critics advanced a "radical economic
treatise, any 'newest economics' to challenge the neo-
Keynesian orthodoxy that is now established in universities, government, and corporations and trade
unions alike."[10]

It must be observed, however, that despite the
spate of criticism which Galbraith's works have received, there are few who would deny his readability.[11]
A certain light-heartedness coupled with a barbed and
somewhat sardonic wit and an unceasing vitality inform
his writing. Additionally, due to his use of active,
colorful language and precise images, he enables the

reader to visualize the events, objects and processes which he describes. The importance of his style is implicit in Paul Samuelson's assessment, which says in part, "if good writing is a crime it is a crime of which most social scientists are quite innocent. But Galbraith is an exception. He does not write for his brethren within the guild. He is par excellence, a noneconomist's economist."[12] In short, "People listen to Galbraith because he talks about important subjects in imaginative and iconoclastic terms."[13] It is this fact which leads Seymour Harris to note that Galbraith is "probably the most read economist of all times." Taking it one step further, former colleague Arthur Schlesinger, Jr. suggests that he is "perhaps the best-known intellectual in the world today."[14]

To many students of American culture, he is the only readable and comprehensive economist since Thorstein Veblen. And like Veblen, and John Stuart Mill before him, Galbraith has succeeded in combining social consciousness with his economics--a blend which may be disparaged as "unscientific," but one which certainly extends his audience far beyond the confines of academia. In his comparison of Galbraith and Mill, William Barber mentions the similarities in purpose, style and method. Both are intent upon "enlightening the public to the inappropriateness of conventional concerns." Both write passionately and both "combine contemporary social criticism with a critique of economics as an intellectual discipline."[15] While Mill accepted much of the economic orthodoxy and sought primarily to undermine the presumption that "laws of income distribution" were immutable, Galbraith, as shall become clear, has launched a more comprehensive critique of the economic pedagogy. Both attempts, however, aim at inducing progressive reform through popular awareness.

It is this ability to reach a broad cross section of the American public which has allowed Galbraith to become an "all-purpose critic in the U.S. and beyond" and which enables Time magazine to identify him as "the most quotable--and possibly influential--critic of U.S. society." He has proven himself, in Newsweek's assessment, "a monumental intellect" with a "forked-lightning wit and an Olympian eye."[16]

Despite his dedication to economics and his recognition of its importance in both national and international affairs, Galbraith has always been somewhat of a rebel. He has refused to restrict himself or his

attention to economics, insisting that a slightly ir-
reverant iconoclasm is demanded by the cultural problems with which modern societies are confronted. He
has thus shaped economics into a tool with which to
probe the current malaise of American society and culture. He insists upon examining economic problems
within their social and political contexts stressing
the interrelationship of the various domains. It is
this interdisciplinary approach which demonstrates his
appreciation of the fact that the conventional separation of politics and economics is artificial and
that it distorts analysis. Only by taking the existence and exercise of power into account can one realistically come to terms with the modern economy. For
this reason, Galbraith, in addition to examining the
power distribution of existing arrangements, has always been willing to take a stand on public issues and
propose alternative arrangements. His ability to use
economics as "a vehicle for achieving broad social
aims,"[17] plus a number of other achievements to be discussed below, has earned Galbraith the distinction of
being dubbed "a man for all seasons and all pursuits."[18]

The validity of this assessment lies in the fact
that Galbraith has, as he once said of Keynes, "crowded
several lives into one....lives, incidentally which
were lived simultaneously."[19] His credentials include
a strange conglomerate of somewhat incompatible acco-
lades and positions ranging far beyond the confines of
economics or academia. Anthony Burgess once remarked,
in a review of Galbraith's only published novel, that
"Galbraith scorns any inner devil that whispers about
the prudence of setting a limit to talent; he will
venture across any intellectual frontier, whether he
has a visa or not."[20] A brief overview of his accomplishments confirms this assessment.

The presidency of the American Economic Association followed close on the heels of his chairmanship
of Americans for Democratic Action--two seemingly
strange bedfellows in the absence of an understanding
of the political implications of economics. That Galbraith understands this relationship is evident from
the potpourri of his publications. In addition to
writing several unlikely best sellers dealing with the
modern industrial scene (American Capitalism, The
Affluent Society, The New Industrial State and Economics and the Public Purpose), he has produced an
historical interpretation of the 1929 stock market
crash (The Great Crash), a history of pecuniary

institutions and policies (Money: Whence It Came, Where It Went), countless essays dealing with a wide range of follies, foibles and personalities (many collected in The Liberal Hour and Economics Peace and Laughter), a collection of relentless political satires (The McLandress Dimension), a novel lampooning the State Department (The Triumph) and, more recently a 13-part series for the BBC and an accompanying text (The Age of Uncertainty).[21]

Additionally, he has co-authored a book on Indian art (Indian Paintings), produced guidebooks for controlling the military (How to Control the Military) and for refurbishing the Democratic Party (Who Needs the Democrats and What It Takes to Be Needed), penned a somewhat wistful autobiography (The Scotch), insightful quasi-travelogues (A China Passage and Journey to Poland and Yugoslavia), a playful but incisive recollection of his years as Indian ambassador (Ambassador's Journal) and a number of varied analyses (America and Western Europe, Beyond the Marshall Plan, Recovery in Europe, Economic Development in Perspective, Economics and the Art of Controversy, Marketing Efficiency in Puerto Rico and A Theory of Price Control). This listing, it should be noted, excludes a vast amount of writing which has appeared in any number of magazines. Bernard Collier rightly notes, "in any single year few periodicals of quality and taste are deprived one of his fascinatingly evil essays or the delicate sarcasm of his criticism."[22] Between 1959 and 1968, his secretary estimates, he published at least 54 book reviews, 32 articles, 35 letters to the editor, 8 introductions to others' books and countless lectures.[23]

His "service" record is no less extensive or diverse. In addition to teaching at Harvard, he has served as Indian Ambassador and economic advisor to the National Defense Advisory Committee, conducted innumerable speaking tours, advised Presidents from Franklin Roosevelt to Lyndon Johnson, written speeches for Presidential hopefuls from Adlai Stevenson to George McGovern and led the vanguard of the Vietnam opposition. (His proposals for withdrawl from Southeast Asia were published in How to Get Out of Vietnam.) When not in Cambridge, Washington or England, he can most often be found either in Newfane, Vermont or Gstaad, Switzerland doing what he most enjoys--writing.

Earlier in his career, he served various

government commissions, including the Office of Price Administration, the Strategic Bombing Survey and the Office of Economic Security Policy and acted as consultant to the Department of Agriculture, the National Resources Planning Board, the Council of Economic Advisors, the National Security Resources Board, Selective Service Administration and the American Farm Bureau Federation.

Perusing this list, one is tempted to recall Keynes' opinion that "the master-economist must possess a rare combination of gifts. He must be mathematician, historian, statesman, philosopher--in some degree." Keynes continues, "No part of man's nature or his institutions must lie entirely outside his regard. He must be purposeful and disinterested in a simultaneous mood; as aloof and uncorruptible as an artist, yet sometimes as near the earth as a politician."[24] That Galbraith has managed to fill this bill is part of his prowess. He has availed himself to a myriad of opportunities while becoming captive of no one position.[25]

Significantly, Samuelson, calling him the "Sage of the Mixed Economy," notes that Galbraith "is part of our affluence."[26] It is in this sense that one must see Galbraith's work as an outgrowth of American culture; he is an American phenomenon. Colin Clark has suggested that without the dominant position of the American economy it is likely that the British would have maintained their lead in the field of economics.[27] But, just as technological developments and affluence have given American industrialists the power to affect countless overseas markets, they have given American academics an increased interest in understanding the system and maintaining our affluence.

Additionally, since American development has gone furthest, American economists have been able to analyze the most advanced stages of capitalism which has enabled them to command an international audience. More important, as Galbraith explains, "It is the good fortune of the affluent country that the opportunity cost of economic disucussion is low and hence it can afford all kinds."[28] It can even afford a Galbraith. David Halberstam calls Galbraith "a unique American phenomenon." He explains: "In America, where there are so many things to oppose, he was an oppositionist, but in our largess even the oppositionists are affluent."[29]

Unquestionably there is a certain awesomeness associated with the range of credentials which Galbraith
boasts. Few men, and fewer academics, have commanded
attention from so many diverse quarters simultaneously.
In attempting to understand the characteristics which
have enabled Galbraith to accomplish so much, one immediately envisions an extremely disciplined man, with
a far reaching mind and a seasoned sense of decorum.
While all of this has undoubtedly played a part, it
does not satisfactorily explain his prominence. His
destiny, if you will, seems deeply rooted in his early
environment; the Iona Station milieu, for all its
harshness, would seem to have made possible, if not
probable, the direction in which he would later move.

Born October 15, 1908, in Iona Station, a Scotch
farming community on the Canadian northern shore of
Lake Erie, young Galbraith received an early education
in the power of vested interests and conflicting
values. The Scotch, who were predominantly rural,
rallied behind the Liberal Party in opposition to the
urban Tories who had inherited the conservativism of
the original Family Compact. Beyond the simple ethnic
differences between the Scotch and English, the rivalry
was partially a question of political interests.
(Protective tariffs, for example, were to the Tories
a means of stimulating Canadian commerce; to the
Scotch, they were a prime cause of higher priced farm
machinery.) But more important than politics was a
question of economics. As the struggling farmers
watched the merchants prosper, they became increasingly
suspicious. Many suspected price gouging and resented
the fact that so easy a task as managing a store should
bring such a high return. Herein lies the crux of the
matter--a rivalry between two life styles and sets of
values. Galbraith characteristically defines the
issue as one of superiority, ascribing to the Scotch's
belief that the honor should go to them. "They considered agriculture an inherently superior vocation. It
placed man in his fit relation to nature; it abjured
the artificialities of urban existence. It gave him
peace and independence. It was morally superior for it
required manual labor."[30] Thus the conflict in many
ways revolved around the question of the quality of
life--a concern which remains primary in Galbraith's
vision of the "good life."

Even within the Scotch community this issue proved
to be of marked importance. Despite an egalitarian

appearance, the community was divided into three distinct classes in accordance with one's abilities and
character. By far the largest class was the unexcep-
tional middle class who were well regarded but had
little influence upon community opinion or politics.
At the bottom were the disenfranchised whose opinions
were more or less discounted. Unless one owned at
least 100 acres he would fall into this grouping.
(Since the original inheritance was 50 acres and land
was plentiful, this requirement was largely a measure
of diligence and economy.) Unneighborliness or dis-
honesty could also cause a man to be excluded as could
excessive drinking--a habit which earned an individual
the dubious distinction of being an "honorary abor-
igine" and made it unlawful for him to purchase
alcohol. Laziness and, more interestingly, ignorance
could also cause a person to lose his position. The
Scotch shrewdly suspected that there was no direct
equation between education and intelligence and had
"total lack of hesitation in ascribing ignorance to
demagoguery."[31] Perhaps, as Galbraith has suggested,
this is the root of his candid dismissal of many ideas
espoused by the so-called scholar.

At the top of the social structure were the "Men
of Standing" who more or less shaped community opinion.
These were the men who sought practical applications
for the knowledge they possessed and attempted, in this
way, to increase the well-being of the community. Galbraith's father, William Archibald Galbraith, a
teacher turned farmer, was among this elite group and
served as county auditor. As a clan, the Galbraith's
were known for their "industry, for their breeding
ability with livestock, and for their height."[32]

Being affiliated with the Liberal Party rather
than the Toronto Tories, William schooled his son well
on the limiations of excessive allegiance to the
establishment. In his mind, the royal prerogatives
were indefensible since they reflected "the purest
accident of parentage." As he reasoned, legitimating
this accident merely "helped sanction even the pre-
tensions and possibly the prices of the local dry goods
hierarchy in Dutton itself."[33] Thus, kings and princes
ought to be subject to open competitive examinations
to insure the highest caliber rather than the longest
lineage among leaders. Raised with such views, young
Ken was taught to view established institutions
circumspectly.

Nor was this the end of it--the critical perspective was not sufficient by itself; one had to actively employ it in order to lay the foundation for change. Due in part to the fact that the most prestigious clans regarded education highly and "regarded the people of the towns not with envy but amiable contempt,"[34] the Scotch were extremely active in politics. Thus it was that William, according to his son, "for around half a century was the leading Liberal of the community."[35] With characteristic modesty, Galbraith explains his father's prominence with reference to the "superior confidence which people repose in the tall man"--a confidence which is justified by the fact that size affords visibility which means the tall man "is much more closely watched. In consequence, his behavior is far better than that of smaller men."[36]

In any event, it was from his father that Galbraith received much of his political education. According to his recollections, he began accompanying his father, who was a "prodigious orator" from the age of six or eight. "It was of some educational value, and I learned, among other things, the use of humor."[37] One such lesson which Galbraith relates occurred at an auction. His father, mounting a large manure pile, appologized for speaking from the Tory platform. Later the boy congratulated his father for his wit and ability to hold the attention of the audience. His father replied: "It was good but it didn't change any votes."[38] This lesson is one that has served Galbraith well during his stints at speech writing.

Humor notwithstanding, Galbraith was raised in an atmosphere of stark, unrelenting Calvinism. The Galbraith's belonged to a sect known as the Old School or hardshell Baptists and from his recollections, the church well deserved its name. As Galbraith depicts it, Veblen could well have had this very church in mind when he observed that "If any element of comfort is admitted in the fittings of the sanctuary, it should be at least scrupulously screened and masked under an ostensible austerity.... making the fitting of the place a means of mortifying the flesh, especially in appearance."[39] And so it was in Iona Station. The structure itself was a bleak building, completely unadorned. The church, likewise, "contained nothing, literally nothing, but square oaken pews and a plain wooden pulpit. Church doctrine forbade a choir, organ--in fact music of any kind."[40]

Even weekly collections were forbidden, "not to protect the worshipers from some momentary impulse to generosity....Money was the weekday faith. To keep it out of church was to show that Sunday was sacred to a different deity."[41] Further, with their uncompromising creed of predestination, there was little need for money. It could not save the giver nor was it necessary to convert the heathens who "presumably all had been born damned."[42] The whole ordeal has left its mark upon Galbraith who compares the sermons to "exercises of the most acute pain," and comments that "For thirty years I have not been in a church for other than architectural reasons or to witness a marriage or funeral, and it is partly because I associate them to this day with torture."[43]

The attitudes of the church also affected the conduct of daily life. It was a life without frills in which hard work was the norm. "They did not ask God for anything they could do for themselves."[44] Propriety and morality regulated all activity. As Galbraith recalls, "We were taught that sexual intercourse was, under all circumstances a sin. Marriage was not a mitigation so much as a kind of license for misbehavior."[45] Once, recalls Galbraith, after having read one of Anatole France's more explicitly provocative novels, he chanced to be strolling with the golden-haired girl of his affections. Passing through the orchard, they climbed a fence rail and watched the grazing cows, one of which was a white bull who happened to be "serving a heifer which was in season." Noticing the interest on his companion's face, young Galbraith remarked: "I think it would be fun to do that." She replied:"Well, it's your cow."[46]

Schooling was viewed by many as a "necessary but burdensome and even somewhat dangerous supplement to a strong back."[47] But, for the more elevated clans, it was seen as having an independent utility as preparation for a profession. Somewhat disenchanted by the long, tedious hours of farming, the young Galbraith became an insatiable reader. His independent progess plus a scarcity of students enabled him to pass through Willey's School in five years and enter Dutton High School at the age of ten.

Dutton, a "gaunt two-story building" situated in an undersized and barren lot, was overseen by Mr. Thomas Elliott, who served as principal, taught geography, spelling, zoology, physics and chemistry, and proved himself "grossly uninformed" about everything save, possibly, spelling. "Old Tommy" as he was "unaffectionately" known, did much to reinforce the town-country division. He was fully allied with the townspeople. As Galbraith recalls, "No New Yorker out of O. Henry, Horatio Alger or Damon Runyon was more passionately devoted to the urban way of life and the town partly controlled the school."[48]

Sharing the townsmen's low opinion of the rural Scotch, Old Tommy did his best to resign them to their inferiority. He had learned "that equal laws, unequally applied, can also be quite discriminatory and he did not hesitate to resort to such outright favoritism when that was indicated."[49] Similarly, his opinions were invariably those of the Tories and aimed at instructing the Scotch of their backwardness. Both efforts, however, did more to strengthen the Scotch's beliefs in the injustices and ineptitude of the Establishment than to convince them of their own failings. Again, the daily struggles with Old Tommy merely served to teach young Galbraith the value and necessity of social criticism.

III

After high school Galbraith, aided by $300 from his father, entered Ontario Agricultural College intent upon studying animal husbandry. Finding that no such field existed, he switched to agriculture and attained his B.S. in 1931.[50] During these years, however, the boy received reinforcement for his belief in the value of criticism. As Galbraith puts it:

> At OAC students were expected to keep and also to know and cherish their place. Leadership in the student body was solidly in the hands of those who combined an outgoing anti-intellectualism with a sound interest in livestock. This the faculty thought right. Anyone who questioned the established agricultural truths, many of which were wildly wrong, was sharply rebuked and if he offended too often he was marked down as a troublemaker.[51]

Needless to say, Galbraith was in the latter grouping.

In the fall of 1930, however, he spied an advertisement for research assistantships at the

29

Giannini Foundation of Agricultural Economics at the University of California. Some time later, to the surprise of both himself and his professors, he received word that he had been accepted. It was the Great Depression, according to **Business Week**, which saved Galbraith from being "just one more Canadian farmer." When he graduated in 1931, "farming was in a slump, and the best-paying job he found was for graduate study in agricultural economics at the University of California in Berkeley."[52] The annual stipend was $720 which, in Galbraith's words, "if not princely, was by far the best offer of any kind I had."[53]

Accordingly, Galbraith borrowed $500 from his aunt and "almost literally, set sail for California." Following a steamer voyage from Port Stanley to Cleveland, he met another graduate student and began what turned out to be a long, expensive journey. The 1926 Oakland in which they were traveling was in terrible condition and "almost immediately got worse," burning about a quarter gallon of gas and a half pint of oil per mile. Arriving somewhat behind schedule, Galbraith immediately became entranced with the splendor of Berkeley. "From that day on, the University of California has engaged my affection as no other institution--educational, public or pecuniary--with which I have ever been associated."[54]

Additionally, Galbraith's spirit was immediately captured by the intellectual fervor so unlike the passivity of Ontario. Galbraith found instructors who were not only receptive to criticism but encouraged it. From Henry Erdman, head of the agricultural economics department, and Howard Tolley, director of the Giannini Foundation, he learned, not unhappily, "that a professor might like to be informed on some subject by a graduate student--might not just be polite but pleased."[55] Galbraith then, as now, took full advantage of this invitation and "never stopped informing people thereafter."[56]

There were others, as well, who gave the intellectual milieu a dynamic previously lacking in Galbraith's education. Leo Rogin, one of the early disciples of Keynes, conveyed a sense of urgency about the subjects he discussed; Paul Taylor and Charles Gulick passionately defended the rights of the small farmer and the farm workers, while Robert Brady defended the consumer and other underdogs. All told, the atmosphere was one well suited to Galbraith's temperament; it was one which catered to and expanded his social conscience, reinforcing his belief in the need for criticism and increased social justice.

Additionally, during the heart of the Depression with Hoovervilles right next door, there was much intensity and tragedy which was not lost among the graduate students. Those with whom Galbraith was associated were, he recalls, "uniformally radical and the most distinguished were Communists."[57] That he shared their sympathies there can be little doubt. His reasons for remaining outside of the Party are by no means clear. One explanation which he offers is that he feared rejection. His agrarian background from which he had only recently loosed himself, he reasoned, left him, according to strict Marxist doctrine, among the politically immature. "I sensed this bar and I knew also that my pride would be deeply hurt by rejection."[58]

He suggests one other explanation which seems to have a bearing on the direction his life would later take. "Although I recognized that the system could not and should not survive, I was enjoying it so much that secretly, I was a little sorry."[59] This affection, it seems, has remained with Galbraith to this day. Although he can see the limitations of the status quo and the need for change, he can still not accept the need for complete replacement. He remains a rebel, a radical rebel perhaps, but still not a revolutionary.

During his second year at Berkeley, his stipend was increased to $840 and during the third year, he was sent to Davis. At the time Davis was the center of agricultural research and, commanding a salary of $1800, Galbraith was made head of the Department of Economics, Agricultural Economics, Accounting and Farm Management. He laughingly recalls that "with the exception of one elderly dean who gave lectures to nondegree students, I was also the total teaching staff in these disciplines."[60] Despite this load, he managed to complete his dissertation, "California County Expenditures, 1934," and was awarded his Ph.D. in 1934 in Agricultural Economics (M.S., 1933).

When in 1933 an offer from Harvard for the following year arrived, Galbraith had no intention of

accepting it or of leaving California. The instruc-
torship would bring a salary of $2400, so Galbraith
reasoned that he could use the offer as a ploy for a
pay increase at Davis. His encounter with the Dean,
however, dashed this plan as the Dean "congratulated
me warmly on my offer, gave me the impression that
he thought Harvard was being reckless with its money
and said that of course I should go." At that point,
says Galbraith, "I realized to my horror I had no
choice. I couldn't now plead to stay at two-thirds
the price. The great love of my life was over."[61]

His regrets notwithstanding, the Harvard which
Galbraith entered was a veritable hub of excitement,
for it was through Harvard that John Maynard Keynes'
heretical analyses gained entry and acceptance in the
United States. While the "old economics was still
taught by day....in the evenings and almost every
evening from 1936 on, almost everyone in the Harvard
community discussed Keynes."[62] With the arrival
from Minnesota of Alvin Hansen, who had studied under
both Commons and Mitchell, the fervor only intensified.

Hansen, who valued economic ideas largely for
their usefulness (a lesson which Galbraith learned
well), was well received by Harvard's young, ideal-
istic economists. Most, Galbraith suggests, not only
felt that they could change the world, but that Keynes'
theories and proposals offered a means of both preserving and altering the system. To Galbraith's way
of thinking, "Keynes triumphed not because he provided a platform for radicals but because he provided
men who did not really want to be radicals with a
plausible form of conservatism."[63]

"By the end of the thirties, there were two
Cambridges advocating revolution in economics."[64] And,
as Hansen's repute grew, so did his following. In
time, he even attracted a regular stream of policy
makers who "took Hansen's ideas, and perhaps even more
his sense of conviction, back to Washington."[65] This
victory, however, was not easily won. In 1937, the
somber men of orthodox view held sway. Just as economic recovery seemed within grasp, they deemed it
time to cut spending, raise taxes and move toward a
balanced budget. Despite the protests of the
Keynesians, the more orthodox view held the day.
Subsequently, "As the budget moved toward balance,
the recovery came to a halt. Presently there was a
new and ghastly slump, a recession within the

Depression. It was entirely as Keynes predicted. The men of sound judgment had made our case."[66] This sense of the power of ideas whose time has come has been among the most durable notions in Galbraith's vision.

During this same period, Galbraith also met and married Catherine Atwater, formerly a Smith College valedictorian, who had come to study comparative literature at Radcliffe. The day after their marriage in September, 1937, the Galbraiths set sail for Cambridge University where Galbraith was to study under Keynes as a Social Science Research Fellow and Catherine was to teach German. The former never materialized due to the fact that Keynes was taken ill; the year abroad, nevertheless, proved profitable for the emerging scholar. It broadened his theoretical groundings and placed him at the heart of the Keynesian revolution.

Although he has never commented at length on this experience, he remarked on one occassion that he was at Cambridge while Piero Sraffa was working on the Ricardo papers. The importance of this coincidence lies in the fact that it provided "an invitation, rare in modern times, to steep oneself in Ricardo, Malthus and James Mill and to go back to Smith and on to John Stuart Mill and, more superficially, his contemporaries."[67] Not only did this exposure advance Galbraith's understanding of the history of economic thought but it also broadened his understanding of the specific circumstances which had guided the early economists' formulations and proposals.

While at Harvard, Galbraith also had the benefit of being exposed to the ideas of Joseph Schumpeter and John D. Black--two men who profoundly shaped the direction of his thoughts. Surely the severity of Schumpeter's critique was not entirely without effect on the young scholar. His appreciation of the organic unity of society and his prediction of the eventual demise of capitalism were not to be lightly dismissed. More important, however, was "Black's pragmatic approach and his interest in using theory to solve practical problems."[68] From the former, Galbraith came to appreciate the need for an evolutionary perspective and from the latter the need for a realistic rather than a theoretical orientation. Both blended well with his Keynesian bent.

Theory and industrial organization became increasingly important to Galbraith. In 1938, with New England industrialist Henry S. Dennison of the Dennison Paper Manufacturing Company in Framingham, Massachusetts, Galbraith published Modern Competition and Business Policy. Dennison, it should be observed, was one of those outspoken, humanitarian businessmen who had a strong interest in social justice and social reform. Even at this early date, he regarded unions and social insurance not as a threat but as a solvent for social tensions.[69] Also of significance is the fact that even in this early publication, Galbraith's skepticism regarding the competitive model and antitrust policy was evident. Already, Galbraith had come to see the need for a more comprehensive policy of corporate regulation. This was equally evident in his early articles which appeared in The Quarterly Journal of Economics and The Review of Economics and Statistics.[70]

Moving from Harvard to Princeton in 1939, Galbraith spent as much time away from the campus as he did as assistant professor. In 1940, due largely to his previous publications and his Keynesian orientation, he became economic advisor and assistant to Chester Davis, agricultural member of the National Defense Advisory Commission. His appointment was largely arranged by Lauchlin Currie who was seeking a committed Keynesian. While serving in this capacity, Galbraith circulated a paper containing proposals for dealing with inflation which were in accordance with the ideas Keynes had been proposing. "It was an inspired action, for, as a consequnce, in the spring of 1941, I was put in charge of price control, one of the most powerful economic positions of the wartime years."[71] In 1942 he became deputy administrator of a staff which grew from a dozen to some sixteen thousand employees.

His flexibility and responsiveness as a thinker--those qualities which have allowed him to bring his own interpretations and proposals into line with changing realities--were evident even at this point in his career. Finding his own system of controlling prices which had been enacted in the Emergency Price Control Act of 1942 to be unworkable, he quickly abandoned it in favor of a system which did work, not only during World War II, but also during the Korean War. The new system embodied in the General Maximum Price Regulation, rather than relying on taxation augmented by control of consumer credit and business borrowing and viewing price control as a measure for dealing with particular equilibrium situations on a case by case basis, sought to fix all prices. "It flatly reversed the earlier design for price control policy. It made no pretense to deal with particular disequilibria....Events had forced the step that economists, in the main current of economic theory, had so long viewed as unwise or impossible, or both."[72]

The job, however, proved to be a thankless one and soon his enemies outnumbered his friends. In his recollection, "I did everything the exact reverse of what I had [previously] written. Naturally I felt a good deal of moral indignation against my critics, who were still guided by my original articles."[73] He continues to explain that as a result he soon mastered a highly refined technique of turning people down-- "the absolute maximum of tactlessness, which managed to turn them against me personally and not the government."[74]

On May 27, 1943, businessmen appearing before the House Interstate Commission demanded his ouster. As a result, he resigned May 31, 1943 and Roosevelt gladly accepted his resignation. "It was," says Galbraith, "the most popular single thing he did that entire term." The whole experience, again brought home to Galbraith the important role which vested interests and distorted understandings can play in the reception of any policy measure.

Temporarily unemployed, he offered his assistance to the Armed Forces but was rejected because of his 6'8" height. Consequently, he joined Henry Luce's forces and served as an editor of Fortune magazine from 1943 to 1948. It was here that Galbraith learned to write with clarity and to avoid the use of pro- fessional jargon "because you were writing not just for your own audience but always for Harry (Luce) and Harry's curiosity transcended his ideology--he would accept unfavorable ideas, but only if they were very clear."[75] Yet, since Luce had a penchant for elimin- ation of what he considered to be unnecessary words, it was only after leaving Fortune that Galbraith de- veloped the fluid style for which he has become so well known. As he has commented, "It took me a long time after I left Fortune to discover that I could say things and exploit the possibilities of language that Harry never could have allowed."[76]

During this period he did take time off to return to government work under the auspices of the U.S. Strategic Bombing Survey which he headed. It was his job to study the effects of air attacks on the economies of Germany and Japan. In 1949, he returned to Harvard as professor of economics, a post which he has held more or less continually since that time.

IV

Upon his reentrance to academia, Galbraith published a number of scholarly articles summarizing his experience as a governmental servant and analyzing the position of agriculture within the larger economic system. His early work which included A Theory of Price Control (1952) and a number of technical essays gave him entry into the field, but brought him little acclaim. Myron Sharpe concurs with Galbraith's judgment that A Theory of Price Control was his best book and goes on to suggest that the "trauma" of having it virtually ignored, "led Galbraith to resolve never to write a book for economists again. He has never deviated from this resolution."[77] Galbraith himself lends credence to this interpretation pointing to the fact that a mere five, or, at best, ten people actually read this book. It was this, he claims, which led him to resolve to force other economists to listen "by having the larger public say to them 'Where do you stand on Galbraith's idea of price control?' They would have to confront what I said."[78]

This explanation, however plausible, seems somewhat simplistic. The implication, to many, is that Galbraith could not handle the demands and strictures of academia. A more convincing explanation seems to lie in Galbraith's belief that economic ideas do indeed possess political implications and that theoretical predispositions often frustrate needed policy. As early as 1952, in A Theory of Price Control, Galbraith was acutely aware of the need for price controls in dealing with persistent inflation. Concurrently, he realized that the failure of economists to appreciate this reality was linked to their fascination with the free, rather than the controlled, market. It was for this reason that toward the end of this book, he reminded the reader that "in the incommensurable task of governing this Republic, we often do in practice what we only later find to be justified in principle."[79]

36

Given these views, the accepted methods and
theories of economics imposed immeasurable constraints
upon his vision. As noted, he had already realized
the problems inherent in the competitive model which,
to his way of thinking, ignored very real changes within the economic system. He came increasingly to see
that this reluctance to admit changes was maintained
by arbitrary restrictions as to what type of study is
permissible and what type of method definitive. He
later expressed it thus: "Neoclassical or neo-Keynesian
economics, though providing unlimited opportunities
for demanding refinement, has a decisive flaw. It
offers no useful handle for grasping the economic
problems that now beset the modern society."[80]

That this conviction was at least partially responsible for his turning to a different style of
writing receives support from the fact that American
Capitalism which is generally taken to signal his
shift appeared the same year as A Theory of Price
Control. In other words, he had, in all likelihood,
chosen to direct his writing to a popular audience
prior to the publication of the latter book. Just as
his earlier publications suggested disenchantment with
accepted conceptualizations and policies, so his later
works attempted to propose alternatives and come to
terms with these problems. Additionally, David
Halberstam suggests that Harvard afforded both a
shield of respectability and a political base for
both Galbraith and Schlesinger. Because of this, they
"could propagate their liberal views, introduce
writers to politicians, New Dealers to younger liberals, columnists to professors, and serve as links
between the practicing and theoretical worlds of
politics."[81]

It was, in any event, Galbraith's subsequent
books and articles aimed at a popular, nonspecialized
audience which won Galbraith his reputation. It is
these works which demonstrate Galbraith's rebel-
liousness and indicate his ability to adapt economics
to social purposes. The issues he raises--counter-
vailing power and its effects, the collision between
full employment and price stability, economic affluence and the quality of life in the United States,
social imbalances and their implications, the
functioning of the "industrial state," the "technostructure," and the government and the roles of women
and the market economy--are questions which are not
confined to the sphere of professional economics but,

in fact, have sweeping implications for the nature and direction of American society. In all his writing he emphasizes the importance of culture and social institutions in economic matters.

Throughout his career it has been obvious that he recognizes the value of social criticism and is forthrightly dedicated to provoking and persuading his audience. He appreciates the impact which ideas have upon the outcome of social processes. For him, social criticism is "an engine of change:"

> In the United States, as elsewhere, political division turns on attitudes toward change. On the one hand are those who by temperament, inertia, vested interests, or nostalgia are disposed to protect the present or retrieve the past. And on the other side are those who by compassion, disposition, or from discontent seek change, in the conviction that it will mean improvement. To the first group, social criticism is unwelcome, save perhaps as it serves to recover the past. For those who seek change, criticism is an essential instrument of political action. To the first group, criticism is gratuitous, unwise, and even defamatory. To the second group, it is a welcome resort to truth.[82]

It will become increasingly clear as we examine the ideas which Galbraith has espoused that he is staunchly within the second group. Although some conservatives view him as a socialist ideologue and some radicals view him as an apologist for monopoly capitalism,[83] Galbraith is a man dedicated to a dynamic understanding rather than a set ideology. His task throughout his career has been to debunk those notions which are no longer functional and to replace them with ideas which can come to terms with existing institutions.

As this chapter has attempted to make clear, his early background prepared him well for these tasks. Born of Scotch descent in the midst of a predominately English region, he fast became aware of the need for social criticism. Similarly, entering the United States as an immigrant he was almost immediately cast into the position of outsider and could view the processes around him from a certain distance and with a comparative perspective. As the next chapter will attempt to demonstrate, his heterodox orientation separated him from the orthodox economists and thus again cast him into the role of critic.

38

PERSPECTIVES AND PREDECESSORS

If, as Galbraith has suggested, ideas can serve as engines of social change, it is equally clear that they can (and do) thwart change and can blind men to new situational imperatives. As noted in the introduction, once a set of ideas becomes institutionalized, it attains a hold upon the individual's way of seeing and thus serves to legitimate existing arrangements.[1] Insofar as the institution serves as an agent of socialization, it insures its own survival. This, it should be noted, is as true of the body of received beliefs which constitute a particular academic discipline as it is of the society at large.

Normal science, Thomas Kuhn reminds us, "is predicated on the assumption that the scientific community knows what the world is like." He continues to note that "much of the success of the enterprise derives from the community's willingness to defend that assumption, if necessary at considerable cost."[2] In effect, then, the discipline functions in a manner reminiscent of a tribal group. Membership is restricted to those who exhibit the appropriate credentials and abide by the rigorous standards and prescriptions established within the group. In the case of economics, a high ranking defense department analyst has testified, "The reason Ph.D's are required is that many economists do not believe what they have learned until they have gone through graduate school and acquired a vested interest in marginal analysis."[3] In short, due to its exclusiveness, "the tribe becomes the world to its members. Its limits and the mental horizons of its members are coterminous."[4]

Grounded in certain primary assumptions, the discipline thus establishes and refines a set of esoteric canons which are couched in sophisticated terminology and constitute the boundaries of the discipline.[5] Members are expected to conduct their research in accordance with those specifications and employ appropriately rigorous methods to verify their results. Training in a specialized discipline may, therefore, be constrictive insofar as the very questions the members pose are conditioned by their group affiliation. Technical problems, rather than the less definitional problems of the external world tend to be awarded the most attention. In fact, Assar Lindbeck suggests, "The choice of topics has often been determined more by consideration of available analytical techniques than by substantive problems."[6]

This tendency, it should be noted, is not unique to any one discipline. Nor is it without certain significant advantages. Many important conclusions have been propounded by those who Robert Solow denotes as "little thinkers"--those who devote their energies to systematic elaboration and refinement of existing models and construction of more sophisticated analytical techniques. In point of fact, much of the prestige of the social sciences can be directly attributed to these efforts. Within economics, Wilkins and Friday point out, the tools and models have been "refined and fortified" by generations of economists: "From Ricardo to Marshall, one after another orthodox economist accepted the general framework of their intellectual forebears, corrected any failings in the logic, and added new methods to increase the rigor of the analysis."[7] Econometrics, for example, has allowed the economist to formulate economic theories in mathematical form and to subject them to quantitative empirical tests.

In so doing, economics achieved a high degree of sophistication and complexity which virtually assured its status among the social sciences. Concurrently, specialization safeguarded its academic independence since it had divorced itself from practical considerations and "from the influence of other fields of scholarship with the exception of mathematics and statistics."[8] Consequently, the discipline rather than being dynamic and in touch with social and cultural developments had a tendency to perpetuate the established doctrines. For instance, when Edward Chamberlin and Joan Robinson proposed their theories of imperfect competition, "theories that would analyze more realistically modern market structure, many economists resisted on the grounds that such modification would destroy economic theory!"[9] Significantly, Richard Gill's study of the economic profession indicates that in spite of methodological innovations, such as the use of game and decision theory, the problem of oligopolies persists. Hence, the tenacity of the competitive model:"Competititve theory remains the only truly systematic general theory of value and distribution which economists possess."[10] It is this situation which has allowed

economists to defend the competitive model in terms of
its "robustness," the "extent to which its conclusions
survive under changes in the assumptions from which it
is derived."[11]

The advantage of such strict adherence to a given
paradigm is that by focusing exclusively upon economic
considerations, economists have been able to construct
a complex model of economic society. This model revolves around the scarcity of the means of production
and the necessity for choice between various objects,
methods and recipients of the production.[12] In theory,
the individual, whether consumer or worker, strives to
maximize his/her rewards just as the privately owned
and operated business firm attempts to maximize profits. Both ends are best realized through the competitive market which consists of a large number of impersonal buyers and sellers, none of whom has the power
to influence either supply or demand. Freely moving
prices are portrayed as the principal factor in economic decision making. Both the individual and the
business firm are presumed to minimize their costs
and maximize their profits. In consequence, marginal
utility and marginal costs are accorded a central
position in neoclassical economic analysis.

The Keynesian system laid Say's Law to rest by
indicating that there could be oversaving and hence
a shortage of demand. Further, it introduced fiscal
policy into the economists' paradigm so as to make
the level of output and employment dependent rather
than independent variables. Neither alteration, however, undermined the neoclassical faith in the market.
Hence, Galbraith's felt need to chide the Keynesians
for their belief that supply and demand "found the
equilibrium after the requisite management of demand
at a higher level of output than before. The mechanism
by which demand and supply were brought into equilibrium, prices established and resources distributed
among uses remained unchanged."[13] This reliance upon
the market system as the most efficient allocator and
distributor of income as well as goods and services
has allowed economists to escape charges of subjectivity, to concentrate on the means of achieving economic
stability, growth and efficiency and to establish
their discipline as "value free."

Scientific purity has not, however, been attained
without cost. In concentrating upon highly complex
statistical models which abstract variables from their

41

social context, economists have often found themselves in the uncomfortable position of defending their models against the charge that they ignore the import of economic power, the need for government regulation and a host of other social considerations which do not lend themselves to quantification.[14]

Following a brief overview of the criticism which the neoclassical model has received, we will be prepared to explore in more detail the development of Galbraith's dissent, focusing on his perspctive as well as on those thinkers who have most significantly influenced his thought. Before pursuing this examination, one caveat should be offered. The point of this chapter is not to discredit the orthodox perspective but, rather, to explore the manner in which the heterodox orientation deviates from the more conventional point of view.

The relative merits of the two perspectives are less important for this purpose than the distinct motivations of the two schools of thought. Whereas orthodox thinkers have sought to establish economics as a paradigmatic science, the heretics have sought to transform economics into a vehicle for broad-angled social evaluation. Accordingly, while the critics acknowledge that marginal analysis may well constitute the most fruitful means of assessing and predicting the import of peripheral socioeconomic change, they hold that it is inherently conservative. They base this claim on the tendency of marginalists to abstract social institutions from their sociohistoric context and to avoid assessment of the legitimacy or underlying dynamic of existing institutions. Thus, the debate between orthodoxy and heterodoxy revolves, as will become evident, largely around the purpose and inclusiveness of economics. The validity of the two stances remains a moot point, beyond the scope of this discussion. Accordingly, my aim is to explicate rather than resolve the issues which are involved.

II

In reviewing the New Left's critique of the economics profession, Assar Lindbeck observed that its complaints revolve around the charge that academic economists have studied the "wrong" problems. In this regard, he identifies five major areas which the orthodox perspective is said to neglect: the distribution of income, wealth and power; the allocation of resources among the various sectors of the economy; the

qualitative or social conditions of the society; the
qualitative changes within the economy; and the interaction of economic and political factors.[15] In essence,
he concludes, the revolt revolves around questions of
"the priorities the economists as a group have as-
signed to different components of the workings of the
economy in their collective choice of topics for research."[16] The gist of the criticism aimed at orthodoxy is well expressed by Allan Gruchy:

> The insistence on making and keeping economics
> exact has tended to cause economists not to cul-
> tivate those areas where the mathematical ap-
> proach is not fruitful. As a result the scope of
> economics has been unduly narrowed to accomodate
> those who refuse to go beyond equilibrium
> analysis.[17]

So long as economists posit the competitive model
as a working hypothesis, prices can be expected to
gravitate toward an equilibrium and corporate activities can presumably be regulated by market forces.
Although many orthodox thinkers admit that the market
is susceptible to failures, that firms can become
too large and can engender various diseconomies, that
certain services are not profitable and thus won't
attract investment, and that other profitable areas
of investment may command a superfluity of resources,
they staunchly deny the systemic roots of these disparities. As an outgrowth of their belief that competition or symmetrical oligopoly offers the most efficient and "freest" system, they insist that minimal
interference and/or regulation can redress imbalances.
Broader-angled governmental intervention would, in
this view, involve imposition of value-laden judgments
and, hence, transcend the limits of economics proper.

In short, what has been sacrificed is an appreciation of the importance of evolutionary change.
So preoccupied are the orthodox economists with refinement of the system and construction of sophisticated measuring devices, that they have failed to come
to grips with the dramatic changes within the social
and economic landscape. This preoccupation, as suggested above, has led to a fundamental shift in
emphasis. Hugh S. Norton, for one, contrasts those
who were attracted to economics in the past with
those being drawn to it today. The former, he sees
as "searching for solutions to problems," with
methodology as a secondary concern; the more recent
entrants, he feels, are "much more interested in

the solutions than the problems" and give the impression "that the aggregate subject matter is of little importance."[18] Even defenders admit that the real world is seldom as neat as their theoretical systems would seem to suggest. But, it is argued that "While our theory has many inadequacies, it is, nevertheless, the best we have at present and it does... add to understanding."[19]

One thus senses an ever-increasing gap between economic theory and economic reality and a consequent dearth of innovative policy formulations. Rather than risk one's reputation by advancing an unpopular measure, economists continue to propose the same remedies which proved effective at an earlier time. In this sense, it is not hard to understand the ongoing reliance upon fiscal and monetary controls despite their ineffectiveness in checking inflation and their perpetuation of economic strain.[20] The situation, according to Galbraith, is an outgrowth of the "persistent and never-ending competition between what is relevant and what is merely acceptable. In this competition, while the strategic advantage lies with what exists, all tactical advantage is with the acceptable."[21] In short, ideas and interpretations which have been previously accepted have an intrinsic advantage over those which are innovative and unfamiliar. The late John F. Kennedy expressed it thus: "The great enemy of truth is very often not the lie--deliberate, contrived and dishonest-- but the myth--persistent, persuasive and unrealistic."[22]

Herein lies the explanation for the fact that social theory, more often than not, emerges as the conservative, and sometimes reactionary, handmaiden of an outmoded idea system. Given the intrinsic relationship between social theory and public policy formulation, this tendency can hardly be overlooked or pardoned, even if it can be explained. The importance, Galbraith notes, stems from the fact that economics, unlike mathematics, "deals with matters which men consider very close to their lives."[23] Thus, since economic policy is the province of specialists, "what economists believe or wish to believe...are not matters of passing detail. They are decisive."[24] Economists should, therefore, be attuned to situational and institutional changes rather than shackled to abstractions and traditional verities.

44

Recognizing the static nature and conservative impact of ideas, Galbraith has repeatedly taken it upon himself to challenge what he terms "conventional wisdom"--a term he uses to refer to the familiar and accepted economic platitudes which guide our thinking and dictate national priorities and policies. Along with other reform-oriented social scientists, he has charged that the competitive market model espoused by neoclassical economists obscures the exercise of unrestrained market power by the mature corporation. In so doing, it serves as an ideological defense of the status quo. In a similar vein, Michael Harrington has argued,

It has been the special genius of capitalism that its injustices were supposed to be the unavoidable consequences of the working of impersonal forces. In this myth the corporate executive and the worker both had to submit to the laws of the market. Therefore to suggest that society impose its own values upon the economy was dangerous, for it involved tinkering with a marvelous mechanism which automatically vectored a myriad of private greeds into a common good but only on the condition that it be left alone.[25]

In rejecting this conception, Galbraith has come to appreciate the need for active government intervention above and beyond the monetary and fiscal measures endorsed by the orthodox economists.[26] Additionally, he has argued the indispensibility of social services for individual and social welfare. It is in this sense that he must be viewed within the genre of social criticism outlined in the introduction.

As early as 1952, in the foreward to _American Capitalism_, he made his purpose explicit when he classified his book not as a polemic, ideological tract, but within the genre of social criticism. Since the primary goal of criticism is demystification of outworn ideas, he explained that he would "pass under review ideas that are strongly held and positions that are warmly defended and, with some, at least.... take vigorous issue. Even though they are, as here, the ideas of men I respect, this is the way of progress."[27] His rationale, he explained was tied to the fact that economic ideas have a tendency to crystallize into dogma and that "neither liberals nor conservatives have a very good record of weighing challenges to accepted concepts and doctrines with critical detachment."[28]

Before examining his particular indictments of the conventional wisdom, subjects of subsequent chapters, it seems best to place his thinking within a personal and intellectual context. Only in this way is it possible to appreciate his work as an expression of a larger movement within the field of economics-- a movement which has attempted to broaden the perimeters of the discipline and make economics responsive to evolving social change.

III

Given Galbraith's background it is not entirely surprising to find him often taking issue with the economics profession or the elected officials. Schooled in a somewhat isolated rural community which emphasized hard work and practicality, he developed little patience for cant and an overriding skepticism of the established order and its self-interested justifications. Despite the privileges and prerogatives claimed by the townspeople on the basis of ancestral links with the old ruling class, Galbraith recalls being "taught to think that claims to social prestige based on such vacuous criteria were silly."[29] This attitude was carried over, as well, in the clansmen's attitudes toward the Crown. Although they never saw themselves as disloyal, they maintained that "one could be loyal and still have grave misgivings about the royal establishment."[30]

Similarly, Galbraith's relationship to the economics profession has been somewhat circumspect. Entering the field through the portal of agricultural economics, Galbraith soon recognized a prestige and status system as invidious as those rankings with which he was raised.[31] Upon reaching Berkeley, he was again a "second class citizen" in the eyes of the non-agricultural economists. Although highly practical and applicable, the prices of peaches and prunes, the problems of irrigation, and ethnic preferences for sage, orange blossom and clover-flavored honey were accorded less than meritorious standing. To reach the higher rungs of the departmental ladder, one was expected to abandon exoteric knowledge and matter of fact methods for esoteria and statistical sophistication.

Although Galbraith, under the tutelage of Ewald Grether and M.M. Knight, amply demonstrated his ability to master economic theory and "other branches of impractical knowledge," one suspects that his early

training predisposed him to concentrate the bulk of
his energy upon practical questions and pragmatic
solutions. This interpretation receives support from
the nature of his early publications which, as will be
evident shortly, were aimed at concrete problems and
practical remedies.

His proclivity for dealing with actualities rather
than refinements of an obtuse economic model well
suited him for the upheavals which were to beset the
field of economics during his training period. It was
at about this time that the impact of America's departure from the principles of laissez faire economics
was reaching crisis proportion. In his chronicle of
the evolution of economic thought, Richard Gill observes that by the early 1930s the gap between economic theory and economic reality was "too vast to be
accounted for in terms of exceptions or patchwork
corrections. It needed to be dealt with within the
central body of economic theory, a goal which would
obviously require a substantial reconstruction of what
had long been accepted."[32] Thus, as Norton indicates,
"economists who came to maturity during these years
were naturally influenced in their thinking by serious
cyclical problems which were so apparent during this
decade."[33] Corporate concentration, a persistent decline in agriculture, labor unrest and consumer protests all signaled a breakdown of the allegedly self-
adjusting and self-equilibrating system.

Confronted daily with the problems of migratory
labor, Hoovervilles, attempts to form producer coop-
eratives and the legacy of the I.W.W. movement, Galbraith grew increasingly wary of the accepted economic platitudes. In many ways, the Depression seemed
to be a vindication of the Veblenian gloom and Galbraith recalls the excitement with which he and his
fellow graduate students encountered the savant's
works.[34] It was well nigh impossible for them to
suppose that the system was operating effectively or
equitably or to overlook the scarcity of practical
prescriptions offered by the orthodox economists.
Wilkins and Friday offer a similar view:
    The Institutionalists made a sizable impact on
    orthodoxy, but they made almost no inroads on
    the major policy proposals. They served as a foil,
    helping the neo-classicals to sharpen their tools.
    The formulation, for example, of the theories of
    monopolistic or imperfect competition is largely
    the result of Institutionalist prodding. But the

47

policy prescriptions remained unchanged: do not
tamper with profits, and try to make the real
world more competitive. The problems created by
the great inequalities that pervaded the society
and which were a major concern of the heretics
were brushed aside by the orthodox economists as
necessary, although perhaps temporary, facts of
life.[35]

IV

From the outset of his career, Galbraith displayed a
tendency to break away from the boundaries imposed
by orthodox economics and to entertain questions which
appeared to have a pragmatic import for the future of
economic society. Even then, he was challenging what,
to him, seemed dubious classifications and interpretations. In his first article published in 1935, for
instance, he not only expressed concern over the unrealistic nature of certain categorizations within the
economic pedagogy but, more importantly, displayed
much interest in the practical implications of certain
standard interpretations, suggesting that

it may be that a failure to appreciate the pres-
ent-day importance of trade as compared with
industry holds serious possibilities of an over-
estimation of the extent to which reemployment
measures should be planned for the industrial
rather than the commercial population. These
values of the present estimates remain despite
the fact that they involve, as indicated, many
arbitrary definitions and assumptions...and a
certain number of gaps and guesses.[36]

What this suggests, is an awareness that the development of the various sectors of the economy will not
necessarily be uniform and that positive action may be
needed to correct the resulting imbalances. This
article also reveals a concern with the interdependence of the various segments of the society[37] and
seems to indicate early leanings toward a holistic[38]
orientation, a point to which we shall return.

That the Chamberlin-Robinson revolution, augmented
by the studies of Berle and Means,[39] left a marked
impression upon the young scholar can hardly be denied.
Unlike his orthodox colleagues who reluctantly acknowl-
edged the existence of the imperfect market and continued to believe that oligopolies would respond to
market influences,[40] Galbraith was intent upon re-
assessing public policy in terms of the market power

at the disposal of the oligopolies. He rejected the
neo-classical faith in antitrust litigation since he
felt that dissolution of the giants could do no more
than "establish a condition of duopoly or oligopoly,"[41]
which in no way diminished the firm's ability to
wield monopoly power[42] or sacrifice profits in order
to maintain existing price arrangements. Thus, as
early as 1936 he was clearly aligned with the heterodox economists who insisted that the modern corporation
could not be understood within the confines of the
old competitive model. Further, he held that the large
firm could no longer be expected to pursue profit maximization since it was controlled not by the owners,
but by trained managers.

On these and other issues to be dealt with
shortly, Galbraith, following his penchant for pragmatic realism, parted ways with his more orthodox
brethren and gradually arrived at a holistic philosophy of economics. Rejecting the block universe
defended by the neoclassicists, he advanced an open-
ended, dynamic system which took cognizance of the
continually changing cultural context within which
economic institutions and ideas functioned. It was
this orientation which led him to see the importance
of flexibility and innovation on the part of the
economist. Rather than defend conceptions which
latently functioned to justify the status quo and to
perpetuate its disparities, Galbraith opted to join
the heretics in their overt campaign to formulate a
"realistic" system which was responsive to socio-
economic change.

His departure was evident as early as 1936 with
the publication of "Monopoly and Price Rigidities"
which placed him at the center of the imperfect competition controversy and identified him with heterodoxy's camp. Following a qualitative analysis of
various factors which contributed to price rigidities
in imperfect markets, Galbraith briefly examined a
series of policy implications which his study suggested. The primary need, of course, was to recognize
the various forms of monopoly power as normal rather
than special cases. Only in this way, he held, could
policy makers advance proposals which were capable of
dealing with the mature corporations.

Also of importance was a more realistic appraisal
of factors inducing price rigidities among oligopolies.

Simplistic equation of monopoly power and rigidity, he charged, overlooked many of the more subtle influences which were operative. Since rigidity was at least partially an outgrowth of the oligopolies' calculations of the risks and costs of price reduction, Galbraith chided that perhaps an educational program centered around the "proper" uses of cost analysis in relation to price policy could be organized. As he observed, "So far the Government has deemed it necessary to educate the farmer, consumer, laborer, even the banker. But the American businessman has been credited with an omniscience which places him above the need for such attention. This assumption may warrant reexamination."[43]

Finally, he suggested that economic stability might be enhanced by increasing the economic power available within competitive industries. Citing as precedent various agricultural programs, he argued that this might put an end to drastic fluctuations in prices and production and hence prove beneficial. That casting aspersions on the competitive principle was heresy, there is little doubt. Nevertheless, although time and changing conditions have modified his position, Galbraith has remained a firm advocate of increasing the power available to the small firm, a point to which we shall return.[44]

V

Galbraith's dissension, it should be recalled, came during the wake of the Keynesian revolution which laid to rest the assumption that left to itself the economy would find equilibrium at full employment. Keynes made the government an active participant in economic affairs by strengthening the relatively passive monetary policy with the addition of fiscal policy, through which the government could stimulate or retard economic growth. His success stemmed, in large measure, from the fact that the Depression had proven the inability of the orthodoxy to propose solutions for a troubled nation. It was a time when the profession could "no longer evade anomalies that subvert the existing tradition of scientific practice" and is thus forced to "begin the extraordinary investigations that lead the profession at last to a new set of commitments."[45] Or so it appeared.

The advent of Roosevelt's New Deal intensified the crisis situation as it ushered in a new philosophy which held that "society as a whole,

functioning through government, must protect itself
and its members against the disruptive forces inherent
in an industrial, market-oriented economy."[46]   In
effect, these developments overthrew the theory of
laissez faire economics and made government, in theory
as well as practice, an active participant in the
mixed public-private economy. Yet, with miraculous
staying power, the neoclassical economists managed to
accomodate Keynes within their system without dis-
membering their theoretical orientation or revamping
their discipline.

Textbooks continued to expound the neoclassical
model; the standard unit of economic analysis remained
the firm, run by the owner who directed its operations
toward profit maximization. The market remained unchanged; control of the system remained lodged in the
hands of the consumer who determined how much of what
would be produced by expressing his/her desires to
purchase various commodities. Prices continued to be
seen as self adjusting and consumer controlled. In
retrospect, Galbraith has observed that
>If Keynes seemed radical to his time, he was, in
>one important respect, completely orthodox. The
>economic structure which he assumed was that
>which economists had anciently avowed--that of
>competition, freely moving prices and the ulti-
>mate, uninhibited control of economic behavior by
>the market. There were unions but they made rel-
>atively little difference to Keynes. Corporations
>and corporate power made no real difference at
>all.[47]

Although an early convert to Keynesian economics,
Galbraith became increasingly convinced that Keynes
had not gone far enough. The market oriented perspective, he came to realize, ill-prepared the individual to deal effectively with the realities of the
modern industrial complex and, more important, made
him/her hostile and suspicious of those policies which
were necessary to deal with the persistent problems
of inflation, environmental blight, agricultural
underdevelopment, power or poverty. To come to terms
with these problems, Galbraith argued, one had to
appreciate that oligopolies could not be understood
as if they were either monopolies or competitive
firms. Their orientation as well as their practices
had to be understood as an outgrowth of their unique
market structure which allowed them to set their own
prices in accordance with the overall interests of
the industry.

The degree of Galbraith's departure from orthodoxy was clear in 1952 when he expressed the belief
that price and wage control had an important, if not
indispensable, role in inflation control. That such
a belief was not widely accepted he attributed to the
restrictiveness of the orthodox perspective. Thus he
charged that instead of evaluating price controls "for
their utility or disutility in preventing inflation
or facilitating mobilization, professional economists
have shown a disposition to dismiss them as uniquely
evil in themselves."[48] This dismissal, he contended,
was an outgrowth of the orthodox economists' belief
that prices, the rationing and allocating mechanism
of the economy, equalize supply and demand and "guide
resources from less to more important uses. Obviously, if prices are fixed, they can no longer perform these functions."[49] In Galbraith's mind, such
a view would not do.

His own experience with price control during
World War II had convinced him of the market power at
the disposal of the large corporation. Following
Gardiner C. Means, he had come to see that the prices
of oligopolies were "administered" and that oligopolies could and would raise prices long before full
employment had been achieved.[50] This, in fact, had
been the reason that the Office of Price Administration, as noted in chapter two, had rejected the
Emergency Price Control Act in favor of the more
comprehensive General Maximum Price Regulation. It
was this understanding which made him ready to
sacrifice theory for practical action.

Sievers' assessment is well taken: "Galbraith's
vision focuses on economics as a tool for social
diagnosis and prescription, and not as mere analytical
physiology."[51] This is not to say that he discounts
the value of theoretical analysis or detailed empirical research, but rather that he finds these useful only as a means of achieving a social organization
which protects the rights of all rather than favoring
the powerful and provides those social services which
lie outside the reach of the individual. It is this
stance which leads Ben Seligman to comment:
> While Galbraith has conceded that technical de-
> velopments such as national income accounting,
> input-output matrices, and the refinement of
> index numbers have been useful, he has chided
> economists for failing to accomodate their per-
> fect market-wage doctrines to the existence

of trade unions, or to assimilate the corporation into the main body of economic theory.[52] It is for this reason that he has taken it upon himself not only to explain the social system but to persuade his readers that the time for reform has come.[53]

VI

In attempting to persuade, Galbraith has rejected the notion of value free methodology and assumed the stance of an advocate. The value of such an undertaking is, of course, debatable and may well revolve around one's agreement or disagreement with Galbraith's conclusions. This, however, is unfortunate insofar as one need not agree with Galbraith's prescriptions to acknowledge the importance of the questions which he is raising. One can hardly dismiss urban squalor as a social, rather than an economic, problem any more than one can deny the disparities in power available to the defense industry as compared to that at the disposal of the housing industry. One can, of course, choose to disregard such questions in the name of scientific purity. This, Kuhn avers, is one of the advantages afforded a mature discipline, since paradigms can serve to "insulate the community from those socially important problems that are not reducible to the puzzle form, because they cannot be stated in terms of the conceptual and instrumental tools the paradigm supplies."[54] Herein lies the apparent basis for eminent economist Robert Solow's claim that economists "are determined little-thinkers....not likely to be much helped or hindered in their activities by Professor Galbraith's view of Whither We are Trending."[55]

Solow's glib discounting of Galbraith's probing into the economic superstructure is reminiscent of orthodox dismissals of his academic ancestors, especially Marx and Veblen, to whom Galbraith acknowledges his greatest debt. What all three men have in common is a holistic economic orientation which is diametrically opposed to the mechanistic thinking of the orthodox economists. Each is primarily interested in the sources and consequences of institutional change and expresses an appreciation of the organic unity of society. Rather than standing in awe of the self-regulating capacity of the market system, all three have dared to delve beneath the veneer and investigate its inner workings.[56]

What most impressed not only Marx and Veblen, but

all of the institutional[57] or holistic economists was
the dynamism of the system. In their awareness of the
central importance of social change and evolutionary
development, they insisted upon viewing economics as
a cultural science. Gruchy explains:

> In reconstructing their science the holistic
> economists have not sought to duplicate the
> formalistic science of their orthodox prede-
> cessors and contemporaries. Instead they have
> endeavored to create an economics that is a
> "cultural" rather than a "formal" science....
> which gives too much attention to the shape or
> form of its theorizing, and not enough con-
> sideration to the content of that theorizing
> and its relation to the real facts of economic
> life.[58]

Insofar as the holistic economist values content
over form, he must sacrifice a good deal of his rigorous methodology in order to accomodate the non-
quantifiable and thus settle for less scientific purity. But in shying away from formalism, he is more
apt to stay attuned to the social and political developments which may be producing a very different
reality. Alvin Gouldner defines the "pathology" characteristic of the classicist as "the danger of ritu-
alism, in which conformity to the formal canons of
the craft is pursued compulsively to the point where
it warps work, emptying it of insight, significant
truth, and intellectually viable substance."[59] Just
as the rejection of Say's Law led to a recognition
that demand could be insufficient, it seems reasonable
to predict that critical examination of the doctrine
of consumer sovereignty will allow economists to
broaden their frame of reference and to consider alternative institutional arrangements which rely less
upon market constraints to promote consumer welfare.
The point, as Robin Marris has expressed it, is that
"the notion of consumers' sovereignty, essentially an
economic theory, retains very considerable political
force in defense of the status quo."[60]

Herein lies the importance of Galbraith's criticism. Only by examining the broader context with which
economic theory interacts can the legitimacy of
existing institutions and economic policies be called
into question. So long as the consumer is thought to
be the prime mover of the productive forces, it is
reasonable to assume that economic growth constitutes
a means of extending the effective range of consumer

opportunities. If, however, the corporation has gained the ability to shape consumer demand, "it is not correct to speak of the market as acting to adapt the given resources of the economy to meet the material requirements of society."[61] This being the case, it would fall upon the economist to concern himself with the costs of market-controlled growth and to evaluate new institutions and policies as possible means of promoting consumer welfare.

Rejection of formalism enables the holistic economist to take into account the ever-changing cultural context in which social organization, human nature and economic progress must be viewed. Rather than approaching economic behavior from a mechanistic point of view, it can be viewed as a cultural phenomenon. Herein lies the fundamental difference between the heterodox and orthodox perspectives. Hamilton observes that "the reason institutionalism differs so radically from classicism with regard to change and thus in total outlook is because institutionalism is built on the culture concept....The dynamic element of culture is what is subject to evolutionary development. This evolutionary development of culture is economic progress."[62] In consequence, change, rather than stasis, is the pivotal point of institutional theory.

So long as one remains preoccupied with paradigm refinement and measurement of synchronic changes, analysis tends to be ahistorical, dissolving the connection between the particular object of study and its context.[63] The net result of such a division is an inability to understand the import of more basic, diachronic changes which may have altered both the structure and the underlying dynamic of the economic system. Thus, rather than assuming that the mature corporation which is subject to managerial control maximizes profits in accordance with the traditional theory of the firm, economists should subject this proposition to rigorous tests.

Although some studies have been conducted along these lines, their results have not been conclusive. This has allowed orthodox economists to rely upon the normative concept of "workable competition" to interpret corporate behavior. Almost by design, this notion vindicated traditional faith in the market since it asserted that all industries are "acceptably competitive, unless concrete disproof were given, including a showing that a specifiable alternative system would yield superior result."[64]

Yet, as Marris has argued, no one familiar with the statistical relationships relating to the growth, financing, and internal rates of return in mature corporations "can honestly claim that these are easily explained by the hypothesis that the corporations are generally attempting to maximize the present value of their equity." He continues, "to say that the latter is still the best hypothesis we've got is to say that we have no satisfactory hypothesis at all."[65] Also of significance is Simon's observation that the "satisficing model" and the dynamic theory of firm sizes have "quite different implications for public policies" than those of the "maximizing model" or the equilibrium model.[66]

Lacking an appreciation of developmental change, one's model presupposes a universality of certain concepts and relationships. Thus the viability of private enterprise under existing arrangements is never seriously examined. Human nature, no less than social organization, is viewed as given and, hence, static. Man becomes an "extraordinarily fixed and limited animal whose nature is absolutely constant."[67]

The importance of change as it bears upon economic thought transcends particulars and informs the individual's entire conception of economic science. Given a mechanistic understanding of change, Gruchy has argued, "economics becomes a narrow discipline which is mainly concerned with the study of economic equilibrium."[68] As a result, economists pay little attention to institutional change "save possibly when such changes can be demonstrated to improve efficiency, a sacred object of all good marginalists."[69]

In the evolutionary view, on the other hand, diachronic change is central to economic study. According to this perspective, the rise of the large and complex corporation invalidates many of the presumptions which have long guided orthodox economists' study of the economy. Accordingly, they maintain that "at some stage in growth and in power, a clear, clean break with the economics of the private firm in the classical market" transforms the large corporation into a public institution.[70]

Again we find Galbraith aligned with economic heterodoxy, attempting to broaden the scope of the field to include an appreciation of institutional change. Just as Marx saw the world as "an historical product, the result of the activity of a whole succession of generations...developing its industry and its intercourse, modifying its social organization according to the changing needs,"[71] so Galbraith is prepared to argue that what confront the theorist are historical imperatives rather than ideological choices. It is in this sense, that he sees the rise of the mature corporation as an organic response to vast changes wrought by recent technological developments.[72]

His emphasis upon the importance of technological innovation should not be equated with technological determinism. Galbraith places too much stock in the individual's ability to transform both himself and his environment to subscribe to such a doctrine. Note, for example, the amount of latitude which he grants the technostructure in the management of the aims and activities of the large corporation. Their behavior must be seen as adaptive rather than determined.[73] For him, it would seem, technological innovation merely constitutes an altered set of objective circumstances with which the individual must deal. Given the vast commitments of time and resources required to exploit new potentials, size becomes imperative. With size comes the need for complex organization and, therefore, the need for some form of planning and/or anticipation of market demand.[74]

Similarly, in his view, the New Deal must be seen not as a subversive plot aimed at undermining the market economy, but as a spontaneous social response to a changed economic landscape. By the 1930s, the emergence of the mature corporation (to be discussed in chapter four), which was guided by wholly different priorities and goals and organized in a manner antithetical to that of the market economy, had destoyed the practicability of laissez faire capitalism. Given the vast disparities in power between the individual entrepreneur and the large corporation, it was unreasonable to allow the system to produce its own somewhat attenuated equilibrium.

Galbraith's interpretation of the New Deal is significant insofar as it reflects his longstanding belief in the possibility of progressive change.

Unlike many recent social scientists who speak as
Leftist critics of American historiogrphy,[75] Galbraith
has found no need to discredit the original intent of
the Roosevelt era reforms. The limitations of the
labor legislation and the regulatory commission, in
Galbraith's view, stem not from original error (or
businessmen's design) but from new objective conditions
which have frustrated their effectiveness. Accordingly, Galbraith contends that with new policies which
come to terms with the new sources of economic and
political power, it is still possible to achieve the
ideal of affirmative democracy by which popular interests are given priority and virtual control over
private power.[76]

One final example of Galbraith's concern with
developmental change and/or adaptive responses might
be mentioned. In his treatment of management-labor
relations, he again emphasizes the formative process
more than the end result. Even when advancing his
optimistic notion of countervailing power which portrayed the rise of labor unions and large retailers as
a form of consumer protection, his emphasis was upon
the process through which these weaker groups recognized the need to organize to protect their own interests.[77] In a similar vein, the unions and the technostructure within the large corporation are portrayed
as having increasingly adjusted their goals and behavior, producing a symbiotic relationship, due to a
shared recognition that harmony, rather than dispute,
is, in fact, more beneficial to both parties.[78]

VII

In an attempt to free themselves from the restrictions
of the neoclassical model, the holistic economists
have abandoned the belief that the market, allowed to
operate freely, can guide the economy. The free
market cannot, they charge, be assumed to produce what
the consumer wants, to distribute products justly or
to maximize social welfare. Nor can the price system
be reliably expected to move resources in accordance
with shifts in consumer demands. In this connection,
Ayres observes that
> "Wants" are not "primary data," and the alterna-
> tive to "consumer sovereignty" is not dictator-
> ship. The glorification of consumption in stand-
> ard theory is a logical corollary of the con-
> ception of the economy as "market guided"....But
> "effective demand" (the only kind that counts)
> means purchases; and since purchases are sub-

stantially influenced by advertising and even
more by the "pecuniary canons of taste" which
Veblen identified, this has long seemed one of
the weakest links in classical theory.[79]
That Galbraith has reached the same conclusion will be
evident when we consider in more detail his view of
society and his view of the individual. For the time
being, it is sufficient to note that Galbraith, like
the earlier holists, rejects the view of individuals
as "contemplative, calculating beings living and
working in what Marshall described as the stationary
state."[80]

Given this conviction, it is not surprising to
find him and his heterodox brethren often affiliated
with the reform liberals.[81] As part of their task,
the heterodox economists accept the need to advance
certain policies which are in keeping with social
goals and normative standards. They apply their values to real situations and advocate specific remedies.
In their behalf, Sievers describes their actions as a
"legitimate function of the political economist to
criticize the uses of consumer credit, for example,
and to advocate a remedial policy consistent with the
functioning of the economic system."[82] Only by
reacting in this manner, can the heterodox economists
break the hold of the conventional wisdom and espouse
policy which is in keeping with the new situational
imperatives.

Although for this reason their analysis is often
value-laden, advancing specific reforms and adjust-
ments, it is their belief that orthodox economists,
although more covertly, are equally prone to endorse
value-biased measures. The assertion, for instance,
that the free, competitive market should be strength-
ened because it insures individual freedom, reflects
a very pronounced set of values. Similarly, the
equation of a higher gross national product with social betterment discounts the importance of statistical
difficulties which "make it impossible to construct
an index of the gross national product which faithfully
records changes in our material well-being."[83] That
individual freedom and individual consumption have
long been revered as worthy social goals makes them
no more value-free than the demands for a more equitable and environmentally safer society advanced by
the heterodox economists.

Echoing both Marx's and Veblen's charge that "men's present habits of thought tend to persist indefinitely, except as circumstances enforce a change,"[84] Galbraith has repeatedly argued that the "enemy of the conventional wisdom is not ideas but the march of events."[85] His task, therefore, is to devise policy formulations which are in keeping with the new organization and function of society, rather than the conventional wisdom. In his attempt to convince the public that economic growth and full employment for their own sake are no longer relevant, realistic or even desirable goals, he has advanced his thinking beyond the strictly economic to the socio-economic questions of how to attain more even development and how to foster more equitable relationships within the society. He has been unwilling simply to accept the affluence of the United States and has, instead, insisted upon considering its implications and possibilities. In his words:

> The myopic preoccupation with production and
> material investment has diverted our attention
> from the more urgent questions of how we are
> employing our resources and, in particular,
> from the greater need and opportunity for in-
> vesting in persons.[86]

His suggestion, once more, is that concrete changes demand a new perspective conducive to adaptive response. Before considering the specific responses which he feels are justified, it is important to gain an understanding of the manner in which he views the society and the individual, the subjects of chapters four and five respectively.

Throughout his career, Galbraith has displayed a profound respect for American capitalism and has marveled
at its ability to increase productivity and production
at unprecedented rates. The basis for this admiration
is most clearly seen in American Capitalism which projects, in Myron Sharpe's judgment, an "aura of complacency" as it attempts to explain why the system
works despite its deviation from the prescriptions of
orthodox economics.[1] The beauty of the system, in
Galbraith's mind, is its ability to adapt to changes
and to endorse policies which come to terms with problems even when such policies lack theoretical justifications. For this reason, he persistently reminded
President Kennedy that "the glories of the Kennedy Era
will be written not in the rate of economic growth or
even in the level of unemployment....Its glory and reward will be from the way it tackles the infinity of
problems that beset a growing population and an increasingly complex society in an increasingly competitive world."[2] It is, to Galbraith's way of thinking, flexibility which gives the system its vitality
and spontaneity as well as its progressive orientation.

Yet, even as Galbraith praises the system, he
cannot overlook the inherent contradictions between
American ideals and persistent imbalances within the
economy. As this chapter will attempt to demonstrate,
Galbraith sees the rise of the mature corporation as
having significantly altered the socioeconomic landscape and as having produced a condition of extreme
inequality of opportunity (and performance) between
the large corporation and the small firm.

While irony has come increasingly to color his
writing and has left some readers extremely skeptical
as to his ideological leanings, the fact to be borne
in mind is that Galbraith is both a reformer and a
pragmatist. This orientation effectively predisposes
him to campaign for improvements in those areas where
he perceives grave injustices or unrealized possibilities. The historical record has further convinced him
of the defensibility of his stance, since
        those who see themselves as the strongest de-
        fenders of the system, those who proclaim them-
        selves the most stalwart friends of free enter-

prise, even capitalism, will be most fearful of measures designed to conserve the system. They will be the most antagonistic to the action that will improve its performance, enhance its reputation, increase its capacity to survive.[3]
Hence, his preference for "stating moderate positions in abrasive form" in order to arouse people and promote positive policies.[4]

In order to move America closer to his conception of the "good life," Galbraith has often been one of the most severe critics of this society--not because he is un-American but, in fact, because he places great stock in American ideals. Accordingly, he is committed to the notion of progressive reform which, in his view, can only be engendered by criticism. In a rapidly changing society, he contends, rigid allegiances to past laws and policies may well obscure the impact of recent developments and thus penalize those groups whose positions have prevented them from exploiting new opportunities and/or establishing a power base through which to enhance their positions. Thus, he has insisted, "We raise the minimum wage only by noting that the income of those groups affected is extremely inadequate. We improve the position of the aged only after enlarging on the poverty imposed by their positions."[5] And his list goes on.

The point to be appreciated is that improvements are won only by severe condemnation of the status quo. So long as all appears to be well, there is little impetus for change. As a result, social inertia tends to perpetuate existing disparities and, hence, to block needed innovation. A case in point is the post-World War II market revival which provoked Galbraith to write The Affluent Society.[6] Its impact upon Galbraith's vision can best be appreciated by a brief examination of its contours and Galbraith's responses.

II
In the aftermath of the New Deal, businessmen, politicians and a war-wearied public ached for a return to normalcy, a return to laissez faire economics. Government intervention into the economy bespoke a drift toward statism and thus seemed both dangerous and unnecessary. Left to its own design, it was argued, the market would provide the needed goods and services and, thus, insure the rights and liberties of the individual. Hence the renewed enthusiasm for the theory of perfect competition among economists. Shepherd

explains that the interplay of theory and reality
served to convince economists "that actual market
activity (except perhaps for a few special cases)
does approximate neoclassical competition in all
essentials....the analysis of full-cost pricing
assumed away interdependence among rivals and possible
rigidities and joint action among them."[7] The government, accordingly, was instructed by conservatives
to keep its distance (except in those areas such as
defense expenditures which could be defended in terms
of the greater good--defense against communism).[8]

Even liberals came to endorse this arrangement
because their commitment to Keynesian policy channeled
their attention to maintenance of an adequate level of
employment and production, and away from considerations of the relative production of the various
sectors of the economy.[9] So long as demand could be
stimulated, economic growth and, by extension, individual welfare seemed assured. The liberals justified their position by noting that expenditures for
public services could always be substituted for military expenditures. Yet, in point of fact, Galbraith
reminds us,

> following World War II, the Keynesian Revolution
> was, in effect absorbed by the planning system.
> thereafter government policy reflected closely
> the planning system's needs. Public expenditures
> were set at a permanently high level and exten-
> sively concentrated on military and other tech-
> nical artifacts or on military or industrial de-
> velopments.[10]

Consequently, the practical import of the market
revival and the Keynesian shift was not to check the
growth of big government as its defenders suggested.
Instead, it served to restrain government initiative
and to discourage new forms of public spending. Federal policies which were in the interests of the
mature corporations were accepted as necessary; those
that were not, were repudiated as unnecessary governmental interference with the private economy. Thus,
public education, public housing, public medicine,
pollution control, welfare and a host of other social
services came to be equated with the loss of individual liberty.[11]

Galbraith's involvement with the problems of
agriculture led him to an early appreciation of the
limitations of the Keynesian remedy. As noted in

chapter three, his experience with price control had
convinced him of the inability of either monetary or
fiscal policy to curb the inflationary tendencies of
the oligopolies' pricing policies without direct controls. Farm prices, on the other hand, continued to
behave as prices were "supposed" to behave. They fell
demonstrably during periods of tight money and slack
demand. The resulting disparity was especially visible
during the 1950s when the prices secured by farmers
and small entrepreneurs responded quickly to the price
squeezes initiated under Eisenhower while corporate
prices continued to climb.

Such uneven performance could not be lightly dismissed in a society which prided itself on concern
for the welfare and rights of all individuals. Initially, what seems to have most impressed Galbraith
about this development is that despite phenomenal
increases in aggregate productivity and production,
there remained islands of egregious poverty in the
rural United States. Seeking the causes for the
perpetuation of poverty, he realized that the poor
remained poor not because of their innate deficiency,
but because of their inability to gain access to
essential public services. Thus, he came to argue:

> economic growth will not solve all economic prob-
> lems. On the contrary, it leaves us with a hard
> core of poverty which is unrelieved by the gen-
> eral advance. Part of this is in the cities; it
> consists of the individuals or families who are
> physically, morally, or mentally unable to adjust
> themselves to the demands of highly organized
> economic society....More striking is the problem
> of rural poverty. In both Canada and the United
> States progress leaves great islands of such
> poverty in its wake. This is not the poverty of
> individuals, it is the poverty of whole areas,
> and one cannot explain it away on the grounds of
> individual inadequacy or misfortune.[12]

The inattention awarded poverty seemed to reflect
a national preference for private goods over public
expenditures as well as a failure to assess social
progress in any but aggregate monetary terms which
blurred disparities between the economic sectors. As
a result, he argued, underinvestment in education,
housing, health, recreation and community development
effectively denied those outside the mainstream a
chance to meet the requirements of a technologically
sophisticated society. Growth alone, he argued,

could not solve this problem.

To deal with these issues, Galbraith found it necessary to step outside the traditional boundaries of economics and to challenge the Keynesian preoccupation with expansion and growth in order to promote redistribution of resources among the various sectors of the economy. According to his recollections, "The writing, accordingly, involved a heavy effort to detach myself from my own past beliefs. I discovered how difficult that could be."[13]

It seems that Galbraith's affiliation with Kennedy's campaign, in addition to being an outgrowth of a friendship with Kennedy begun in the 1930's at Harvard, was an expression of his belief that if Kennedy were elected, his administration would campaign for social change. And in some ways, he was not disappointed, since its advent brought about the open espousal in Washington of Keynesian economics. "In the Kennedy and early Johnson years the total output of the economy expanded at a steady rate. The resulting employment increased more rapidly than the labor force; in consequence, unemployment went steadily down. And by modest direct effort prices were held stable."[14] Equally salutary, was the fact that the price guidelines constituted an admission of the fact that prices and wages were subject to corporate and union control-- an admission staunchly opposed by both orthodox economists and corporate spokesmen.[15] These achievements again served to vindicate Galbraith's faith in America's ability to adapt to situational imperatives.

Yet, the tax policies enacted under Presidents Kennedy and Johnson failed, in Galbraith's estimation, to come to terms with pressing social problems.[16] He had relentlessly urged that rather than reduce taxes, the government should stimulate the economy by financing educational grants, home loans, youth programs, and community development programs. But, as Lekachman has observed, it may well have been national preference which led both Kennedy and Johnson to place "a large bet on the capacity of business to produce the right goods in the right quantities and to distribute them to the right people."[17] This choice seemed counterproductive to Galbraith.[18]

That the ineffectiveness of his prodding had a marked effect upon Galbraith's vision is beyond doubt. Significantly, he has spoken of The Affluent Society, which first laid bare the problems of the poor, as "a window to a room" in the sense that his study of poverty and his subsequent efforts to strengthen remedial actions led him to appreciate the implications of recent social and economic developments as they influenced both the structure and function of the economy.

In order to understand his criticism and proposed remedies to our economic and social dilemmas, it is necessary to explore this room in order to come to terms with his conception of American society. For this reason, the next sections of this chapter will attempt to recreate and analyze the boundaries and dynamics of American society as they have been perceived by Galbraith.

III

The focal metaphor in the Galbraithian vision is unevenness. The economic terrain emerges cluttered with contradictory images and edifices. While recognizing a continuum, Galbraith depicts an economy consisting of two general economic groups--those with full range of power, freed from competition and the uncertainties of the market, and those without these powers and prerogatives.

The power of the former--the mature corporations-- derives in large measure from their size, their technological complexity, their organization and their control over resources and output. The impotence of the latter--the entrepreneurial firms--stems, accordingly, from their simplicity--a simplicity which leaves thum unable to stabilize the competitive market, to command their own resources, to take advantage of technological developments, or to exert influence upon the government.

Given his holistic orientation, Galbraith cannot easily dismiss the fact that this type of bimodal development effects the overall functioning of the economy, according special treatment to those who have access to seats of power and penalizing those who lack it. The point to be reckoned with is that this dualistic development "is unrelated to need; the inequality in income bears no necessary relationship to production or efficiency. Both are the results of unequal deployment of power. Both are socially damaging."[19]

In this sense, current disparities between the mature corporation and the market-oriented firm cannot be written off as ephemeral or simply ignored. Rather than rationalizing the difference in performance between, say, the automotive industry and the housing industry by reference to market preferences, those differences must be seen as systemic, hinging upon the amount of power available to the various groups.

Despite assertions that power and society itself are pluralistic and that power "does not significantly cross the boundaries of each sphere in which it is created,"[20] the fact remains that power has become concentrated in a relatively small number of institutions which have an inordinate amount of influence upon national priorities and policies.[21] Although quite aware that pluralism is more conducive to our egalitarian ideals, Galbraith contends that economic and political power have become concentrated in such a way as to make them the real forces which mold our national development and determine the "proper" areas for research and expansion.[22]

While acknowledging the importance of the thousands of small businesses which remain subject to competition and the demands of the market, Galbraith contends that the key characteristics of the modern economy are located elsewhere--among the five hundred to one thousand mature corporations which are responsible for over two-thirds of all industrial sales and three-fifths of all employment in the mining and manufacturing sectors of the economy. A similar recognition led to the organization of the conference on Corporate Accountability held in the fall of 1971 in Washington D.C. As its organizer, Ralph Nader, observed, "Our large corporations are unparalleled as buffers shielding their executive decision-makers from public inquiry and accountability. A supposed democracy should not suffer from the exercise of such uncontrolled power."[23]

It is in the mature corporation that one finds the advanced technology and complex organization which have come to characterize the advanced industrial nations. It is here, too, that one finds corporations which have managed to diminish both competitive pressures and the risks and uncertainties of the market. In consequence, they have greatly expanded the scope of corporate decision making just as they have

multiplied the strategies at their command. Following
World War II, the corporation, according to Andrew
Hacker, became the epitome of the American institution.
The importance of this development is that it "has
made time-honored theories of politics and economics
irrelevant, and its explosive growth has created new
breeds whose behavior can no longer be accounted for
by traditional rules of conduct."[24] Herein lies the
significance of Galbraith's concern with the mature
corporation rather than the entrepreneurial firm.
Only by understanding how it functions, can one
appreciate the importance of power in the modern
economy or the disadvantages under which the competitive, market-oriented firm operates.

IV

Although unequal power has long been central to Galbraith's view of society, it is significant that
prior to the publication of The New Industrial State
(1967), he focused largely upon imbalances between the
private and public sectors of the economy rather than
those between large and small businesses. This shift
in emphasis reflects his growing awareness of the systemic roots of the imbalances with which he was
dealing.

    Significantly, he has indicated that prior to
going to India he felt that The New Industrial State
was almost finished, locked it in a bank vault and returned to find it was hardly begun. The import of
this admission seems to be related to the fact that
it had been almost 15 years since he had served a government agency. In that time, both the organization
and the temper of the State Department had been radically transformed.

    During the New Deal era, he recalls,[25] his col-
leagues had been unassuming civil servants, there had
been little "make work," the White House had always
been accessible and relations between foreign countries and Washington had been respectful and polite.
After World War II, however, increasing world responsibility necessitated an increasingly complex organization in Washington. Accordingly, there developed
an intricate bureaucracy, the members of which gained
their power through their positions and their ability
to expand the scope of their particular agency. Consequently, there was a marked rise in the number of
people involved in any particular decision and an increasingly powerful array of agencies and subagencies.

This shift left a marked impression upon Galbraith:
  The far more serious problem is that the State
  Department is simply too large and with size has
  come an inflexibility that is as inevitable as it
  is incredible. The reason is simple: there are
  more people on C Street than there are problems.
  Nothing is so serious for a crypto-Tallyrand as
  unemployment. By common understanding, therefore,
  everyone insists on, and by common consent everyone is accorded a finger in every important
  pie.[26]
Witnessing the new-found power of those within the
organization, Galbraith was forced to reassess his
understanding of the process of decision making as
well as his understanding of the nature of power in
the modern industrial society.

     As noted in the previous chapter, his perspective
predisposes him to see the rise of the large corporation as an organic response to an altered structure
of opportunities. Thus, he argues that in order to
take advantage of sophisticated technological developments, a corporation must expand in order to accomodate an increasingly specialized work force. Additionally, vast resources must be made available to
underwrite the costs of research, development, production and marketing. Again, size is of the essence
since only the large corporation, by retaining a
healthy share of earnings,can reap the compensatory
advantages of internal financing and thus free itself
from inflated and/or unstable interest rates.

     Although at times Galbraith is unclear as to
whether the key variable is the sheer size of the
firm or the structure of the various industries[27] in
which it operates, he seems to view the two as mutually supportive characteristics. Another confusion
occurs due to his frequent use of the defense industry
corporations (which function largely in a single
product market) as illustrations of the tendencies
which he describes. This emphasis has led Bruce Scott,
for one, to argue that Galbraith's argument "takes
account of only one of the two technological trends
which have been shaping corporate strategy." According to Scott, "he has failed to consider the
other aspect of modern technology which has influenced
the corporation--namely the development of new
products via research."[28] Yet, as will become clear
in section six, Galbraith accords a central position

to technological virtuosity which is, by and large, equivalent to Scott's reference to "the impact of R & D on the creation of new products and new markets."

Walter Adams who, with a good many other economists would accept Galbraith's analysis insofar as it equates corporate growth with economies of scale, asserts that since it is the plant rather than the firm which can be said to benefit from large scale operations and integrated behavior, "there is little technological justification for combining these functionally separate plants into a single administrative unit." He continues, "United States Steel is nothing more than several Inland Steels strewn about the country, and no one has yet suggested that Inland is not big enough to be efficient." In fact, argues Adams, conglomerate size may well be a mask for inefficiency insofar as the diversified corporation can apply gains in one industry against losses in another and thus has a constant margin for error or inefficiency.[29]

While acknowledging the plausibility of this argument, Galbraith takes these same observations and weaves them into a somewhat different mesh. His evolutionary perspective leads him to view mergers and conglomerates as purely natural developments. The corporation, he argues, is only interested in efficiency _per se_ as it bears upon its own ends. What this suggests is that given the opportunity, the corporation will "mind the main chance," if you will, and expand into new fields and increase existing operations in order to protect its own interests. Planning, rather than efficiency, is what goads corporate behavior.[30]

Planning in Galbraith's view consists not only of foreseeing required steps to initiate developments and of determining how much of each particular commodity will be produced, but also of effecting and stabilizing the market response. The primary distinction between this type of planning and the planning of the small firm is that in addition to determining product line, plant location, manufacturing techniques, scale and organization of production and output level, the mature corporation also exerts immeasurable influence on both the cost of inputs and the price of outputs, a prerogative denied the small firm. It is also clear that the large concerns have a much greater leaverage in bargaining with suppliers and influencing purchasers.

70

Given its vast commitment of both time and resources to each production process, the large corporation cannot afford to subject itself to the uncertainties of either competition or the market. It must be able to calculate far in advance just how much capital must be set aside. It also must be relatively sure that there will be a suitable level of demand for the particular product.

Both of these needs can be satisfied to a large extent by the combined use of several available techniques for stabilizing the competitive market. Suppliers can either be directly owned or adopted as satellite firms; long-standing contracts can insure that the desired quantity is available at the desired price. Diversification can protect the corporation against slack demand for any particular product.[31] The market can be controlled by a quasi-collusive policy of price stabilization whereby prices are set by the largest corporation in the industry.[32] Additionally, labor can be placated by conceding its demands since the union contract allows management of the product.[33] Finally, demand can be generated through advertising and/or government contracts. All told, security can be maximized insofar as "Competition in prices, the key to the classical code, is vitiated or wiped out entirely."[34]

Galbraith's point, then, is that the corporation by taking advantage of the extant opportunity structure can further its own ends by eliminating the uncertainties of the market.[35] In this sense, the rise of the large corporation "is in the service not of monopoly or economies of scale but of planning. And for this planning--control of supply, control of demand, provision of capital, minimization of risk--there is no clear upper limit to desirable size."[36] It is this interpretation which sets Galbraith's analysis apart from that of the more conventional economists who attempt to understand the large corporation within the context of the competitive market. Even Myron Sharpe, in his largely negative critique of the Galbraithian vision, concedes the importance of Galbraith's approach.
The uniqueness of Galbraith's view on monopoly and competition is to be found in his emphasis on technology. Most economists discuss the suppression of patents, but they do not acknowledge the need to protect existing investments in plant and machinery. They carefully scrutinize large

71

firms which hold back innovations from public
use; they say nothing of industries in which
small firms and competition are typical and in
which innovations do not take place at all. Galbraith's recurring theme is that the slight decline of efficiency in concentrated industries
is more than offset by large gains from technological development.[37]

Due to Galbraith's level of generalization, he
never addresses himself to the issue of whether it is
the large or medium sized corporation which originally
initiates the technological advancement. According
to his scheme, what is important is that largely all
changes take place within the oligopolistic sector of
the economy as opposed to the less well organized
market sector to be discussed in section five. Herein
lies at least part of the reason for his dismissal of
the oft-heard proposal to stimulate competition among
the oligopolies by transforming them from assymetrical
to symmetrical structures (with comparably sized firms
instead of one leader and two or three medium sized
followers).[38] In his view, this would not significantly reduce the giants' advantage over their much
smaller and highly competitive suppliers and distributors.

Galbraith's view that the rise of the large corporation is natural and progressive should not, as is
often the case, be taken to indicate a preference for
powerful cartels and monopolies over competition and
economic freedom.[39] Nor should it be seen as a reflection of "his contempt for hard work and his un-
mistakable dislike of the conscientious small businessman who has a passion for 'self-exploitation.'"[40]
Given his holistic perspective, he views change as
both inevitable and necessary; with changes come a
host of new historical imperatives. Thus, the planning of the mature corporation is not willful, but
inherent to the whole matrix of development. It is
for this reason that Galbraith labels this segment of
the economy as the planning system to differentiate it
from the market system.

Although Robert Fitch asserts that Galbraith is
an ideologist "who would do for monopoly capitalism
what the Jesuits did for Catholicism--establish its
compatibility with humanity,"[41] the point to be appreciated is that the mature corporation can be
brought into the service of the public only by under-

standing its organization and operation. In an attempt
to understand and analyze the mature corporation, Galbraith has emphasized not its efficiency and humanity,
as Fitch contends, but rather the disparities resulting
from the unrestrained power afforded by the emergent
corporate structure. His concern with the social
import of this transition becomes clear in his discussion of corporate manipulation of the consumer and
his analysis of the resultant diseconomies, the subjects of chapter five. It is equally clear in his
analysis of the powerlessness of the market-oriented
firm discussed below.

Before turning to Galbraith's analysis of the
small firm it may be useful to consider the influence
of Marx and Veblen upon his analysis of the modern
industrial society. He concurs with them regarding
the implicit tendencies toward corporate concentration
but uses this as a springboard for a quite distinct
conclusion. He rejects Marx's prediction of the
growing misery of the workers, seeing them instead as
becoming more and more enmeshed in the organizational
matrix and more than able to satisfy their basic needs.
Although spiritual misery there may be, material misery has been eliminated to a large degree for the
majority of workers. Poverty, although by no means
unimportant, is no longer the common condition.

Equally untenable in Galbraith's mind is Veblen's
prediction of the denouement of business industry at
the hands of the machine process or the dynastic
state.[42] Instead, Galbraith posits a pattern of development which leaves the corporation with unrestrained power, free from the constraints of the
market. By emphasizing production (by workers),
prices (of materials and goods), policies (of government and regulatory agencies) and consumption (by
the public), the mature corporation insures its own
longevity by conditioning people to a way of life
which serves corporate interests and perpetuates
corporate power.

V

On the other hand, there remain at least twelve million small firms which have been excluded, almost by
definition, from participation in the "planned"
economy. Although they provide half of the private
economic output they must, being small, maximize their
profits in order to survive the competition of related

73

firms. Yet, even given profit maximization, because they lack the ability to save, they remain dependent upon the uncertain financial market. This, in turn, retards their ability to finance technological innovation; it also disallows expensive campaigns to manipulate the consumer or influence the state.

These are the firms which conform to the neoclassical model and serve to justify faith in the free enterprise system. On occasion, a small firm may by wit or guile secure a virtual monopoly of a given market in a given geographical location, but it is generally a tenuous command, circumscribed by the ease of entry, the ability of a motorized population to elude unreasonable subjection by transporting its business to another location and by the inability of even the monopolistic small firm to exert its power over its own costs. The point, then, is that although the small firms may well attempt to escape from the constraints of the market, they lack the resources available to the mature corporations. They must, therefore, concentrate on differentiation of their products and services rather than control of prices, costs and demand. While the mature corporations can turn to other suppliers in order to obtain more favorable prices, the small firm lacks alternatives. Similarly, while the financial distress of the mature corporation (e.g., Lockheed) is often offset by a sympathetic government agency, the demise of the small firm is accepted as a natural result of ineptitude in the face of shrewder competitors. Further, the ease of entry into their product fields denies small firms the chance to gain control of the market or to establish tacit agreements over pricing arrangements.

Since prices are established and maintained through competition in the market sector of the economy, it is not surprising that Galbraith's analysis of their performance has evoked little negative criticism save the charges that his analysis bespeaks contempt and casts competition into the role of the primary enemy.[43] It has, however, been argued that Galbraith underestimates the amount of technological innovation within the market economy. The small competitive firm, it is suggested, often has greater motivation to innovate in order to gain an advantage within the market.[44] While not disputing this point, Galbraith's claim is that most of the technological dynamic of the market oriented firms comes from external sources.

Agriculture, for instance, is progressive largely because of the research sponsored by government funded
institutions such as the experimental stations or
extension councils. Similarly, he cliams, technical
improvement among small firms "is underwritten by
large firms or...it is the overflow of work that has
come out of the universities or it is sanctioned by
(say) the Atomic Energy Commission or some other
agency of the government."[45]

By and large, what Galbraith calls the market
economy consists of firms or persons whose tasks are
geographically dispersed and whose activities are
limited or unstandardized. Typical in this regard
are farmers, service representatives, retailers, small
manufacturers and artists. Characteristically, their
activities are limited to small scale, require only
low levels of technology and are not conducive to
organization. Lacking organization, they also lack
power over costs, output and prices and, thus, remain
subject to market constraints.

Participants in the market system who want
stabilization of their prices or control of their
supply must act collectively or get the assistance of the government. Such effort is highly
visible and often ineffective, unsuccessful or
inefficient. Voluntary collective efforts can be
destroyed by a few deserters. Legislators do not
always respond--even to farmers.[46]

Compounding their weakness is their intrinsic
relationship with the mature corporations which, as
indicated, effectively dominate their economic envi-
ronments. Since those in the market system are often
dependent upon the planning system for resources and
sales as well as consumer items, it follows that there
is an ineluctable bias built into the economic system.
While in theory all firms pay the same prices for
their inputs, costs generally reflect the buyer's
bargaining power (or lack of such power). This is
particularly evident in the case of finance capital
which is much more readily available to the large
firm. The lower unit cost of loans to the mature
corporations reflects not only the lower bank-cost in
making such loans, but also the relative security of
the loan. Both the size and the proven reliability
of the large corporation accord it a favorable position
in applying for external funds. In consequence, Galbraith argues, the "central problem of the modern economy is unequal development."[47] This, as suggested

earlier, spawns grave inequality of income which is unrelated to either productivity or efficiency.

Galbraith freely concedes that the world of the small firms is by no means homogeneous. Its heterogeneity, however, by no means invalidates the claim that the overall performance and general tendencies of the market system reveal a marked dissimilarity from those of the planning system. Significantly, Galbraith emphasizes the fact that some of the participants have been more successful than others in exerting control over their economic environment. Yet, even the most successful lack the power afforded the mature corporations. It is with this understanding that one must consider Murray Weidenbaum's charge:

> The "downtrodden groups," those in the sectors of the economy not dominated by a few large firms, comprise a heterogeneous array. The largest group, the services, ranges from hamburger countermen to physicians, from gas station attendants to lawyers, domestics to dentists--not all quite the wretched of the earth.[48]

The point to be borne in mind when considering this critique is that doctors, dentists and lawyers are unique in their access to professional organizations-- the AMA, ADA and ABA--which safeguard their interests and control entry into the field. This control, however, is not comparable to that exerted by mature corporations, since the nature of their services precludes extensive reliance upon complex organization. Since a premium is placed upon personal service, it is not possible to reap the economies of large scale or to institute technological innovations which could improve efficiency and reduce costs. Similarly, the professionals' command over external economies--the price of materials--is limited due to their lack of bargaining power with their suppliers.

One finds a comparable situation within the construction industry. Whereas commercial builders can be relatively sure of a steady demand, no such advantage is afforded residential builders. Thus, while electricians, carpenters and plumbers in concentrated metropolitan areas are able to unionize, those in the outlying areas find organization much less rewarding. Not only is unionization frustrated by the seasonal nature of their work, but also by the unreliability of demand. To unionize would effectively deny them the ability to fill openings which arise in nonunionized firms and, hence, impair rather than improve their situation. Their weakness is compounded by the sheer number of firms which are forced to compete for the limited supply of work. Thus it is that Galbraith argues that unevenness is the central characteristic of the modern economic system.

His primary emphasis is upon the fact that whereas the planning system can absorb wage increases due to its control over its own prices, the market system, still dependent upon profit maximization and competitive pricing, lacks this latitude. Given the planning system's prices and costs, the problem must be seen as systemic. Comparing this inequity to Third World Imperialism, Galbraith maintains that both reflect the same power disparity and that protesting imperialism while overlooking the weakness of the market-oriented firm is to perpetuate very real injustices. It is also to misunderstand the causes of the exploitation which are linked not to cultural chauvinism but to the indifference of the planning system to the rights and needs of all weaker sellers and buyers which can be bent to serve its ends.[49]

In essence, then, while the corporate evolution described in the previous section remains beyond the reach of some twelve million business concerns, its impact upon their existence has been profound. It has reduced them to the position of pawns at once denied access and subject to the demands of the planning system. They are forced to compete among themselves in order to remain economically viable and yet their costs and prices are controlled not by an impersonal market but an all too personal corporate network.

That their plight goes unrecognized is largely due to the hold which orthodox thought has upon the perceptions of economists and politicians.[50] Taught to view free enterprise and the competitive market as the most socially beneficent organizational form, they tend to be more interested in studying specific diseconomies than in entertaining the possibility that corporate evolution may, in fact, have invalidated accepted policy and introduced very real power disparities into the socioeconomic system. Similarly, their proposals reflect their belief that more strenuous competition within the market is the surest means of promoting economic welfare.

Equally telling is the emphasis which economists place upon aggregate economic indices. What is emphasized is the effect upon <u>total</u> demand, <u>total</u> employment and <u>total</u> production. So long as these are rising, it is assumed that a general improvement in economic performance and, by extension, in the quality of life is taking place. This is not to suggest that economists are insensitive to the fact that the market has limitations and deficiencies, but, rather, that in their professional analyses, they tend to award structural variables a secondary role as compared to aggregate measurements. Thus, the differential impact of policies on the planning and market systems is never called into question. In consequence, one detects an inconsistency between avowed values and actual practice.

> The small businessman and the competitive sector of the economy are deeply beloved in principle; their fate, however, inspires no particular concern in practice except, perhaps, as it may be tied to historic symbols such as the antitrust laws. In considerable measure the liturgy of small business serves as a substitute for action.[51]

To understand this is to understand much of the existing injustice. Yet, a full understanding depends on an appreciation of the manner in which the mature corporation functions and the goals it pursues.

VI

Although Galbraith's emphasis upon the importance of power in the modern society might seem to place him among the defenders of an elitist theory of American society, the manner in which he deals with its location suggests a somewhat different interpretation. This is not to say that he depicts a pluralistic arrangement, but merely that he rejects the notion that power is confined to the top echelon of managers and militarists. Instead, he suggests that power, although lodged in a relatively small number of institutions, has become diversified. In a sense, it has passed <u>into</u> the organization rather than being imposed from without.

Galbraith's analysis is predicated on the much discussed managerial revolution, spawned by increasing specialization and the widespread distribution of stock holdings, which multiplied administrative problems manyfold and effectively severed ownership from control.[52] These structural changes, as is widely agreed, had a profound impact upon both manpower requirements and administrative organization. The result, as Max Weber characterized it, was the creation of an "iron cage of bureaucracy." The tendency which Weber foresaw was the increasing replacement of the moneyed elite by trained specialists. Education and training rather than status and privilege were becoming the basis for appointments; rules rather than traditions were coming to sanction behavior.[53] Statistically, the trend has long been clear: whereas the number of persons involved in independent business enterprise increased a mere two and one-half times between 1870 and 1940, managerial employees increased fourteen times and technicians increased forty times.[54]

Galbraith's reentry into the State Department, as suggested earlier, made him sensitive to the fact that power was no longer the province of the top echelon but had, in fact, come to penetrate the bureaucracy at all levels of decision making. Each group passed its judgments to its superiors who used these inputs to formulate their own assessments. It was this development which prompted Galbraith to observe that "No sane man should ever take a staff position as distinct from some line of responsibility in Washington. One should get his power, not from above but from the job below."[55] This, he came to believe, possibly because of his own dependence for information during his Ambassadorial stint,[56] was an organizational imperative. With increasing diversification and specialization, no one individual could acquire the needed knowledge about all aspects of an issue or situation to formulate a decision.

This recognition seems to have had a profound impact upon his understanding of corporate organization. Thus, he argues that decisions are made by diverse groups of specialists--researchers, designers, accountants, lawyers, economists, engineers, personnel specialists, public relations agents and other experts--who pool their knowledge in order to determine and advance corporate goals. The members of the technostructure, as Galbraith calls this group, derive their power not from personal qualifications, but from their participation in their various institutions. Only as they pool their varied knowledge, talents and experiences can decisions be made. It is thus organized intelligence rather than individual excellence which commands power.[57]

The point, of course, is not that top management has no power, but that it has only partial power since it must depend upon men much further down the corporate ladder for information and judgments. So long as these individuals perform in such a way as to facilitate moderate gains and preserve the corporation's standing within its field, top management has no reason to interfere.

This aspect of Galbraith's analysis seems to bear the imprint of his experiences as chief price administrator during World War II. Significantly, he recalls being confronted with requests drawn up by teams of technical experts of all kinds. As he has commented, "To have checked any of these claims would have required a comparable team of experts who, in fact, could probably only have been obtained by robbing the corporations who were engaged in producing the goods."[58] It is for this reason that Galbraith argues that "nearly all powers--initiation, character of development, rejection or acceptance--are exercised deep in the company. It is not the managers who decide. Effective power of decision is lodged deeply in the technical, planning and other specialized staff."[59] In this view (to be analyzed more fully below), top managers have become pivotal adjuncts to an increasingly populated structure. While they retain prerogatives over their own salaries and bonuses, they consistently yield to the specialists when it comes to specific issues and policies.

Not surprisingly, this aspect of Galbraith's model has not been well received by more radical economists who link managerial prerogative and monopoly capitalism to an elitist theory of social organization. Accordingly, he has been charged with blurring the distinction between top management and middle level executives. Ackerman and MacEwan, for example, have argued: "By confusing the two groups, Galbraith makes it sound as if management power comes from technical expertise rather than by virtue of being at the top of the corporate hierarchy."[60] In contrast, they hold that control is still firmly wielded by the corporate elite which commands controlling stock interests.

A middle ground is suggested by Robert Heilbroner. He concurs with Galbraith insofar as he sees power being increasingly commanded by a professional elite, but suggests that Galbraith's claim that this shift has been completed oversimplifies the situation. The

importance Galbraith grants the experts, Heilbroner
maintains,
> masks the fact that there is going on within
> American capitalism a contest between the forces
> of science and technology and the older forces
> of wealth and ownership....the tensions between
> the Old Guard and the New needs to be brought to
> the fore, not hidden behind the undifferentiated
> screen of the technostructure.[61]

The point which must be emphasized is that the
debate revolves around the definition of effective
power. To Galbraith, it is not plenary power, but the
ability to shape decisions and formulate policies
which is important. He freely admits that the top
managers retain the "power of casting personnel, initiating major changes, reorganizing the bureaucracy,"
but insists that the "power of substantive decision
passes into the technostructure."[62] Herein lies the
essential disagreement between Galbraith and his
critics. By taking a functional view of power, Galbraith rejects the notion that the corporation remains
primarily in the service of an elite class of managers
and directors.

In fact, argues Galbraith, the technostructure,
in its allegiance to the corporation, maintains a set
of priorities which are geared to maximize success
rather than profits. The technostructure, as Galbraith depicts it, is a self-serving bureaucracy which
seeks, above all else, its own security and expansion
and, consequently, practices what might be called a
pacification policy: by maintaining a secure minimum
of earning, it is able to placate stockholders with
dividends and managers with reinvestable earnings.
> Whatever serves this purpose--the stabilization
> of prices, the control of costs, the management
> of consumer response, the control of public
> purchases, the neutralization of adverse tenden-
> cies in prices, costs or consumer behavior that
> cannot be controlled, the winning of government
> policies that stabilize demand or absorb undue
> risk--will be central to the efforts of the
> technostructure and the corporation.[63]
Having achieved this security, however, it can abandon
its altruistic mantle and begin advancing goals designed to insure its own survival.[64]

Like any organism, the technostructure is obsessed
with growth; it must expand its perimeters lest it be

forced to make concessions which jeopardize existing
positions within the corporation. To the individual
expert, expansion spells "more jobs with more responsibility and hence more promotion and more compensation."[65] Thus, by developing new markets or expanding existing markets, the individual can further both
corporate and personal interests. Additionally, he
can prove himself and his worth to the corporation by
displaying his technological virtuosity through the
development of new products and the "improvements" of
existing products.[66] Again, the goal is increased
output rather than increased consumer satisfaction.

The importance which Galbraith attaches to the
rise of the technostructure again seems to reflect
his reformist disposition. So long as power is
wielded by an educated elite, rather than a moneyed
elite, change is possible. To humanize corporate behavior, if you will, requires only that specialists
begin to redirect their energies into areas of development which further consumer welfare. Since the
technostructure is not primarily interested in
pecuniary reward (as were the entrepreneurs), it is
more responsive to proposals for social innovation
and/or reform. The cost, conveniently, can be passed
forward (to the consumer) or backward (to the stockholder). Further, given the corporation's thirst for
qualified talent, the "educational and scientific
estate" acquires an elevated status which serves as
a potential source of power and can, as Galbraith
argued in The New Industrial State, be "the necessary
force for skepticism, emancipation and pluralism."[67]

                           VII
While Galbraith places less emphasis upon the role
of the intellectual in his later books, his faith in
education as a means of emancipation of belief remains
unshaken. Although an analysis of his propsed vehicles
of emancipation must be withheld until the sixth
chapter, it seems appropriate to explore his felt-
need for emancipation at this point in order to round
out the discussion of his view of American society.
As noted, what most intrigues Galbraith is the persistence of chronic imbalances which could be eliminated. To understand the roots of these imbalances
requires an appreciation of the power which the
planning system has acquired over public policy.

Government presence within the economy is by now
a more or less accomplished fact. Galbraith's anal-

ysis of this development places him in a middle
position between the libertarians and the Marxists.[68]
He sees government intervention not as a counter-
revolution, as it is depicted by the libertarians, or
as an attempt to check the anarchy inherent within
capitalism, as claimed by the Marxists. Instead, he
sees this development as a pragmatic response to an
increasingly concentrated economic structure. The
large corporation's acceptance of government intervention, a development documented by Monsen and
Cannon,[69] is depicted in a similar manner.

Significant in this regard is the fact that Galbraith initially viewed the differential impact of
monetary and fiscal policy upon the market and planning system as the coincidental outgrowth of dissimilar market structures.[70] Of late, however, he has
come to argue that these disparities are intentional
insofar as the planning system, which has a great
influence upon public policy, only endorses those
policies which favor its particular situation. Thus
monetary and fiscal policy are accepted largely because they stabilize demand and diminish market risk,
both of which facilitate planning and corporate
growth. That their impact upon the entrepreneurial
firm is less salutary comes as no surprise. These
firms are much more dependent upon the external
financial market and hence feel the impact of inflated
interest rates to a much greater degree.

Additionally, the large corporation has become
the primary recipient of government exemptions, research grants, contracts and preferences. Increasingly, government expenditures are devoted either to
military or technical developments. It is this
development which has allowed the mature corporation
to establish a virtual symbiosis with the government--
an advantage far beyond the ken of the smaller, less
powerful market-oriented firm.

While some have charged that the regulatory
agencies constitute a bar against the very symbiosis
which Galbraith describes, the facts seem to favor
Galbraith. It has been estimated, for example, that
"inefficient and unfair regulation costs the average
American family $2,000 a year" largely because busi-
ness "has the power and resources to make their
positions known to the agencies that regulate them."[71]
Thus it was that in 1972, the Federal Aviation Administration was persuaded by McDonnel-Douglas to make

the requirements to repair a faulty cargo door on the
DC-10's permissive rather than mandatory; the cost
was clear in 1974 when one of them crashed near Paris,
killing 344 people. In another instance, concessions
by the Federal Power Commission to natural gas companies   to increase prices in 1974 cost consumers $3-$5
billion; the six year delay in instituting a prohibition against the use of flammable materials in
children's sleepwear resulted in thousands of serious
burns. Without unnecessary multiplication of examples,
it seems reasonable to concur with Nossiter's finding
that "the overwhelming testimony is that the regu-
lators in time become the captives of the regulated,
that the commissions become the captives of the industry they are supposed to police."[72] This has been
the record of virtually every agency instituted
since 1887.[73]

     This tendency is amply illustrated by both the
increasing financial bonding between the two net-
works and the recurrent exchanges of personnel between
them.[74] The importance of this situation is that it
effectively eliminates the line between the government
and the private enterprises which are supposedly being
regulated. As members become more or less inter-
changeable, "each organization comes to accept the
other's goals....Each organization, accordingly, is an
extension of the other."[75]

     Just as the representatives of the industrial
system serving on commissions and councils reach conclusions supporting the need for more military expenditures, these same foundations award grants and
sponsor research in areas which best further their own
interests. As Galbraith has argued:
          That defense requirements are set purely by nat-
          ional interest, that they are independent of any
          needs of the industrial system, is a useful form-
          ula. It sanctifies expenditures that could not be
          defended if they were specifically for support to
          the industrial system. It likewise lends credence
          to the belief, important for the autonomy of the
          technostructure, that a deep chasm separates state
          and private business.[76]
Galbraith became acutely aware of this development
during the Bay of Pigs debacle which seemed to reflect
the growing power of both the military interests and
the CIA upon foreign policy.[77] The Vietnam conflict
again reflected the power of those intent upon

increasing our military involvement and hence our
military expenditures. The problem, as Galbraith has
come to define it, is inherent in bureaucratic organization which seems to possess a propensity for continuing extant policies and preoccupations. Thus,
argues Galbraith, "the inertial dynamic of the bureaucracy" is the major explanation of the disasters of
the sixties. "At the Bay of Pigs, in the Dominican
Republic, in Vietnam, Laos, Thailand (as again in
Cambodia), the bureaucracy showed its power to sweep
the leadership into disaster against all the councils
of common sense."[78]

The irony of the current relationship is that the
government manifestly favors the large corporation at
the expense of the less organized and more vulnerable
segments of the economy. As Galbraith once observed,
The Government can go into West Virginia and
sink $50-or 70-million into an electronic mon-
itoring apparatus which doesn't work, and this is
dismissed as a minor error. But spend $5,000 on
some dead-end youngster and you're really in
trouble. Anything done on behalf of the poor
arouses the passion of one dismal kind of
political critic.[79]
Similarly, when a corporation such as Lockheed, Consol-
idated Edison or Penn Central announces a state of
financial distress, the government, in the name of
preserving free enterprise and achieving economic
stability, ignores the possibility of public ownership and opts instead to stabilize the industry
through loans and grants. Meanwhile, poverty program
budgets are curbed because they are said to constitute
an inflationary impetus.

A further irony emerges as orthodox thinkers defend subsidizing the mature corporation while they
vehemently deny that such action effectively transforms these concerns into public institutions. But,
argues Galbraith, if the distinction between the
private and public sectors of the economy is to retain any meaning, it is essential that those firms
which have evolved beyond the entrepreneurial stage be
taken for what they are. Pragmatic response to the
new relationship between the corporation and the state
requires a new understanding which facilitates direct
intervention into corporate policy. Currently, Galbraith argues, "where there is a clash between corporate goals and the public interest--as with the safety
of products, industrial effects on the environment,

the effect of price and wage settlements on the economy, the equity of profits, or the appropriateness of executive compensation--there is no natural right of the corporation to be left alone."[80] Hence, the need to view the large corporation as a <u>public institution</u>, and to reassess national goals and policies in order to determine whether they are in the service of the technostructure or the larger population.

Given pressing social needs, Galbraith contends, our obsession with increasing production and private consumption--goals which directly serve the interests of the planning system--become less and less defensible. We fail to consider their implications for the individual, the environment or those firms which remain subject to the constraints of the market.

So long as the planning system determines when, where and how much investment should be initiated, this neglect is likely to persist. Subject to no effective regulation, these corporations are able to set the order of priorities on national growth, technological innovation and expansion and conformity.[81] They are also able to deny those outside the planning system access to power and, hence, force them to operate at a disadvantage. Thus, provision of welfare, housing and urban services are undervalued because their recipients lack a power base through which to exert influence upon the government. In fact, with the possible exception of commercial agriculture, "the distribution of public resources reflects the power of the planning system over the state."[82]

To understand the impact which this development has had upon the individual and the environment, it now becomes necessary to explore in some detail the notion of consumer sovereignty and the rise of the advertising industry. Following this discussion, it will be possible to understand the manner in which social goals and priorities have come to serve the interests, not of the individual, but of the mature corporation.

Implicit in the Galbraithian philosophy is a voluntaristic conception of history. The individual, although sometimes deluded by outmoded thought systems, is viewed as an active agent capable of directing and determining the type of social organization which best suits his/her needs. Human nature, far from being static or innate, is viewed as emergent and situationally determined. In consequence, Galbraith depicts the system as an outgrowth, not of capital investment, but "improvements in men and improvements brought about by highly improved men."[1]

Herein lies the importance of the aforementioned development of advanced technology and specialized knowledge; it has allowed the mature corporation to transcend the market and achieve a productivity and power beyond the reach of the entrepreneurial firm. Thus, the power resident in the technostructure must be seen as the result not of conspiracy, but of evolution. That such an evolution has been beneficial in terms of increasing economic growth and raising the standard of living, Galbraith freely concedes. His concern, however, is with the resultant disparities which have accompanied these increases.

In a society keynoted by powerful economic institutions, the traditional balance of power which enabled the individual to test his mettle against others and expect at least to break even has been invalidated. The individual entrepreneur is no longer the key agent in the capitalist process any more than consumer welfare is the spur to economic development. Instead, one finds powerful bureaucracies advancing their own goals and conditioning the public to relinquish personal values and ends.

The importance which Galbraith attaches to this transformation must be seen as a reflection of his progressive orientation. Believing that society is meant to be a vehicle through which individuals realize their own goals and find a sense of fulfillment, he is intent upon creating a system which safeguards individual liberty. It is for this reason that he emphasizes the importance of asking not whether the system is working, but whose interests it is serving.

Although his rationale is largely an extension
of Jeffersonian values, the means he advances are
essentially Hamiltonian. Increasingly, he has come
to appreciate that individual liberties are contingent
upon increasing centralization and nationalization.
The task is to identify and strengthen the weakest
participants in the economy rather than to attempt to
restore competition. Additionally, there is the need
to bring the technostructure into the service of
public, rather than corporate, goals and to provide
for those services which the individual cannot provide
for him/herself. In short, there is a need to achieve
a balance between public services and private services,
between what is shared collectively and what is con-
sumed individually. Galbraith's point, then, is "that
you do not have liberty in the absence of law and order
or in the absence of a good educational system, which
liberates the mind; that there isn't much advantage in
having freedom if you can't breathe the air; that there
isn't much advantage to go swimming if the water is
lethal."[2]

Irving Kristol has suggested that Galbraith's
emphasis upon government intervention to rectify imbalances bespeaks an implicitly anti-capitalist ethos
which has transmuted the ideological substance of the
"Progressive-reform" tradition while retaining its
rhetorical emphasis. Accordingly, Kristol argues,
his proposals and those of a group Kristol calls the
"New Class" of professionals, involve a subversion of
liberal institutions.
Though they continue to speak the language of
"Progressive-reform," in actuality they are
acting upon a hidden agenda: to propel the nation
from that modified version of capitalism we call
"the welfare state" toward an economic system so
stridently regulated in detail as to fulfill
many of the traditional anti-capitalist aspirations of the Left.[3]
Kristol's argument is provocative, but it obscures the
imbalances in economic and political power which allow
the mature corporations to free themselves from the
risks of competition and to shape consumer response.
In fact, although he offers no evidence, he asserts
that Galbraith's view of the industrial system is a
"wild exaggeration."

His case is based upon the assertion that private enterprise is the most beneficent system and that it alone can safeguard individual liberty. The argument thus becomes somewhat tautological, since it assumes that institutions that were once liberal are, by definition, still liberal. The problem inherent in Kristol's position is that his static view of traditional rights and liberties makes him unable to understand the manner in which these have been divested of their critical import. Free enterprise means little to those people who, by virtue of age, incapacity or injustice, are unable to participate in the system and are, hence, unable to secure a subsistence level of income. It also means little to those who must transact business with mature corporations from positions of weakness. Enterprise can no longer be considered free when the giants have the power to set both their own prices and those available to their suppliers and distributors.

In large measure, economists and politicians wedded to the values of free enterprise, have overlooked these issues by concentrating their attention upon aggregate indexes. In so doing, they have been able to ignore persistent imbalances and, hence, to overlook existing disparities. Further, by equating increased production with social advancement, they have obscured the importance of the composition and distribution of aggregate output. For this reason, Galbraith argues that

> neoclassicism doesn't come to grips with the unevenness in growth--as between, say the housing industry and the automobile industry; it doesn't come to grips with the growing inequality in income and distribution; it doesn't come to grips with the problem of coordination of the different sectors of the economy now celebrated as the energy crisis...with the problem of environmental disharmonies. It--notably--does not come to grips with the problem of controls--or even admit to their need.[4]

It is for this reason that the paradoxes of our society have come to assume a focal position within Galbraith's vision. His holism predisposes him to consider the interrelationships between the various sectors of the economy, just as his pragmatism leads him to discard ideas which no longer seem to be facilitating responsive adaptation.

He recognizes, however, that those in positions
of power are deeply committed to preservation of the
status quo and tend either to ignore inconvenient analyses or to stigmatize them as "eccentric, unscientific,
lacking in scholarly precision or repute or otherwise
unworthy."[5] Thus, he has aimed his appeal at a broader
audience--an audience, incidentally, which in the
1970s has shown great concern over such issues as military involvement, environmental disharmony and persistent inflation. It is to those people who, however vaguely, have begun to sense that something is
amiss that Galbraith has directed his writing.[6] Significantly, he has repeatedly denied the charge that
he has "popularized" economics and has indicated that
he writes only for the discerning reader. He explains,
"I am prepared to say that only one-twentieth of 1 per
cent of the American people read books carefully. But
that's one hundred thousand people, and that's all
I ever ask for."[7]

In the main, one suspects that Galbraith's audience is concentrated in academic communities and consists primarily of those who are young and, hence,
more open to new interpretations.[8] Although many who
lack contact with academia have doubtless been exposed
to his ideas through the mass media, it seems unlikely
that the details of his analyses have had a major impact upon the thinking of the "unwashed masses," whose
plight he portrays. Instead, he has geared his appeal
to those who are (or may be) in positions from which
they can affect the plight of those denied equitable
treatment.

That Galbraith has chosen such a tactic is not
wholly surprising. The Scotch Liberals, like the
American populists, molded their political strategies
around the interests of the common people rather than
the respectable community, suspecting that anything
espoused by the latter group would doubtless serve the
interests of the elite at great expense to those outside its perimeters. The effectiveness of these early
efforts on the part of the populists and social democrats, both here and abroad, seems to have impressed
Galbraith with the general public's capacity for skepticism, as well as the importance of what might be
called the climate of opinion. Doubtless, his involvement with the Vietnam protests served to reaffirm his
belief that in an open society popular disillusionment
can very decidedly shape the course of events. This
experience also reinforced his faith in the ability of

professionals--academics, journalists and politicians--
to act as leaders of community opinion.

Being a student of history, however, Galbraith is
keenly aware of the ability of those in command to
safeguard their positions by endorsing a philosophy
which equates their activities with the welfare of the
society. Thus, while the populists rallied against
the rise of the robber barons following the Civil War,
businessmen propounded an ideology which wedded democracy to capitalism and proclaimed that business was
the surest source of the advancement and betterment of
the whole. Their success, in John Cawelti's assessment, was due, at least in part, to a blind spot in
American culture regarding the political import of
economic power. "Americans tended to make a basic
distinction between political and economic power, to
fear and restrict political power, to regard economic
power as essentially benevolent."[9] Consequently, the
American business creed has assumed a revered status
with competition and individualism "held both to explain the success and to provide the moral justification for American capitalism."[10] As Arthur Johnson
indicates, "the nineteenth century capitalist, competitive rationale, which fitted the corporate system
loosely even in that era, has continued to be articulated by business spokesmen (and until recently,
accepted by the public) with sincerity."[11]

In large measure, Galbraith argues, the success
and persistence of the business ideology can be attributed to the theoretical support it received from
neoclassical economics. Despite massive technological
and social changes, businessmen have clung to the competitive model formulated at a time when the typical
unit of production was small, local, individually
owned and owner operated. Despite the differences in
past and present economic structure, this model has
remained the defense of corporate prerogative.

Among other things, the competitive model solved
the problem of power by denying its very existence.
"Given the rigorous prescriptions of competition, there
was very little need for the exercise of private economic power and none for its misuse."[12] That this was
in keeping with American values and ideals, there can
be little doubt. Just at the time when the individual
was being subjected to the demands of a burgeoning
corporate structure, the ideology seemed to provide an
answer--the corporation remained subject to consumer

demands and, hence, insured consumer welfare. The very simplicity of the model, according to **Business Week**, appealed markedly to both businessmen and economists. "It calls for no intervention by the state, no centralized planning....provides an answer to anyone who charges business with abusing its power....No one has enough to abuse."[13]

As indicated in chapter three, Galbraith became disenchanted with this conception at an early stage of his career; he sensed that, rather than serving as a description of reality, the model had become a mere justification for the status quo.[14] Additionally, he came to believe that acceptance of the business ide-ology functioned to frustrate popular awareness of the massive changes which had affected the operation of the economy. In this sense, he felt it served to frustrate needed changes and dissuade people from engaging in constructive protest. The problem, as Galbraith defines it, is:

> The forces controlling belief have not been sufficiently identified. Nor the purpose of the control. Nor the techniques for such control. And, finally, it has not been seen that escape from the discipline of the planning system in-volves escape not from discipline altogether but a transfer to the greater discipline of self.[15]

For this reason, Galbraith, like Marx, has centered his attention around the construction of an alternative image of social organization--an image which he feels is more in keeping with present realities. It is his hope that once a new vision of society is available, the general public can gradually free itself and the system from unrealistic goals and policies.[16]

Of pressing importance to Galbraith is the need to revamp the criteria by which we measure our success and evaluate our public policies. In order to under-stand Galbraith's analysis of the position of the individual within contemporary American society and his rejection of the time-honored notion of consumer sovereignty, it is imperative that we first examine his critique of the primacy accorded production and mass consumption in this society.

II

Central to his vision is the increasing affluence which characterizes our society. Post World War II America has achieved a degree of richness unequalled by previous generations. Rising incomes plus a general availability of consumer credit have provided the consumer with seemingly limitless opportunities to increase his/her consumption. Yet, with all its wealth, America has not proven capable of solving the fundamental problems of economic life--inequality, insecurity and instability.

For the millions of Americans who continue to suffer from the deep-seated and pervasive misery spawned by poverty, the affluent society "ceases to be a reality or even a hope; it becomes a taunt."[17] The extant disparities are captured graphically by Robert Heilbroner.

> The uneasy coexistence of poverty and abundance--
> of prodigies of space exploration and pinched
> programs for education, of magnificent office
> buildings and squalid tenements--becomes even
> less defensible as our sheer productive capac-
> ity makes mockery of the age-old claim that
> poverty is a fact of life thrust upon us by the
> immovable presence of scarcity.[18]

The persistence of poverty amidst plenty, a phenomenon quite visible to the agricultural economist who is ever confronted with the powerlessness of small farmers, serves as a poignant reminder that economic forces do not have an equable impact upon all parts of society. Of comparable import is the inability of those who remain subject to the constraints of the market--those in agriculture, service, retail and small industry--to wield a countervailing power against the mature corporation.

Although many of those within the market system live above the subsistence level, and are thus free from the stigma of poverty, their existence is far from secure. What allows the small, unorganized firm to survive, according to Galbraith, is the persistence of exploitation, especially self-exploitation by which "the individual is induced, by his relative lack of economic power, to work for relatively less return than the economy generally pays for such effort."[19]

The point, then, is that the problem lies not with technology, but with our existing socioeconomic organization which is keynoted by a sharply skewed distribution of power and a markedly unequal distribution of income and wealth.[20] These two character-istics are, of course, mutually supportive. So long as one has power, one can more or less dictate one's own compensation; without power, no such opportunity exists.

Although these disparities have been rationalized by functionalists[21] as a reflection of the higher remuneration accorded those who make superior contributions or display unusual ingenuity, such a defense becomes increasingly untenable in the face of our unprecedented affluence. It is similarly weakened by the diminishing importance of the individual within the corporation. The committee has, in large measure, superceded the individual, a development which leads Galbraith to the following observation:

> It is the nature of organization that it takes men of average ability but diverse knowledge and combines their efforts for a result that is far better than any individual could achieve. To a marked extent it provides a substitute for exceptional talent--something that is recognized in practice in the total indifference of the stock market to changes in command in the great corporation and the Stygian obscurity into which the greatest entrepreneur disappears on the day he retires.[22]

Thus, to excuse disparities on the basis of individual differences is to overlook structural changes and to perpetuate very real injustices.

Another inherent weakness in the functionalist position is the fact that in a heterogeneous society, what is functional for one group is more often than not dysfunctional for other groups. Using poverty as a case in point, Herbert Gans, with tongue in cheek, has demonstrated that functional analysis can as easily be used to unmask the differential impact of various phenomena as to defend the status quo. In his study, he identifies fifteen sets of positive functions which are fulfilled by the persistence of poverty. Not surprisingly, these are functions which serve the interests of the affluent at great expense to the poor. Following a discussion of various functional alternatives, Gans concludes,

> that social phenomena which are functional for affluent groups and dysfunctional for poor ones persist; that when the elimination of such phenomena through functional alternatives generates dysfunctions for the affluent, they will continue to persist; and that phenomena like poverty can be eliminated only when they either become sufficiently dysfunctional for the affluent or when

the poor can obtain enough power to change the
system of social stratification.[23]
Herein lies the explanation for the fact that the
majority of orthodox thinkers continue to rely upon
a general increase in the standard of living--a solution which very often fails to improve the situation
of those with incomes below the subsistence level--to
lessen social inequalities and tensions.

In effect, increased production has come to be
seen as a panacea and as an "alternative to redistribution or even reduction of inequality."[24] This conclusion is borne out by the criticsm which The
Affluent Society has received for ignoring the need
to increase production in order to improve the position of the poor. Leon Keyserling's critique
is representative in this regard. He maintains that
"in the final analysis, their incomes can rise
significantly (except for those employed by the government) only through the expansion of those parts
of the economy which provide private employment and
wages and salaries." These, he continues, "must come
from a rapid increase in total production and total
national income."[25] As this criticism indicates,
typically it is production which is emphasized as the
means of reducing and possibly eliminating poverty
and inequality. Poverty programs are deemphasized
not because the problem has abated, but because the
conventional wisdom holds that increased production,
rather than redistribution of income, is the surest
means of achieving a "classless" society.

Creative measures geared to enhance economic
security and stability for those outside the planning
system have also been deemphasized. Economic insecurity, once viewed as central and/or inherent in the
self regulating business cycle has, according to Galbraith, been eliminated to a great extent for the
mature corporation. This has been facilitated by the
planning system's ability to reduce risks, obtain government subsidies and placate labor. Depression remains as the only serious threat since it alone might
impair the effectiveness of the elaborate network of
micro-measures which protect the planning system.
Hence, "prevention of depression remains the sine qua
non for economic security."[26]

To guard against a depression, a decline in aggregate demand must be prevented at all costs. As a
result, the mature corporation has gradually come to

embrace the tenets of Keynesian economics as a means of furthering their own interests. They have used the national commitment to full employment to justify unrestrained corporate growth as the surest means of insuring employment, income, security and stability. The difficulty of such a stance has, of late, become clear. The acceptance of the Phillips curve which designates an inverse correlation between prices and unemployment has led even the staunchest defenders of monetary and fiscal policy to admit that one must either accept inflation or unemployment as necessary conditions.[27]

The problem seems to stem in large measure from an absence of debate as to the goals of our economic efforts or the content of our economic future. In his study of the "harried leisure class," Staffan Burenstam Linder is struck by our tendency to "speak with amazement and admiration of the consumption miracle, conceiving of it as assuming ever larger proportions over the decade, without having any counterpart in another miracle--that of complete material satisfaction."[28] Although we will have occasion to return to this argument, for present purposes, it is important to emphasize that despite the persistence of poverty and insecurity among those barred from the planning system, we continue to measure our economic performance in terms of aggregate performance. This has had the effect of creating visions of a general affluence and obscuring the attendant disparities in distribution and production. It has also functioned to deemphasize the social and environmental diseconomies generated by increasing production and consumption.

The irony of this development is implicit in the assessment offered in 1972 by the Commission of Population Growth and the American Future. Rather than focusing upon aggregate production they conclude,

> we can also identify and measure the limiting
> factors, the inequalities of opportunity, and
> the environmental hazards that give rise to
> such limitations in the quality of life--for
> example, inadequate distribution of and access
> to health, education, and welfare services;
> cultural and social constraints on human per-
> formance and development associated with race,
> ethnic origin, sex and age; barriers to full
> economic and cultural participation; unequal
> access to environmental quality; and unequal
> exposure to environmental hazard.[29]

The problem, then, seems to be that our obsession with
growth has muted debate over the purpose of our economic activity and left us captive to the "thralldom of
a myth--the myth that production by its overpowering
importance and its ineluctable difficulty, is the
central problem of our lives."[30]

III

Galbraith's point is not that national prosperity is
unimportant, but that it is not a solution for poverty
or systemic imbalances. It is significant in this
regard to recall that Galbraith was extremely involved
in the drafting of the War on Poverty initiated under
the Kennedy Administration. Also of importance is his
campaign against tax reduction. The two are part and
parcel of his conviction that increased prosperity
"is not a remedy for the distress in our cities. And...
that the problem of the cities grows from a very bad
sense of priorities on the part of the Federal Government."[31] More specifically, he argued in 1964:

> The case for tax reduction rests on the need to
> reduce the dampening effect of taxation at high
> levels of output and income and thus insure that
> these levels are maintained. The further effect,
> it is argued, will be increased tax revenues
> from a better functioning economy. Whatever the
> merits of this case, it provides no support for
> the contention that needed tasks of government
> should be held back to facilitate the cut.[32]

As might have been anticipated, however, the 1964 Tax
Act and subsequent monetary and fiscal policies conjoined with increasing military expenditures have had
the effect of diverting funds from social services
and, hence, perpetuating existing disparities.

Echoing Keynes' prediction that the economic
problem is not "the permanent problem of the human
race," Galbraith has persistently emphasized the
diminishing relevance of increasing production for
its own sake. Instead he urges that we turn our
attention to humanitarian ends and attempt to work for
a better, more balanced society in which every individual has the freedom to shape his/her own destiny
and provide for his/her own basic needs. It is for
this reason that he, although far too Calvinistic to
endorse the drug movement, has applauded the efforts
of American youth to establish a viable, permissive
counter culture. Individual liberation, in his view,
rather than increased consumption and a rising stan-

dard of living should now be our primary social goal.

Keynes' prediction in 1930 was "that the standard of life in progressive countries one hundred
years hence will be between four and eight times as
high as it is today."[33] From this he reasoned that
the goals of personal fulfillment could at last be
substituted for those of increased production. In
many ways, argues Galbraith, this prediction has been
fulfilled much more quickly than Keynes expected or
could have expected. Heilbroner's figures bear out
this assessment.

> By 1944 we were spending more for war production
> than the entire value of GNP in 1933--and output
> and employment boomed accordingly....Gross Nat-
> ional Product which had reached a level of $213
> billion in 1945...reached $234 billion in 1947;
> $259 billion in 1949; $280 billion in 1950; an
> amazing $329 billion in 1951; $400 billion in
> early 1956; $500 billion in 1960; almost touched
> $750 billion in 1966; and triumphantly attained
> the unimaginable height of $1,000 billion--a
> trillion dollars--in the first years of the
> 1970's.[34]

Even given inflation, at least half of this increase
can be attributed to real increases in the available
quantity of goods and services.

This being the case, it is difficult to understand our continued obsession with increased production. Difficult, that is, if one fails to consider
the benign implications of the time-worn doctrine of
consumer sovereignty which constitutes the heart of
the orthodox philosophy. Breit and Ransom explain:
"The individual is imagined in a constant process of
delicately balancing his marginal expenditures and
marginal utilities."[35] The theory of consumer sovereignty thus has the effect of vesting the individual
with the ultimate power of decision in the economic
system. This is especially reassuring, observes Galbraith, "in a culture which sets a high and even
mystical store by the individual and which may suspect
that, somehow he is being threatened by organization."[36]

It is significant in this regard to observe that
James Roche, past chairman of General Motors, has
charged that the critics (a group he never delineates
with any precision) of consumer sovereignty have
attempted to undermine free enterprise and alienate
the consumer. Consumer legislation is, in his mind,

largely superfluous and wrong-headed and serves to shed doubt on the system's workability. In his estimation, "The entire success of free enterprise can be traced to the vitality it gains by competitive striving to satisfy the discriminatory customer. To destroy the concept of consumer supremacy is to destroy free enterprise."[37] The problem with this stance is not one of sincerity, but one of credibility.

The theory of consumer sovereignty involves two presuppositions--neither of which is applicable to today's economy. The first is the notion that the urgency of wants does not diminish as more goods and services are amassed. While the theory of diminishing marginal utility posits a decline in the satisfaction of more units of a particular commodity, economists have tended to adopt a neutral position regarding the urgency of new or additional wants. It is assumed that satisfactions will not decline as the individual accumulates more goods and services because the new acquisitions will fill needs distinct from those filled by previous purchases. As Galbraith notes, "The concept of satiation has very little standing in economics. It is neither useful nor scientific to speculate on the comparative cravings of the stomach and the mind."[38] Thus, in theory, the provision of health care is of no greater urgency than the need for longer tail fins and more chrome. Similarly, one cannot, and moreover should not, distinguish between material and psychic needs.

What this overlooks, however, is the distinction made earlier by Veblen, Keynes and other heretics, between absolute and relative needs. In Keynes' words, the difference is between "those needs which are absolute in the sense that we feel them whatever the situation of our fellow human beings may be, and those which are relative in the sense that we feel them only if their satisfaction lifts us above, makes us feel superior."[39] The point, to which we will return, which is often overlooked or disputed by Galbraith's critics, is that while relative needs may indeed be insatiable insofar as they have an invidious momentum of their own, absolute needs are not, since a point is soon reached at which "we prefer to devote our future energies to noneconomic purposes."[40]

The second tenet of the consumer demand theory holds that wants are original with the consumer who votes, as it were, for increased production of a

99

certain kind through his expenditures. Since these
wants are innate, it is not the place of the economist
to evaluate them. Nor is it the place of the government to attempt to alter the distribution of resources
between various sectors of the economy. So long as
the consumer is viewed as supreme economic man, "standards are set by economizing consumers and scarce resources allocated so as to maximize welfare."[41]

Herein lies the explanation for our somewhat selective commitment to production which leads us to
accept the disparate production levels of the planning and market system. Because it is ultimately the
sovereign consumer who decides what is produced, it
seems entirely reasonable to the economist to rely
upon market forces to determine the output of various
firms. The consequence of this attitude is that, in
the main, the emphasis is placed upon private goods.
Significantly, it is private consumption which is reflected in a rising standard of living, the traditional
measure of individual well-being. In emphasizing private consumption and deemphasizing public services
(except those which serve the needs of the planning
system), however, we are led to "view production of
some of the most frivolous goods with pride. We regard
the production of some of the most significant and
civilizing services with regret."[42] This disparity
will be discussed in more detail at a later point.

Galbraith, echoing Veblen, suggests that this
emphasis upon consumer goods is linked, in part, to
our value system which stresses individual success,
mobility and competition. "Because the society sets
great store by the ability to produce a high standard
of living," Galbraith maintains, "it evaluates people
by the products they possess."[43] The impact of Keynes'
emphasis upon expansion of aggregate demand has merely
reinforced this tendency. In effect, Keynesian theory
made increasing production the lodestone of American
politicians and Keynesian policy thus became the new
conventional wisdom. "The question of the distribution
of the products so produced--who gets it--is decidedly
secondary."[44]

IV

Galbraith's rejection of the notion of consumer sovereignty is premised both on the increasing affluence
of American society and the rise of modern advertising.
As noted in the previous chapter, predictable sales are
of cardinal importance to the planning system. In

consequence, the mature corporations have invested
billions of dollars into the creation of an elaborate
network of specialists whose sole purpose is to stimulate a reliable level of demand.[45] Galbraith explains:

> Included among the managers are those who sell
> goods and design strategies by which they are
> sold. And so are many who are thought of as en-
> gaged in the production of goods. The management
> of demand consists in devising a sales strategy
> for a particular product. It also consists in
> devising a product, or features of a product
> around which a sales strategy can be built. Pro-
> duction design, model change, packaging and even
> performance reflect the need to provide what are
> called strong selling points.[46]

Galbraith's point, then, is that with an increasing
superfluity of income, advertising gains its power
insofar as the individual becomes vulnerable to external persuasion or management as to what he/she
buys. Rather than the accepted sequence by which the
individual dictates his/her desires to the producer,
there emerges what Galbraith calls the revised sequence
by which "wants are increasingly created by the process by which they are satisfied."[47]

Herein lies the crux of Galbraith's argument. So
long as wants are not innate but are, rather, contrived, they cannot be viewed as urgent and cannot
be used to justify the ongoing urgency of production.[48]
This is particularly true when wants are created by the
same agencies which fulfill them--not in order to
increase consumer welfare, but, rather, to stimulate
consumption. Significantly, Robin Marris has reached
a similar conclusion. He observes that for the professional manager of the modern corporation, the "concept of consumer need disappears, and the only question
of interest in connection with a proposed new product
is whether a sufficient number of consumers, irrespec-
tive of 'real need,' can be persuaded to buy it."[49]

To raise such objections and question priorites
is, as Galbraith knows, non-objective and leaves the
critic open to charges of subjectivity and elitism.
But to accept the myth of consumer sovereignty is to
"give high moral and scientific sanction to social
indifference."[50] It is also to ignore the fact that
in the absence of the emphasis currently placed on
demand, the individual would be much freer of pressures
to consume.
    No one would have pressed upon them the advantages

of new packages, new forms of processed foods, newly devised dentifrices, new pain-killers or other new variants of older products. Being not pressed by the need for these things, they would have spent less reliably of their income and worked less rapidly to get more....Growth could not then remain a goal.[51]

The time has come, he argues, when considerations of compassion, individual well-being, economic security, humane working conditions and the minimization of social tensions should assume a primary position above strict considerations of productive efficiency and consumption.

To argue, as one reviewer has, that the urge to consume is not to be despised because it affords the individual access to civilization (which is defined as "the opportunity for human development beyond the merry-peasant level"[52]), is to miss Galbraith's main point. Neither manufacturers nor advertisers aim to spread the comforts of civilization. Their goal is to increase their own sales by persuading people that their goods are among the necessary comforts of civilization. In so doing, they divert attention and energy away from human development and induce the individual to raise his/her material expectations, rather than to elevate his/her cultural expectations or appreciations. Further, mere accumulation should not be equated with development. It is far easier to procure a replication of an artistic masterpiece than to gain an appreciation of the culture or tradition in which it belongs. Understanding comes from study, not from acquisition; it is facilitated by education, not manufacturing. Thus, as Galbraith has argued, it is public services such as educational grants and endowments to the arts which can elevate the individual beyond the "merry peasant" level, not private production.

Galbraith's conclusion regarding the import of advertising coincides with the argument advanced by David Potter. Potter argues that advertising has become an agency of social control which sees the individual strictly as a consumer and exploits his/her values, desires and wants with little or no regard for social betterment. Potter contends that as far back as 1900 producers were using advertising not to familiarize the public with their products, but to actively stimulate demand. Significantly, he notes that with the alteration of the function of advertising, "the older factual, prosy notices which focused upon the specifications of the commodity now gave way to a more lyrical type of appeal which focused instead upon the desires of the consumer."[53]

It is in this sense that the objection raised by Allen that Galbraith is incorrect because the consumer is not a catspaw, but rather a conscious decider, misses the point. Allen's argument is that the consumer is now "able to free himself from the conventions and restraints which once confined him to a small number of resorts, and he is now at liberty to exercise his choice among the diverse attractions presented him by rival firms or government agencies."[54] This assumes, not only that the consumer's wants are urgent and original, but also that the consumer can make an intelligent choice between the various brands which he is offered. The reality seems to support Galbraith's claim insofar as the individual, in his reliance upon advertisements, substitutes ersatz information for genuine insights; these stimuli serve largely to justify or motivate selection of particular brands or additional commodities.[55]

To view the consumer, in Veblen's classic words, as "a lightning calculator of pleasures and pains, who oscillates like a homogeneous globule of desire for happiness under the impulse of stimuli that shift him about the area but leave him intact," is to blur the importance of habit and the desire for emulative display and conspicuous consumption. It is also to overlook the wastefulness of current consumption patterns which have facilitated increased demands for production goods. As Galbraith's former colleague and mentor Alvin Hansen noted in 1960:

> A not inconsiderable part of our productive resources is wasted on artificially created wants. Instead of the durable and quality products that are prized more and more as the years go by, we deliberately create things we soon tire of--things that an effervescent scheme of social values quickly renders obsolete.[56]

That orthodox economists, wedded to neoclassical economics, tend to deemphasize this tendency is again indicative of their allegiance to the theory of consumer sovereignty. In its absence, the composition of the gross national product would be divested of its sacrosanct veneer and be subject to evaluation and criticism. This, in large measure, explains the fervor with which Galbraith's challenge has been repudiated by his critics. Essentially, he has demanded that economists broaden their perspective in order to include the issues of affluence; in so doing, he has effectively jeopardized the status and/or importance of the discipline as it is currently defined.[57]

Myron Sharpe has, accordingly, attempted to discredit Galbraith's analysis by arguing that the power of advertising derives from its ability to identify and transform latent needs into conscious wants.[58] This, it should be noted, is essentially Galbraith's claim--that the advertisers exploit consumer values and desires, regardless of their direct linkage with the product which is for sale. Thus, when an advertiser associates mouth wash with sex appeal or cigarettes with idyllic meadows, the latent need is most probably the love and the pristine splendor, rather than the clean mouth and nicotine after-taste. To use Sharpe's own example, the fact that the telephone merely fills the need to communicate does not explain away the massive campaigns for the purchase of touch tone, princess, empress and decorator phones.

In defense of consumer sovereignty, Jean Boddewyn[59] has attempted to dispute Galbraith's claim by arguing that since all needs are the result of socialization or acculturation, the distinction between relative and absolute needs is unimportant. Citing as evidence the initial reluctance of European peasants to use potatoes as a dietary staple, Boddewyn argues that all wants are contrived. Thus he claims, longer tail fins, which Galbraith denounces as nonessential, cannot objectively be said to be any less essential than the legislation of the New Frontier, which Galbraith endorses. The point to be emphasized in this regard is that with an increasing standard of living, accumulation of goods should seemingly become less important and resources should become available to right the social imbalances discussed in section V and the unevenness discussed in the previous chapter.

Another defensive response is offered by F.A. Hayek. Hayek charges that Galbraith's treatment of the dependence effect (the revised sequence)bespeaks non-sequitur logic. Hayek's case is based upon the assumption that few needs are absolute in the sense that they are devoid of environmental influence. Thus,

he maintains that the effectiveness of an advertiser
is contingent "not only on what he does but also on
what the others do and on a great many other influences operating upon the consumer." From this, follows his conclusion that "every particular consumer
still has the choice between all those different
offers."[60]

It should be recalled that Galbraith is not
arguing that producers determine absolutely, but
rather that they effect partial management of consumer
choice. The importance of this distinction stems from
the fact that the theory of consumer sovereignty and,
by extension, the urgency of production hinges upon
consumer-initiated demand. In his rejoinder to Robert
Solow's charge that because producers lack complete
control, consumer sovereignty remains tenable, Galbraith indicated, "It will hardly be suggested that
what is imperfect or incomplete can, as a matter of
sound scientific method be ignored."[61] Hence, to
continue to defend the notion of consumer sovereignty
as the rationale for increasing production seems indefensible.

Closely allied to the process of demand stimulation is the process of debt creation. Just as the
advertisers have instilled new, ever-expanding wants
in the consumer, merchandisers have provided new,
easier means of satisfying them. Given the availability of credit cards and installment plans, it is
no longer necessary to qualify for a bank loan to
satisfy one's desires; it remains necessary, however,
to incur debt, albeit to a different source. "The
rise of consumer credit," Gabriel Kolko suggests, "is
one of the most important keys to understanding increases in the nation's standard of living since World
War II."[62] His statistics indicate a rise of out-
standing credit from 3.7 percent of national personal
income in 1929 to 9.9 percent in 1957, and almost a
tripling of the number of families relying upon such
income. It is this development which prompts Galbraith to take into account the "legacy of wants"--
"the bills which descend like the winter snow on those
who are buying on the installment plan. By millions
of hearths throughout the land it is known that when
these harbingers arrive the repossession man cannot be
far behind."[63] Can, queries Galbraith, "the bill col-
lector be the central figure in the good society?"

The point, then, which cannot be overemphasized is
that we have overlooked the wastefulness of the productive process in order to maintain a high level of
production and a high level of employment. Until
recently, there has been only the dimmest outcry agaist
either built-in obsolescence or destruction of the
environment through pollution. This, in large measure,
is due to our allegiance to growth and increasing
production--an allegiance which has unfortunately di-
verted our attention from questions of equity of distribution and blinded us to the costs of our re-
splendant growth and unrivaled standard of living.

This obsession has also blinded us into believing
that the market is a reasonable and socially beneficent allocator of resources--the argument undergirding
the neoclassical defense of the free market. Under
certain conditions, it is true that the market promotes
maximum efficiency, but given the power and prerogatives of the planning system, large corporations are
able to minimize market risk and woo government bureaucrats in order to win legislation and secure contracts which serve their interests. Further, as the
1972 Commission on Population Growth and the American
Future indicated,

> private market forces....work well in general
> and over the short run to reduce costs, husband
> resources, increase productivity and provide a
> higher material standard of living for the indi-
> vidual. But the market mechanism has been inef-
> fective in allocating the social and environ-
> mental costs of production and consumption....
> Nor has the market mechanism been able to pro-
> vide socially acceptable incomes for people who,
> by virtue of age, incapacity, or injustice, are
> poorly equipped to participate in the market
> system for producing and distributing income.[64]

Given the potential of this society, we can no longer
afford to equate social welfare with productive efficiency. Nor can we afford to rely on the free market
to provide needed goods and services to those who
have been excluded or subjected to an inferior position. It has been this reliance which has created
what Galbraith has identified as "social imbalance."

The predisposition to stimulate the economy
through production of private goods with low levels
of urgency has, in effect, caused a starvation of the
public sector, save where the power of the planning

system is brought to bear upon the state. Meanwhile,
the changing demographic composition of metropolitan
areas conjoined with the shrinking tax base has left
many state and local governments enmeshed in a fiscal
squeeze. Public demands for services are rising
faster than the ability to finance them. To Galbraith's way of thinking:

> Increasing population and increasing density of
> population increase the friction of person upon
> person and the outlay that is necessary for soc-
> ial harmony. And it is reasonable to suppose that
> [a] growing proportion of the requirements of an
> increasingly civilized community--schools, col-
> leges, libraries, museums, hospitals, recrea-
> tional facilities--are by their nature in the
> public domain.[65]

Without federal financing, these services will remain
in short supply. Yet, given the disparities in power
available to the planning and market systems, it should
be no surprise that if expenditures must be delayed,
reduced or foregone to prevent inflation, "it is upon
outlays for welfare, housing, urban services, education, and the like that the curtailment has princip-
ally to fall."[66]

Social balance is loosely defined as a "satisfactory relationship" between the publicly financed
and privately produced goods and services within the
society. Although no precise equation is given, the
essence of Galbraith's charge is that those agencies
which are primarily in the service of the individual
as opposed to the corporate network are discriminated
against when it comes time to allot federal funds.
Significantly, Shepherd indicates that "federal funds
(chiefly through the Defense Department and the space
agency, NASA) have been paying for a majority of the
R&D done by industrial firms; indeed in some of the
fastest-growing major industries, for nearly all of
it."[67] Conversely, as Galbraith explains,

> Such services of the state as the care of the
> ill, aged and physically or mentally infirm,
> the provision of health services in general, the
> provision of parks and recreational areas, the
> removal of rubbish, the provision of agreeable
> public structures, assistance to the impoverished
> and many other services are not of importance
> to the industrial system. In consequence, they
> do badly in competition for public funds.[68]

This tendency is reflected in the 1976 budget
report which projects an increase in defense outlays
from 85.3 billion to 94 billion dollars, an increase
of $278 million in outlays for general science, space
and technology and a reduction of farm subsidies and
acreage restrictions "to encourage farmers to respond
more freely to the forces of the market place." Also
of importance is the allocation of 5.4 billion dollars
to highways as compared to 360 million for Amtrak.
Education, according to this report, will continue to
be viewed as primarily the resposibility of the state
and local governments.[69]

While government funding of social services has
certainly increased since Galbraith presented his
social imbalance thesis in 1958, and defense expenditures have decreased since the cessation of the
Vietnam conflict, it is important to note that government funds still flow disproportionately to the
services which are supported by the planning system.
Educational endowments, for example, have frequently
been circumscribed by industrial writ; available
funds for research, for teaching and for scholarships
are for specified purposes or areas which serve industrial interests.

It should be noted that Galbraith is not the first
economist to have discovered social imbalance. Nor
would he claim otherwise. According to economic
orthodoxy, social investment, if left to the market,
will be inadequate to underwrite necessary public
services. Broadly speaking, this is because provision
of social services is unprofitable and requires that
the company by-pass alternative opportunities in order
to supply public housing, recreational facilities,
or education.

While acknowledging the logic of this position,
Galbraith approaches the issue from a markedly different perspective. He begins by observing that the
imbalance which characterizes the modern industrial
economy is highly selective. That is to say that those
public goods and services which are required by the
planning system or which are made necessary by its
products are provided with much less political resistance than those required by other economic groups.
This, as indicated in chapter four, can be seen as a
manifestation of the symbiotic relationship between
the mature corporation and the state which allows the
corporation to exert pressure and win supportive

services. "Those services that are important for the market system or that have no industrial base--that, like relief of privation, provision of nontechnical education, or administration of justice, serve the public at large--are far less amply provided."[70]

Herein lies the explanation for the fact that we improve our highways to accomodate the increasing number of automobiles while we reduce the federal allocations for poverty programs despite the ongoing misery of those denied access to essential public services.[71] Similarly, this symbiosis explains much of the success of those with interests in automobile and gasoline production in blocking efforts to provide an effective mass transportation system or to manufacture electric cars. Even installation of safety devices such as the much discussed air bag has been forestalled by corporate pressure upon government agencies.[72]

While it has been argued that, on the whole, federal subsidies for private industry are far more compatible with the "American way" than government provision of public services, rejection of the theory of consumer sovereignty casts doubt upon this assertion. It becomes possible to question whether the development of a consumption-intensive society was a reflection of the desire or manipulation of consumers.

Significantly, the suburban exodus following World War II can be attributed, at least in part, to investment choices on the part of land development corporations. Lack of alternative housing choices, conjoined with mass availability of automobiles, contributed markedly to the migration impetus. Also of importance was the imposition of industries' needs upon individual households--an imposition which engendered an "industrial life style--an acceptance of the goals of the organization, of the need to maximize income and consumption in accordance with its persuasion, of a public bureaucracy that reflects the interests and serves the needs of organization."[73] Thus, increased reliance upon electrical gadgetry and the general increase in consumption reflect more than simple convenience and increased satisfaction derived from additional commodities. The impact of advertising, although not quantifiable, has been to reinforce and diffuse the association of additional consumption with personal well-being.

109

Parenthetically, it should be noted that this transition was made possible by women's acceptance of the role of household manager charged with seeing to the necessary upkeep and servicing of commodities. Friedan's "problem that has no name" was, according to Galbraith, a result of the "convenient social virtue" which

> ascribes merit to any pattern of behavior, however uncomfortable or unnatural for the individual involved, that serves the comfort or wellbeing of, or is otherwise advantageous for, the more powerful members of the community. The moral commendation of the community for convenient and therefore virtuous behavior then serves as a substitute for pecuniary compensation.[74]

Thus, Galbraith argues, women were seduced into accepting the role of crypto-servant which alone made possible an indefinitely increasing consumption.

It is in this sense that Galbraith perceives the growth of the industrial state as a threat to society. Our goals tend to be couched in terms of economic objectives--increased production, income and employment--which serve the needs of the planning system. The mature corporation, in Galbraith's scheme, seeks expansion and, thus

> exploits the public faith in what is new at the expense of what works. There is innovation that serves only to make a predecessor product virtually obsolete....Innovation, even if serviceable, is irrationally distributed. It is concentrated often on unimportant things that are the product of strong organization and it is slight for important things, the product of weak organization.[75]

There is, according to Galbraith, little equation between the scope of production and the depth of need. Rather, production is generally great "where there is great capacity for managing the behavior of the individual consumer or sharing symbiotically in the control of the procurement of public goods and services."[76] The issue which Galbraith is raising, then, revolves around what may broadly be called the quality of life--whether unevenness and imbalance, which reflect the power of the planning system, can be overlooked in an effort to preserve private enterprise and individual liberty.

Ironically, the stimulation of private consumption makes the imbalance between the private and public services even less excusable. With increased production and consumption--more automobiles, more disposable packages and more appliances--there is an ever increasing need to expand the much neglected public services and to stimulate the growth of the market sector of the economy. In the absence of such remedial action, "the counterpart of increasing opulence will be deepening filth."[77]

The effect of persistent imbalances can be seen clearly in the case of the housing industry. Given an economic slump, it is housing development which is among the first to be curtailed. Galbraith argues that this is largely due to its need for supportive public services including land purchase and clearance, good neighborhood and city planning, effective zoning, financial aids, research and architectural services and subsidized financing for the lower income families.[78] Thus, the need to extricate the housing industry from the market system and bring it under public ownership, a possibility discussed in chapter six.

VI

Another focal, and related, concern running through Galbraith's discussion of the imperatives of affluence has been the question of environmental conservation. As part of a symposium in 1958--long before the current fervor--he emphasized the low marginal utility of additional goods and argued that it was impossible to "single out waste in a product without questioning the product."[79] Excessive appetite for goods was, he argued, at the heart of the problem. Pollution was an effect, not a cause.

The problem with emphasis upon production is not merely that many industrial innovations are superfluous, but that they are also environmentally harmful. The increasing recognition of this reality is evidenced by the rise of Ralph Nader's consumerism movement. Increasingly, Galbraith argues,
it is believed of innovation that, though it serves its function--though it moves people at supersonic speeds or destroys incoming missiles-- it is impressively negligent of the consequent social damage or public danger. Given a sufficient rate of technical progress, it is increasingly assumed, all the beneficiaries will be dead.[80]
Ironically, one finds corporations which are attempting to grow expanding production of precisely those com-

111

modities with external diseconomies such as automobiles which poison the air with fumes and the living
space with scrapped frames. Similarly, there is increased production and consumption of packaged consumer goods which leave in their wake a trail of lit-
ter. Significant in this regard is the fact that in
the first half of 1970 almost a billion dollars was
spent by the mature corporations to avow their "environmental consciousness."[81]

Thus, the problems of social imbalance and environmental blight cannot be considered as separate developments. They are mutually reinforcing. It is for
this reason that Galbraith has charged the state with
the responsibility of protecting the aesthetic and
social priorites which condition the type of life we
live. The state must become aesthetically conscious
because
    Only the state can defend the landscape against
    power lines, advertisers, lumbermen, coal miners,
    and, on frequent occasions, its own highwaymen.
    Only it can rule that some patterns of consump-
    tion--the automobile in the downtown areas of
    the modern city is a prominent possibility--are
    inconsistent with aesthetic goals.[82]

The urgency of action has now, in large measure,
been recognized, but the accompanying implications
have generally been ignored. While environmentalists
speak of cleaning up the surroundings and reclaiming
the natural beauty, they pay little attention to the
need to restrict production and consumption. This,
as Galbraith has repeatedly urged, is mandatory. So
long as private concerns determine the distribution
of resources and channel them into their own particular innovative schemes, there is little promise for a
balanced social performance.[83]

So long as public services are allowed to lag
behind private consumption, one finds, in Galbraith's
now famous phrase, "an atmosphere of private opulence
and public squalor." In this situation, Galbraith
argues, private goods command. "Schools do not compete with television and the movies....Comic books,
alcohol, narcotics, and switch-blade knives are, as
noted, part of the increased flow of goods, and there
is nothing to dispute their enjoyment."[84] It is for
this reason that Galbraith argues that there must be
a reordering of priorities with increasing attention

being paid to people rather than goods. Given our affluence, the means for curing poverty, ridding the society of the accompanying social and psychological costs of unequal development and protecting the environment are at our disposal if we only have the will to act and the ability to free our minds from outmoded assumptions. "Different goals would lead to a different--and also less predictable--decision with different benefits and other beneficiaries."[85]

It is toward a reformulation of social goals that Galbraith has directed his writing. His belief in the ability and willingness of Americans to formulate and/or endorse policies suited to a technologically advanced and affluent industrial society, is rooted deeply in the democratic tradition. Throughout his career, he has directed his severest criticism toward those who he felt were perpetuating outmoded idea systems which served to distort understanding of contemporary relationships. Hence, his felt-need to offer an alternative theoretical orientation and to emphasize the social problems and therewith the political tasks confronting American society. The reforms which he has proposed, the subject of chapter six, constitute what might be called "Galbraith's American Dream."

The study of John Kenneth Galbraith can be intellectually stimulating and ethically provocative; it can also
be frustrating and somewhat unsatisfying. While his
writing abounds with playful skepticism, barbed wit-
ticisms and caustic ironies, yet the whole connotes
an untrammeled optimism which often seems incongruous
with his own analysis. His insights into the modern
malaise are many, but at times he overreaches, strain-
ing the credibility of his own generalizations.

Overstatement notwithstanding, one cannot but
admire the vision which propels him, the force with
which he flails at his more orthodox brethren and the
tenacity of his faith in the possibility of progressive change. Although not a radical, he has earned
the respect of the young economists involved in the
Union for Radical Political Economics because he has
"published effective ridicule against the orthodox
faith."[1] Many outside the guild have also been capti-
vated by the Galbraithian vantage point. Thus, Edward
T. Chase can argue that "Galbraith's vision is a pragmatic one and he seems boldly optimistic in his belief that proper government action can improve matters.
A pity one can't vote him into high office."[2]

Even a casual analysis of the Galbraithian vision
reveals an active involvement with American culture
and society. Rather than rigid allegiance to a previously formulated ideology, Galbraith has displayed
an acute sensitivity to structural and situational
changes.[3] Nowhere is this more evident than in his
proposals for reform which will be analyzed in this
chapter. Yet, his emphasis has, in two important re-
spects, remained constant. First, he has continually
insisted upon examining the political import of economic ideas and institutions. More specifically, as
Robert Lekachman has observed, "Galbraith's economics
is distinguished from conventional varieties by its
concern with the location and control of economic
power."[4]

It is this concern which has led Galbraith to
analyze orthodox economics in terms of its instrumental function for the mature corporations. It is,

he argues, "instrumental in that it serves not the understanding or improvement of the economic system but the goals of those who have power in the system."[5] Enough has been said in previous chapters to indicate that Galbraith has long been disenchanted with this purpose and has relentlessly insisted that the primary end of economics should be to facilitate understanding of the actual operation of the economy--a point to which we shall return.

Second, as an outgrowth of his expository purpose, he has persistently argued that the socioeconomic environment can be democratized in such a way as to better serve the interests of the entire population. This requires, in his view, reform, not revolution. He concedes that "There are countries where I think revolution is therapeutic, where there may be no alternative to revolution. But the history of the United States is mainly one of successful reform. This being so, I have an unabashed commitment to reform. If reform works, revolution becomes unnecessary."[6] In effect, his belief in the possibility of responsive change is an expression of his voluntaristic conception of history discussed in chapter five.

Just as the individual has rationalized and civilized the workaday world in ways unimaginable to Marx, so Galbraith argues, the public can, and moreover must, take command of the underlying purposes which determine the direction of the system. Rather than increased production, he argues, humanitarian considerations should now be primary. Only by considering the broader economic issues of distribution and allocation can the system be wrested from the dictates of the mature corporations.

> As production ceases to be the goal, the question of who gets the product can no longer be elided-- it can no longer be agreed that this problem is solved by everyone getting more. Income guarantees are part of the answer. So is more widely shared work. So is more employment in the civilian public services. So is a far, far better system of taxation to pay for those services.[7]

To advance these measures, Galbraith advocates "a public state (as opposed to one possessed by the planning system),"[8]

Galbraith's claim that this is a historical imperative, forced by changing circumstances, leads

116

him to call for emancipation of belief. Emancipation, that is, from the conventional wisdom which sanctifies growth for its own sake and equates individual happiness with increased consumption. In large measure, what Galbraith is advocating is a reordering of priorities which is in keeping with a changed reality. Thus the importance he attaches to understanding the economic system as it is rather than as it should be. In his words:

> One does not suppress neoclassical economics; one shows its tendentious function and seeks to provide a substitute. One does not prohibit advertising; one resists its persuasion. One does not legislate against science or engineering; one sees their eminence in relation to the arts as a contrivance of the planning system.[9]

His optimistic faith in the ability of people to look beneath the veneer seems, at least partially, to be an outgrowth of recent developments such as the consumerism movement and the efforts of the Federal Trade Commission, Food and Drug Administration and other agencies to insure truth in advertising and increased safety of products. His confidence also reflects the significance which he attaches to the Vietnam war protests, the efforts of the young involved in the counterculture to return to a simpler mode of life, the rise in cable television subscriptions and, possibly, the demise of Richard Nixon.

He alludes to the efforts of the populists and social democrats and reveals a profound respect for their campaigns against privilege. By the mid-thirties, he notes, the split was overt with "almost all reputable opinion arrayed against Roosevelt and the New Deal. It was part of the popular instinct that this showed that Roosevelt was right."[10] He sadly concedes that in the past thirty years this popular skepticism has waned. Yet, argues Galbraith, there is no need for despair. With proper attention to the causes of the current unrest and dissatisfaction, the structural forces which distort the public purpose and coopt the state can be unmasked. In his view, the power of the planning system over public policy is not plenary.

For instance, in the case of the Vietnam war, which was strongly endorsed by the planning system and the related bureaucracies as the only means of resisting communism, the public could not be convinced.

More recently, observes Galbraith, "similar though
lesser fissures have opened between the public and
the planning system on matters of domestic policy--
notably on the environment, taxation, public support
to such technological innovations as the SST, even on
highway building. These fissures in the future will
become wider."[11] Of significance in this regard is
the recent resurgence of a populist coalition spear-
headed by the "New Populist Front" in Washington D.C.
which stood behind Fred Harris' 1976 Presidential can-
didacy.[12] A similar spirit informed Gene McCarthy's
struggle to insure the rights of third party candidates. Also of importance is the formation of a radical caucus within the economic profession.[13]

   The success of such efforts is less important for
present purposes than the implicit commitment of those
involved to undermine the hierarchy of privileges and
the restrictiveness of orthodox thought. The situation is well characterized by Gibson Winter who urges
the recognition of a "new social reality"--a reality
which he characterizes as follows:
   We are now dependent upon resources and services
   controlled by massive organizations which are
   indispensable to our freedom, our dignity and
   ultimately our survival. The control and allocation of such resources can no longer be left
   to chance and exploitive advantage of private
   interests.[14]

   By this point, it is by no means surprising that
Galbraith has come to see that change must be actively
promoted. Of importance in this regard are his early
allegiance to Keynesian economics and his involvement
with the social legislation of the New Deal. Both
Keynes and Roosevelt initially received a hostile response from orthodox thinkers--not because their proposals were radical, but because they were radically
at variance with the conventional wisdom.[15] Both were,
in fact, steadfastly dedicated to remedial action
aimed at saving, rather than overthrowing capitalism.
In this sense, they were the very anathema of Marx and
their proposals a major alternative to Marxism. As
Richard Polenberg has indicated, even with the "radi-
calization" of the New Deal--the institution of such
measures as the Social Security and the Wagner Acts
and the creation of the Resettlement Administration
and the WPA--the general cast was compromising. Additionally, he observes that "once legislation was on
the books, discontent tended to be channeled into

efforts to improve existing law rather than to alter the system."[16] Nevertheless, orthodox thinkers continued to oppose the innovators.

Through his involvement with both of these efforts to elicit change, Galbraith became aware that solutions did not gain ready acceptance; reforms had to be engineered and promoted by people outside of the dominant perspective. Paradoxically, once the effectiveness of an innovative scheme has been demonstrated, even the most adament critics tend to endorse it out of practical necessity.[17] Hence, Galbraith's emphasis upon the need for reevaluation and experimentation.

> That the economic system has a tendency to perfect itself will, perhaps, not now be believed. Unequal development, inequality, frivolous and erratic innovation, environmental assault, indifference to personality, power over the state, inflation, failure in inter-industry coordination are part of the system as they are part of the reality.[18]

And, given the systemic nature of these disparities, Galbraith contends that it is no longer possible to rely on conventional avenues of reform.

The hold which orthodox remedies have upon the thinking of economic advisors, politicians and orthodox economists makes it necessary to consider the traditional remedies in order to understand Galbraith's counterplans. His various proposals will be considered in terms of their practicality, their workability, their advantages and their disadvantages. In this examination, the most crucial question will be how the various proposals will effect the disparities which Galbraith has identified. The final chapter will attempt to place Galbraith's proposals within their ideological and philosophical contexts.

Before beginning this analysis, one caveat seems in order. Although particular proposals will be rather severely critiqued, my intent is by no means to negate the importance of Galbraith's analysis. Galbraith has not confined his attention to the one-dimensional "social problem" which is easily remedied within the boundaries of the status quo. He has, instead, attempted to promote broad angled reform of the basic structural components of this society. Inherent in such an effort is the temptation to over-value the efficacy of certain measures and, hence, to understate the complexity of the actual situation.

II

The most oft proposed remedies for social imbalances
are antitrust litigation (to restore or enhance competition) and monetary and fiscal policy (to stimulate
or retard the economy). In Galbraith's estimation,
these traditional prescriptions are incapable of
dealing with the existing social conditions. He
charges that, for reasons discussed below, they are
incapable of checking the powers of the mature corporation. In consequence, rather than reducing imbalances and inequality they merely perpetuate existing conditions and insure unequal development between
the coporate network and the small business establishment.[19]

At no point in his career has Galbraith placed
much faith in antitrust policies as a means of recti-
fying economic imbalances. As early as 1936, possibly as an outgrowth of his year of study at Cambridge, he argued that antitrust litigation could, at
best, promote duopoly or oligopoly; it could not, he
argued, diminish the large corporations' power over
prices or profits and, hence, could not induce competitive behavior. By 1952, his argument had matured
but his skepticism remained intact.

At this point he argued that antitrust, rather
than dismantling original market power, was normally
implemented against the emerging countervailing powers.
This belief led Galbraith to take a relativistic
stance and argue that possession and exercise of power
were neither positive nor negative phenomena. Thus,
he reasoned that the necessary questions were "Against
whom and for what purpose is the power being exercised?" In the absence of clear evidence "that the
public is the victim, the antitrust laws, by attacking
countervailing power can as well enhance as reduce
monopoly power."[20]

Instead of prosecution, Galbraith urged the government to nurture the bargaining power of weak
economic groups in order to promote countervailing
power in cases in which it did not arise naturally.
Again, one detects the influence of his agricultural
economics background since he bases his case on the
effectiveness of a comparable policy of subsidies and
price supports which enabled the farmer to compete
more equally with business interests.

In his subsequent treatments, antitrust laws again receive criticism, albeit for different reasons. The inherent weakness comes to be portrayed, not as discrimination against countervailing groups, but discrimination against small, powerless concerns which are still extrmely vulnerable to the risks of competition.

On the one hand, the oligopolistic industries have virtual control over their prices and their level of production. They display little fear of being prosecuted for their inordinate share of sales within a given industry. A recent example illustrates this phenomenon well. With the introduction of the Chevette, General Motors was expected to increase its share of the market by at least three and possibly ten percent of the market as it strove to regain its 1962 level of 52 percent of all automobile sales.

As this campaign--which could devastate its smaller rivals--was launched, GM President Elliott M. Estes denied fear of antitrust action despite GM's already healthy 42 percent of sales.[21] Were a small firm to attempt a comparable maneuver, its actions would inevitably be called into question. Due to the competitive nature of pricing and ease of entry into the domain of the small firm, only vicious price cutting or a series of interindustry mergers could facilitate such a skewed distribution of sales. In the case of the oligopoly, however, sales can be expanded without disturbing existing price arrangements and, hence, without attracting unwanted attention.

Equally telling in this regard is the fact that post-war mergers have, by and large, united a large corporation with a smaller firm in another field. Despite the increase in power afforded by such weddings, they "are more likely to escape the prohibition of the antitrust laws than mergers between two clearly competing firms in the same industry."[22] It was, in fact, this circumstance which allowed ITT to ascend from 34th to 8th ranked American manufacturing company between 1961 and 1971.[23] Although recent rulings have forced divestment of some subsidiaries, ITT has shown little inclination to cease its expansive activites.[24]

Again, the small firms, lacking the resources and organization, are, by definition, unable to pursue such a course. A similar limitation is imposed upon federally controlled concerns like TVA which are denied the prerogatives to innovate and to expand into

new areas regardless of the advantages such action
might have for both the organization and the general
public.[25] This situation has led Galbraith to argue:
> The form is prosecuted; the substance is exempt.
> We discriminate against those who, as a result of
> numbers and weakness must use crude or overt
> methods to control their markets and in favor of
> those who, because of achieved size and power,
> are under no such compulsion.[26]

The nub of Galbraith's argument is that the antitrust
laws, while avowedly protecting the public against
monopoly power, are anachronisms when over half of the
economy is dominated by 500-600 corporations for whom
planning is both possible and necessary.

Since Galbraith views planning as endemic to the
advanced industrial system, he contends that antitrust
activity is largely ineffectual. It serves to quell
public fears and frustrate a small proportion of
corporate expansions, but it does not (and cannot) deal
with the systemic roots of the uneven development of
the economy. He explains wryly that in reality, "government cannot proclaim half of the economic system illegal; it certainly will not do so if the test of sound
policy is what, in general, serves the goals of this
part of the economy." From this he concludes that
"the planning system need fear only peripheral harass-
ment by the antitrust laws."[27]

This is not to say that Galbraith believes that
all kinds of monopolies are good or that remedial
action is harmful. Nor is it to suggest that he contends that "the large and powerful industrial monopolies which he favors should not only decide prices,
but also make their own decisions about what it is convenient for them to produce, rather than trying to
find out what the consumer wants."[28] It is, rather,
that Galbraith views antitrust laws as unworkable and
maintains that reforming them diverts energy from the
far more difficult task of formulation and legislation of alternative policies which can deal with
the mature corporation. A similar conclusion has been
reached by Ralph Nader, who argues that antitrust
legislation has generally been proposed and enacted in
lieu of more comprehensive programs for effective
federal chartering of the corporation.[29] It can also
be demonstrated that the historical relationship between antitrust legislation and concentration of
economic power, rather than being inverse, is, in
fact, quite direct.[30]

While Galbraith's rejection of antitrust solutions
has been constant, his response to the use of monetary
and fiscal policy is more complex. His early commitment to Keynesian economics led him, in 1952, to
urge the government to further economic development
by promoting an expansionary environment. The tools
he proposed were the very tools--monetary and fiscal
measures--which he later came to disparage as being
discriminatory and ineffective. Thus, in **American Capitalism**, the government was to have only a tangential
role in the economy:

> Centralized decision is brought to bear only on
> the climate in which decisions are made; it in-
> sures only that the factors influencing free and
> intelligent decision will lead to a private
> action that contributes to economic stability.
> Thus, in times of depression, increased govern-
> ment expenditures or decreased taxation will
> cause or allow an increase in demand.[31]

More recently, his conclusions have been less sanguine.

Because of structural differences within the economy, the mature corporation is freed from the degree
of dependence upon external funds characteristic of
the small, strictly competitive firms. Thus, while
the planning system can free itself, relatively speaking, from increased interest rates, small firms have
no such option. Similarly, state and local juris-
dictions as well as school districts and public corporations, are adversely effected. Thus, during periods
of restraint or tight money, the brunt is borne primarily by farmers, residential builders, merchants and
small businessmen.

> Any active monetary policy operates by recurrent
> discriminatory reduction in investment in the
> weakest part of the economic system. (The case of
> housing is especially dramatic.) It thus con-
> tributes directly to inequality in income and in-
> equality in development. It intensifies the
> central and most painful faults of the economy.[32]

Hence, the need to reduce forever the use of monetary
policy.

Galbraith's argument revolves around the claim
that the small firms, in their resemblance to the
competitive market prototype, are broadly stable.
Self-limiting fluctuations in output and employment
are also self-correcting. The mature corporations,
on the other hand, are intrinsically unstable, subject
to recession, depression and persistent inflation.

123

Whereas the small firm responds to market pressures and lowers its prices in the face of decreased demand, the mature corporation maintains existing prices and restricts output. Similarly with wage increases, the mature corporation adds the extra cost to the price of its product thus further inflating the cost of living and generating additional impetus for wage increases.

Further, given the complex interrelationships between the large and small firms, the propensities of the planning system have a profound impact upon the less insulated competitive firms. The irony is that the small firm suffers more from recession and inflation than the large corporations which are largely responsible for the instability. Galbraith explains:

> When demand in the planning system falls, demand for the products and services of the market system is reduced. Since there is no protective control, prices, entrepreneurial incomes and some wages fall. Hardship for the small businessman or farmer is severe.[33]

While the small firms can deal with internal fluctuations, they remain highly susceptible to external movements which lie beyond their control. A recent study in the **Wall** Street Journal explicated the impact of this imbalance in no uncertain terms. It indicated that the small firm can be devastated by as little as a five percent decline in the oligopolies' business, since such a drop may, in turn, induce a 50 to 100 percent decline in sales for the small supplier. Further, the small competitive firm can do nothing to prevent a rival from slashing prices far below costs just to remain in operation.[34]

Of particular importance is the inability of Keynesian economics to deal with inflationary pressures spawned by the wage-price spiral. So long as deficient demand is the central problem, the government can stem the downward drift either by tax reduction, federal spending or by reduced interest rates. Given an upward instability, however, no such simple remedies are readily available. True, government spending can be reduced, interest rates can be raised and, with much more difficulty, taxes can be increased. Such action cannot, however, prevent the large concerns from increasing both wages and prices. By doing so, they are able to pass the costs of higher taxes along to the public. Obviously, no such leverage is available to the small, competitive sector of the economy.

124

Several other problems undermine the effectiveness of fiscal policy. Public spending, as indicated in preceding chapters, is disproportionately preempted by the planning system. In this sense, government spending intensifies the imbalances between the various sectors of the economy, distorting both development and income distribution. Second, argues Galbraith, the tax structure has become progressively less responsive to income changes and less efficient in stabilizing income and expenditures due to an increase in the number of exemptions and loopholes available to upper income groups. Third, there is a marked bias toward tax reduction, rather than increased public expenditures, which also disproportionately favors upper income groups.[35]

Herein lies the basis for Galbraith's conclusion that the remedy to contemporary economic problems "begins not with the needs of stabilization but with those of general reform."[36] It is toward this end that he has recently directed much of his attention. Since his proposals are not "one shot remedies," but constitute a system of reform, they must be viewed in relationship to one another. To facilitate this end, I will first examine the contours of his scheme and introduce the vehicles through which he would generate reform and then proceed to analyze his particular suggestions for specific problems.

III

Broadly speaking, Galbraith's objective is to promote greater equalization among the various sectors of the economy--to encourage the development of the weakest participants and to restrain the prerogatives of the strongest. Among those whose positions he would strengthen are, of course, the various firms within the market system. Included, too, are American housewives, who have been shackled with the dubious distinction of becoming "crypto-servants," charged with administering consumption and seeing that the ever-growing batallion of goods receives proper attention and repair.[37] And, of course, there is the public service sector for which Galbraith has long campaigned.

Rather than dismantling the planning system, Galbraith would reorient it toward the public interest, restricting and redirecting its use of resources. He would also transform the mature corporations into de jure public institutions, rather than allowing them the privileges of de facto public corporations with private prerogatives. Finally, he would institute a central planning agency capable of coordinating the various sectors of the economy. These reforms will be examined in detail later; meanwhile, it is necessary to examine the overall drift of Galbraith's program for reform.

Although Galbraith feels compelled to dub his system of reform "new socialism" rather than simply calling it socialism, his intentions seem pure. He shies away from the rubric "socialism" because it connotes oligarchic control and is often associated with theories of monopoly capitalism which are antithetical to Galbraith's conception of corporate organization.[38] Also of importance in understanding his choice of words is his equation of socialism with the extant social structures of the Soviet Union, Cuba, China and Yugoslavia; it is their shortcomings which lead him to call his vision's end "new socialism." In this sense, he has failed to heed Marx's warning against "false brothers," or anti-socialist socialisms which employ socialist rhetoric to achieve totalitarian ends. Examination of current "socialist" structures in terms of Marx and Engles' criteria of who makes decisions and what interests are being served, reveals what Michael Harrington calls "bureaucratic collectivism," the revolution from above.[39] In point of fact, socialism, as Marx conceived it could not have arisen in any of these countries; the material conditions, no less than the unpreparedness of the masses, disallowed the cultivation of the classless society.

The significance of Galbraith's word-juggling lies deeper than mere semantics. In his attempt to engineer social and economic changes, Galbraith has placed a large bet upon "the public cognizance"--the ability of the people to see the inherent contradictions between the priorities of the large corporation and the needs and interests of the public.[40] He sincerely believes that as the people come to understand the means by which the planning system exerts its influence upon the public and the state and to recognize the subsequent diseconomies stemming from this manipulation, they will insist upon substituting broadly social criteria for the "objective" yardsticks of efficiency and growth as a means of assessing economic performance.

Galbraith's faith in popular awareness, although admirable, would seem incompatible with much of his own analysis. He has persistently argued that the public is, because of its own relatively high standard of living, susceptible to persuasion as to what it feels it needs. Additionally, he understands that those with vested interests in the status quo will resist any attempt to undermine their power or influence. Even more damaging to his argument is the rising level of expectations which has led more and more people to demand a greater share and higher quality of goods and services.[41] Thus, to emancipate belief would, it seems, require the ascendence of Charles Reich's consciousness III types who are more interested in personal fulfillment than corporate status.[42] The post-sixties retreat of many a counter culturist lends little credibility to this prospect.

Yet, for Galbraith, the new socialism is "urgent and even indispensable" since "it cannot be escaped except at the price of grave discomfort, considerable social disorder and, on occasion, lethal damage to health and well-being."[43] The significance of this belief is that Galbraith, consciously or not, has returned once more to Marx's analysis of social change. Just as Galbraith insists that the public consequences of production and the people's dependence upon public services necessitate a new social organization, so Marx argued that the growing tensions between the forces of production and the existing relations of production would largely determine the need, the nature and the direction of social change.

Had Galbraith been more receptive to Marx's analysis, he might also have been able to specify various groups which might propel the emancipation of belief. His lack of specificity regarding this issue is, in fact, one of the key weaknesses of Galbraith's prognosis. Throughout his treatment the constituency of his reform-oriented public is left undefined. In The New Industrial State he laid responsibility upon the educational and scientific estate; in Economics and the Public Purpose he provides only ambiguous references to the cognizant public and the emancipated State.

Galbraith's inability (or unwillingness) to specify particular interest groups invites several inter-pretations. The most plausible revolve around his in-attention to the class structure of American society.

127

Perhaps for reasons of political expediency,[44] he omits
any reference to the possible class interests served
by the planning system, and, hence, cannot identify
class-based groups as potential agents of emancipation.

Since he views society in terms of the cleavage
separating the market system and the planning system,
he tends to overlook the importance of the social relationships operating within the corporate structure.
In consequence, he has come to see labor unions as a
supportive arm of the technostructure, which leads him
to the following conclusion: "I do not think that the
workers' movement can be a decisive factor of reform;
at least not the American trade unions, although their
activities could be useful in other spheres."[45] While
the ambiguity of his reference to "other spheres" may
reflect an appreciation of labor's political potential,
other comments which he has made cast doubt upon this
interpretation.

His analysis revolves around the power (and assumed willingness) of the technostructure to placate
labor with increased wages and fringe benefits. This,
he argues, "makes possible a measure of psychic identification of the employee with the technostructure.
The latter is no longer the implacable class enemy."[46]
Such a conclusion, while plausible, does not, it should
be noted, receive support from studies of labor attitudes in various concentrated industries.[47] While
laborers may well be committed to capitalism, they
"are caught between the promise of a widely affirmed
tradition and the realities of the contemporary economic and social order."[48]

Ely Chinoy's study of the automobile workers in
America, for example, reveals the latent frustrations
and resentments which the less open, more hierarch-
ical opportunity structure has engendered among workers
who are denied the chance to make judgments, discharge
responsibility or achieve personal fulfillment.[49]
Herein lies the explanation for the workers' desires
to leave the factory for independent business or
farming. Their bounded opportunities also account for
the fact that "they approach political questions and
parties from a class conscious point of view."[50]

While discontent is currently internalized to a
large extent, there is no necessary reason for assuming
that internalization will continue. In fact, Zeitlin
has presented a convincing argument for the possibility

128

of automation markedly increasing the supply of superfluous workers and, hence, radically transforming the
structure of the working class.[51] This could clearly
alter the nature of the resentment and possibly its
expression. Increasing hostility toward the "Establishment" could, in this sense, make workers receptive
to and active in initiating alliances with other dis-
sidents or displaced persons.[52]

Further, although union organization has admittedly ameliorated the conflicts between labor and management, it by no means follows that they have achieved
a standoff regarding political and economic policies.
The continuing battles between the mine workers and
such mature corporations as Kennecott, Anaconda and
Phelps Dodge, perhaps the most extreme cases, are symptomatic in this regard.[53] Also of importance is the
recent upsurge of grass-root resistances to labor-
management settlements. Increasingly, workers find
themselves "unable to utilize unions with aged organizational structures and a low degree of internal democracy."[54]

The basic interests of labor and management remain dissimilar insofar as workers emphasize control
over the methods and conditions of production which
employers hold to be "unchallengeable and sacrosanct."
The unwillingness of union officials to promote basic
change has generated countless "illegal" strikes and
led to the formation of independent organizations in
many industries. Because workers have been forced to
work outside official union grievance machinery, production, "particularly in heavy industry, is plagued
by slowdowns and minor acts of sabotage."[55]

More generally, as Monsen and Cannon have documented, the orientation of labor distinguishes itself
from that of management because labor emphasizes "that
it is government's responsibility to solve basic
economic problems such as unemployment, unfair distribution of income, and various welfare needs."[56]
Significantly, in both 1963 and 1965 the AFL-CIO endorsed a National Planning Agency to evaluate resources, needs and priorities; it also endorsed a
fifty percent raise in Social Security, a comprehensive
program of urban redevelopment, a national health
care program and a resource conservation policy.[57]
Equally important is the 1970 organization of the Alliance for Labor Action by the UAW, the Teamsters and
other unions; its policy expresses marked concern for

corporate responsibility and urges the formation of
independent review boards for corporate policy. None
of these developments seems to support Galbraith's dismissal of the workers as a decisive factor of reform.

Had Galbraith paid more attention to recent labor
actions, it seems likely that he would have been more
able to identify at least one major force which could
galvanize his proposed reforms. Heilbroner's critique
of Galbraith's use of the power concept is well taken:

> The power that interests Galbraith is the gen-
> eralized power of bureaucracy....What lacks is an
> analysis of the underlying purpose for which the
> technostructure exerts its organizing capabilities
> under capitalism. In particular, what lacks is a
> description of the general class interests that
> are served by the operations of the technostruc-
> ture in a capitalist society.[58]

Had Galbraith given more attention to the social relationships within the corporate structure it seems probable that he could have been more specific regarding
the interests which impede change and even development
as well as the emergent sources of change breeding
within the society.[59]

IV

The ambiguity of Galbraith's analysis becomes even
more evident when one considers the role he awards to
the Democratic Party which relies heavily upon labor's
support. To facilitate more even development within
the economy and to promote a more egalitarian social
structure, he proposes revamping the Democratic Party
so as to shape it into an instrument of reform. Despite his own rather checkered relationship with the
Democratic national organization,[60] he holds that the
Democratic Party, not the Republican Party or third
parties, is the only vehicle which can induce change
because it "is the party that is open to participation
and responsive to pressure."[61]

Historically, he argues, the Democrats have proven
themselves capable of providing a voice for malcon-
tents, be they immigrants, minorities or workers.
There is the obvious example of the New Deal which,
as Harrington has demonstrated, virtually nullified
efforts to organize an effective Socialist Party in
America.[62] Since this time, Galbraith argues, Democratic victories have included five major policy en-
actments: acceptance of Keynesian economics, promotion
of the Welfare State, endorsement of the trade union

movement, commitment to civil rights legislation, and
espousal of responsible international involvement.
Sadly he concedes that of late these distinctive policies have become equally a part of the Republican
strategy and that Democrats have seemingly become mired
in the status quo, unable to formulate much needed
strategies with which to cope with such phenomena as
economic imbalance or urban decay. In a similar vein,
Robert Heilbroner has persuasively argued that:

> our search for new adaptive measures and insti-
> tutions is hambered by a traditional suspicion
> toward government, by the absence of an ag-
> gressive party of the democratic left pushing
> for social goals, and not least by our abiding
> curse of racism.[63]

At least part of the Democratic Party's inability
to promote innovative policies, in Galbraith's mind,
stems from its incompatable constituency. Rather than
attempting to integrate individuals of similar perspective, it has attempted to "bring together men of
irreconcilable views--men of implacable hostility."[64]
Thus, while the party has won the support of the black
community, a large percentage of its conservative
Southern membership is diametrically opposed to improving the position of the black population and is
patently indifferent to the fate of Northern cities.

Equally untenable in Galbraith's mind is the seniority system which constitutes "a planned gerontoc-
racy" and accords an inordinate amount of power to conservative Southern interests. Writing before the 1975
resistance by junior congressmen, he argued:

> the one unified national accomplishment of the
> Democratic Party is to accord power to Richard
> B. Russell of Georgia, John Stennis of Missis-
> sippi, Allen J. Ellender of Louisiana, John L.
> McClellan of Arkansas, B. Everett Jordan of North
> Carolina, Mendel Rivers of South Carolina, Wil-
> liam M. Comer of Mississippi, James L. Whitten of
> the same state, Wilber D. Mills of Arkansas, Otto
> Passman of Louisiana, John L. McMillan of South
> Carolina and William R. Poage of Texas.[65]

That their ability as heads of committees enables them
to more easily secure government contracts for their
districts should not, Galbraith argues, be confused
with serving their constituencies' interests. More
often than not, such action serves the interests of
corporations and agribusiness while diverting attention
from the unmet needs of weaker interest groups.

131

It is for this reason that Galbraith holds that "there should be a presumption not in favor of re-election but against it." This, he continues, "will greatly enhance the likelihood that legislators will reflect contemporary public attitudes."[66] Additionally, Galbraith proposes that moderate and liberal Southern Democrats support Republican candidates rather than rallying behind the Old Guard conservatives who frustrate attempts to forge a unified party. Such action, he argues, is essential if the hold of established politicians is to be broken.[67]

In subsequent elections, he reasons, the Democrats can then run moderate candidates whose views are consonant with the general party line and with the public interest.[68] Although feasible in theory, such a program abounds with practical difficulties.[69] Such action, Dutton has pointed out, will "require raising the proportion of moderate and liberal democrats in the South from their present 15 to 20 percent share of the electorate, plus increasing the black vote from its likely 15 to 18 percent of the actual vote."[70]

Such a plan further assumes, it should be noted, that people are generally attuned to the voting record of their representatives and thus have a basis upon which to fairly judge performance. As Galbraith knows full well, people are subject to persuasion and habitual responses; both of these tendencies predispose them (in the absence of egregious error on the part of a politician) to favor an incumbent. Nor is this proclivity entirely wrongheaded insofar as a seasoned politician has the advantage of knowing the ins and outs of the legislative process, just as the veteran knows the techniques of organizing and running a campaign.

These limitations notwithstanding, it is to Galbraith's credit that he places emphasis upon congressional action, rather than hollow campaign promises. One cannot but wonder, however, how he would respond to similar criteria being applied to academic performance. The tenure system, no less than the political seniority system, insulates the academic citadel from external review and, thus, protects positions of power. In a similar manner, the gate keepers of academic publications are much more receptive to those with security and established names than to fledgling professors who are more apt to challenge accepted interpretations. This parallel, however, goes beyond Galbraith's scheme.

For Galbraith's reforms to be actualized,
a responsive legislature is primary. Sensing that the
President and the sundry professional bureaucrats cannot (or will not) free themselves from corporate manipulation, he charges Congress with assessment of corporate policies and practices and a comprehensive, strategic review of budget proposals. While legislators
may not always be responsive to the public interest,
they are certainly more visible and more easily replaced than "anonymous technocrats who (like any group
of human beings not subject to steady, crucial scrutiny) can slack off, fumble or encroach."[71] And in the
context of Galbraith's other proposals (discussed below) the legislature need no longer be vulnerable to
private control. Reform of the legislature, then,
must be seen as part of a larger strategy with which
Galbraith proposes to emancipate the state, to develop
a long range strategy with which to phase in the future.

V

To enhance the power and competence of the market system in its relationship to the planning system, Galbraith reverts to the general drift of the analysis he
propounded in American Capitalism. Since his goal is
to eradicate the powerlessness of the unorganized
economic groups, Galbraith proposes exempting the small
businesses from antitrust litigation. With freer reign
over their economic environment, Galbraith contends,
they will be able to man a more secure bargaining
position, stabilize their prices and production and
hence attain a relatively secure level of income.

Concomitantly, the government could model its
policies along the lines adopted in dealing with agriculture; with direct regulation of prices and production available to the small concern it would finally
become possible to promote cooperative efforts within
these industries, since no firm would gain from vio-
lating the compact. To protect the worker, Galbraith
urges a campaign to extend unions to the currently
unorganized sectors of the economy.

This latter measure would be complemented by
extending the scope and coverage of minimum wage legislation. This, in Galbraith's view, is the only possible manner by which to discourage self-exploitation
and to stimulate equity between the two sectors of the
economy. "This means," he argues, "forcing those who
patronize the market system to pay the full price for

133

the product--one that reflects an equality of wage return with the planning system--or go without."[72]

To redress the imbalance in technological development, Galbraith proposes increased government investment in the education, capital and technical needs of
the small concern. This, it should be obvious, is an
accomodation to the fact that in a highly concentrated
economy, resources, be they human, material or financial, no longer move freely in response to demand.
Significantly, William Shepherd has argued that "a
wider spread of federal R & D support and of purchasing
could probably have weakened or checked the relative
rise of the very largest firms."[73] While such action
cannot at this juncture reduce concentration, it can
prevent the cleavage between the planning and market
systems from growing wider. Further, as Galbraith indicates, the ongoing underinvestment in the less powerful sectors of the economy has been responsible for
the competitive decline of the United States in such
industries as textiles, shoes, railroads, shipping
and machine tools which "make or render old-fashioned
products or services with obsolete equipment."[74] Redistribution of funds can reverse this tendency and
thus contribute to more balanced economic development.

In assessing Galbraith's proposals for the unorganized sector of the economy, one is immediately
struck by their practicability. His proposed reforms
aim at inducing small firm development which is broadly
comparable to that which propelled the formation of
the mature corporation. Significantly, he would not
alter the property relations which currently give the
entrepreneurs free reign over their enterprise, but
would instead check their abuse through government
regulation of prices and production. In opting for
such an alternative, Galbraith may well be perpetuating a source of inequality, but he is also increasing the feasibility of his proposals. The small
businessman is much more likely to welcome government
action if it promotes security without uprooting
traditional capitalist motivations.

Government supports, both financial and technical,
would greatly enhance the entrepreneur's ability to
expand operations. Additionally, federal aid would
not destroy entrepreneurial autonomy; initiative would
still be the province of the individual. Profit, although more evenly distributed among employees and
employers, would remain as an incentive for action.

Pecuniary gain, according to Galbraith, must remain the
key motivation in those industries which are not susceptible to large scale organization and cannot, therefore, rely upon identification and adaptation as behavioral goads. While the entrepreneur has long
praised the virtue of free enterprise and competition
as the most conducive to individual initiative, a
change in attitude would not be unprecedented were a
viable alternative made available. Even corporate
executives once opposed government intervention into
the economy.

Galbraith freely concedes that one result of such
a program would be increased prices for goods and
services furnished by the small firm. No longer would
it be necessary (or possible) for a company to slash
prices below a level which allowed it to break even.
Neither would the small firm be forced to withhold a
suitable level of income from its employees. Anticipating charges that such a policy would increase the
cost of living, Galbraith argues that the

> effect of higher prices (in the absence of other
> action) will be smaller purchases, smaller output
> and less employment in the market system than
> would otherwise be the case. This must be ac-
> cepted. The market system now serves as an em-
> ployer of last resort.[75]

With concerted effort, he argues, this unemployment
need be only temporary. Until the prices and wages of
the small firm can be brought into relative parity with
the mature corporation an alternative income should be
available to those who lose (or currently lack) employment. Only in this manner can equity be approached.

Unfortunately, his discussion of the guaranteed
income is sorely lacking in specifics which makes its
feasibility difficult to assess. Among the issues
which Galbraith fails to discuss are the level of
coverage, the details of administration and the financing of such a program. It is of more than passing interest whether he would institute a centralized
or decentralized network, whether he would use strictly
federal funds or federal matching. These questions,
however, remain unanswered.

At one point, he does indicate that the guaranteed
income would relieve states and cities of the cost of
welfare. This would seem to suggest the use of strictly federal funding. In view of New York City's recent

financial distress, such action seems both prudent and
sane. Yet, such a program seems likely to raise the
hackles of those city fathers who currently oppose
bailing out New York City for fear of encouraging financial mismanagement on the part of other cities.
As H. R. Gross once expressed this view: "Iowa doesn't
need money for rat control, why should New York City?"

Anticipating criticism that the guaranteed income
will serve as a disincentive to work and reward para-
sitic indolence, Galbraith takes the stance of a moral
philosopher and argues that some forms of degrading
service will undoubtedly disappear if people are not
forced to defile themselves for token wages. But, in-
veighs Galbraith, some forms of unemployment, like that
of the shoeshine operators, should be encouraged in
the name of human dignity. The dilemma is phrased
succinctly by Gibson Winter when he observes that "the
issue is whether we are ready to say that our new
social reality calls for sharing resources so that
each may be free."[76]

Galbraith's affirmative response to this query
goes further than mere provision of income. His concern with the plight of those who have been denied
access to essential public services leads him to call
for public ownership of the housing, health and transportation industries. Again, he marshals evidence of
precedent and circumstance. Government took control
of education, national defense, street cleaning and
water treatment in response to the indispensability of
these services; even now, the various government programs to buoy up housing, medical services and transportation reflect an awareness that the market cannot
provide what is needed. The problem with present
action, as Galbraith sees it, is that it is inefficient
and produces overlap as well as performance gaps. Thus
the need for a unified and concerted effort.
    Only as socialism is seen as a necessary and
    wholly normal feature of the system will this
    situation change. Then there will be public de-
    mand for high performance, and there will be
    public pride in action. This is not vacuous and
    untested optimism; proof is to be found in Europe
    and Japan.[77]

Herein lies the rationale for Galbraith's espousal
of socialized housing, health care and public transportation. Urban land, public housing, hospitals,

railroads and urban transit must be, he argues, publicly owned and operated. Technical innovation and
efficient organization must be actively promoted and
employees must be well-paid employees of the government. The recent trend toward agreement that some
version of national health care is indispensable suggests a growing dissatisfaction with the performance
of medicine within the market sector of the economy.
The uncertainty which is attached to the availability
of medical and hospital care, no less than its prohib-
itive cost, has generated a wide variety of proposals
which, although less radical than Galbraith's, testify
to the need for change.

VI

Perhaps the most crucial component of Galbraith's
dream for the American future is breaking the planning
system's hold over the socio-economic environment. To
achieve this end, Galbraith advances two broad strategies. The first is to equalize wage differentials
within the corporation and to bring them into general
equality with the wages of the smaller firm. More
important is to transfer ownership of the giants to
the federal government. The two aims are mutually
supportive and, in some ways, inseparable. Both are
premised on the assumption that social justice and
economic welfare can be achieved only by constraining
the autonomy and restricting the growth of the large
corporation.

To achieve his goals, Galbraith believes several
reforms are necessary. First, he would stimulate white
collar union formation and make compensation differentials within the corporate hierarchy a key issue of
collective bargaining negotiations. Even as he proposes this measure, one senses that Galbraith places
little faith in its feasibility. Yet, given the recent rise in white collar union membership, the reason
for his skepticism is not entirely clear.

More important, he would reform the existing income tax system in order to make it more progressive;
he would disallow such free compensations as the expense account and club sponsorship and eliminate the
prefered tax-status of capital gains income (by which
the upper income groups' capital gains are assessed at
half of the maximum tax rate).[78] This type of tax
reform has, it should be observed, long been supported
and even proposed; unfortunately, Galbraith offers no

reason to believe that such a proposal will be any
more successful now than it has been in the past.   If
passed, however, it would provide a crucial source of
revenue with which to finance Galbraith's other proposals.

Third, he would institute price and wage control
among the mature corporations. His own experience with
price control has convinced him of the feasibility of
such action in the case of oligopolistic industries
so long as it is supplemented by appropriate fiscal
measures to restrain demand.[79] Significantly, he does
not propose freezing all prices and wages, but suggests
that controls be selective and that the wages of the
lower paid workers advance in accordance with productivity gains in order to narrow income differentials. In this regard, he suggests the possibility
of establishing a maximum permissible range between
average and maximum compensation; equalization would
then develop gradually.

Finally, Galbraith proposes converting the "fully
mature corporations--those that have completed the
euthanasia of stockholder power" and those that conduct more than fifty percent of their business with
the government into fully public corporations.[80] The
means by which Galbraith would effect this end is
through government purchase of extant stocks with
fixed interest-bearing securities. (While not eliminating inequality, loss of stock would at least pre-
clude further dividends and capital gains from increasing rather than narrowing the gap.) Henceforth,
both the board of directors and the senior management
would be appointed by the government.

This final step, it should be apparent, greatly
enhances the ability of the government to monitor employee compensation and move America closer to an
equalitarian structure. It also allows government to
constrain corporate influence upon the consumer and
the legislature by curtailing advertising and lobbying.
Also of importance is the fact that corporate profits,
rather than being retained as a cushion, would accrue
to the government. This would allow the government
to impose restrictions upon corporate growth and to
limit the technostructure's decision making autonomy.
Decisions on plant location, executive salary and promotion standards would become public matters. These
advantages notwithstanding, one must ask how, following

Galbraith's own analysis, a disinterested board of directors which is dependent upon corporate specialists for information will be able to significantly redirect or check the power of the technostructure.

What must be realized in this regard is that Galbraith's aim is not to stymie growth but to restrain it and align it with the public purpose. Social and environmental costs will, for instance, be weighted against the benefits of certain types of production. Again, this evaluation will rest, not with nameless bureaucrats, but with members of the legislature who, in Galbraith's estimation, are less susceptible to corporate bamboozlement.[81]

The legislature is also charged with overseeing Galbraith's proposed public planning authority. This group should not be confused with the aforementioned planning system. The new group is essentially a public protector charged with preventing such occurrences as the recent blackouts, news print shortages and gas shortages. As Galbraith has argued, the "solution is to recognize the logic of planning with its resulting imperative of coordination."[82] Because the corporations have proven themselves incapable of coordinating their efforts, Galbraith argues, an independent agency must be established.[83]

His analysis is predicated on the belief that only government can (will) anticipate disparities between the various sectors and promote interindustry coordination. In certain instances, Galbraith argues, the situation will require retardation of demand and, in other cases, stimulation of supply. Thus, while discouraging the use and production of electrical appliances and designing buildings with better insulation to conserve energy, public authorities would actively encourage the development of new sources and contribute to the improvement of currently unprofitable energy sources.

Galbraith's program recommends itself largely because of its moderation. While his program is far less comprehensive than the indicative planning embraced by Western European nations,[84] this is part of its appeal. The technostructure is allowed to maintain much of its autonomy because, in Galbraith's estimation, "the autonomous corporate organization, is a highly useful device for undertaking and conducting complex indus-

trial tasks."[85] But, under Galbraith's scheme,
autonomy would become a pragmatic decision--given a
clash of interests, the government would intervene
as a matter of course. One wonders, however, whether
workers' protests against management-induced speedups
would induce intervention. Again, Galbraith's lack
of specificity makes his scheme difficult to evaluate.

Yet, the gradualism by which his proposals would
alter the social and economic order is a part of his
plans' practicability. As Michael Harrington has
candidly admitted, "there is neither political support
nor administrative feasibility for the sudden decisive nationalization of an entire economy."[86] Similarly, John Gambs has argued that before comprehensive
national planning becomes possible in the United
States,
> The conventional wisdom must first be the object
> of considerable erosion....We still cling des-
> perately to the myths of individual initiative,
> laissez-faire and private enterprise, and we do
> not tolerate the idea of planning (despite the
> fact that much planning does go on). Our federal
> government, with its tradition of states' rights,
> makes us balk at national economic legislation.[87]
Hence the importance of Galbraith's critique and his
"modest proposal."

Perhaps the most troubling aspect of Galbraith's
proposed reform is his failure to adequately outline
the manner in which it would eradicate the bureaucratic
symbiosis which he has described.[88] While the legislature demonstrated a potential efficacy for controlling the corporate prerogative in its refusal to grant
funds to the development of the SST, it has not always
been so free of bureaucratic pressure. In fact, as
Robert Heilbroner has argued, it seems quite possible
"that nationalizing the armament makers will make them
less, not more, subject to public control by bringing
them under the protective arm of the Pentagon as a
permanent part of the bureaucracy."[89]

Significantly, Galbraith has conceded that his
proposed socialization of the mature corporations is
a change of "form rather than substance,"[90] since they
are already quasi-public institutions. The issue,
then, is whether government ownership affords more or
less control over corporate affairs. While no definitive answer is possible, one must assume that there

is financial advantage to allowing the government to
benefit from profits rather than merely allowing it
to absorb losses as is currently the case. Further,
one should not underplay the advantage of divesting
passive stockholders of dividends and capital gains
which merely compound existing income inequities.

Even granting these advantages, one must wonder
whether leaving corporate and inter-industry structures intact is not counterproductive in terms of Galbraith's intended equalization within the economy.
Currently government subsidies for R & D as well as
government contracts have had the effect of favoring
the leading firms rather than reducing the asymmet-
rical nature of existing oligopolies. In large
measure, this preferential treatment has been a response to the ease and security of contracting with
established and proven firms. Without a radical over-
haul of the criteria by which funds are awarded
this discriminatory treatment seems likely to continue. As Shepherd indicates:

> Even at the high-water mark of competitive pro-
> curement in 1966-1967, much the greater mass of
> purchasing was still on an essentially noncom-
> petitive basis, and not just in aerospace in-
> dustries. This may tend to strengthen leading
> firms, reducing the prospects for mutual ero-
> sion of leading positions via innovative and
> other efforts by lesser firms.[91]

The point to be borne in mind is that new standards
could be formulated. Again what is required is more
definitive legislation stipulating the conditions
under which federal funds will be allocated. This
possibility becomes more likely in the context of
Galbraith's other proposals--Congress would conduct
a comprehensive budget review and would have the
power to redistribute funds among the various recipients; an independent planning authority would
study inter-industry disparities and propose to Congress appropriate means of offsetting these imbalances.

In the final analysis, the practicability of
Galbraith's program is dependent upon popular response
and legislative initiative. The trends discussed at
the beginning of this chapter provide a basis for
hope, but, as Galbraith is in the habit of saying,
history will be the final arbiter and judge.

Having reviewed the major components of the Galbraithian vision, it is now necessary to attempt a general assessment of his contributions to the field of social criticism. Although definitive conclusions are not possible, chapter seven will attempt to place his critique within its ideological and philosophical contexts, noting how it diverges from the orthodox creed and yet remains firmly within the democratic tradition.

A MAN OF GOOD HOPE: THE VISION REVIEWED

Nearly four decades after the culmination of the New
Deal, Galbraith has advanced a prognosis which is
vaguely reminiscent of economist Rexford Tugwell's
1934 prediction that "we are going forward toward a
realm of cooperative plenty the like of which the world
never has seen."[1] Whether Galbraith's proposed reforms
will be any more able than the New Deal legislation to
propel America into this era of cooperation and social
justice remains an open question. Yet, it is clear
that Galbraith has what Schumpeter calls "vision"--a
new perception of old facts, an unconventional interpretation of common sense reality. Galbraith, in John
Gambs' view, "is trying...to make us take a second
look--this time a clear look at reality, not as it is
conceived in the mixture of poetry, myth and self-
deception which is so much part of standard economic
theory."[2]

What distinguishes Galbraith's work from that of
his colleagues is less the originality of his particular insights and interpretations than the inclusiveness of his theoretical system and the circulation
which his works have received. Not content to limit
his analysis to economics, he insists upon delving
into both social philosophy and public policy. As
one reviewer has commented, "Galbraith knows (in fact
insists) that an economic theory implies an ethical
system, a political purpose, and a psychological
hypothesis."[3] His holistic perspective predisposes
him to see the economic system as a dynamic cultural
component which can only be understood by means of
interdisciplinary study.

For this reason, he has often been dismissed by
more orthodox thinkers as a nonscientific popularizer.
In part, such charges can be viewed as an outgrowth
of professional jealousy. (After all, how many economists have published not just one, but several, best
sellers?)[4] But, in a larger sense, this dismissal can
be interpreted as an outgrowth of what may broadly be
called an ideological cleavage--a cleavage which must
be discussed in some detail in order to properly assess Galbraith's contribution to cultural criticism.

Traditionally, social scientists have operated within a perspective which awarded high valuation to individualism, property rights, free enterprise, a limited state and scientific specialization. This creed, which can be traced to the Enlightenment, has long been revered by Americans; it constitutes a major component of the American Dream of success.[5]

It is this frame of reference which undergirds ex-Secretary of of the Treasury William Simon's charge that "Government interventions in the free market, even when done for the most laudable purposes, frequently result in less competition, less incentive for production, higher costs, higher prices, and ultimately fewer goods and services than we need."[6] The fact that low income housing, to cite but one example, is, by definition, unprofitable and hence contradictory to the aims of both entrepreneurs and corporate managers is never seriously considered. According to Simon, the lesson of history is that "the system of free enterprise, despite its many flaws, is the most compatible with the protection of rights and liberties as well as the most productive of material goods."[7]

By now, it should be clear that Galbraith's vision places him in a far different philosophical camp from Simon and those who share his views. Galbraith's primary purpose, in fact, has been to discredit this perspective and to challenge the priorities which it sanctions. His significance is tied to the fact that he has offered the reader a new way of perceiving the structure, function and interconnection of social and economic phenomena as well as a means of rethinking the individual's position within the larger institutional network.[8]

In order to understand Galbraith's distinctiveness, it is imperative to consider his attitude toward the five key components of the traditional perspective mentioned above. Only in this way is it possible to understand his critique of the ideological underpinnings of American society (section II), the transition which has characterized his thinking (section III) or his espousal of increased government intervention as a means of realizing progressive and/or Jeffersonian values and ideals (section IV).

II

It has long been Galbraith's claim that the vast social changes which have keynoted our history have undermined the appropriateness of the orthodox faith in free enterprise and have transformed the socioeconomic system into a vehicle which frustrates individual aspirations. No longer is society dominated by the traditional Horatio Alger prototypic individual. Instead, as Monsen and Cannon have indicated, people are being forced more and more to work within the confines of organized institutions in order to gain a sense of accomplishment and achieve personal goals.[9] Technology, to Galbraith's way of thinking, has radically altered the structure of society; economic and political power have enabled the corporation to dictate national priorities and to determine what goods and services are available and what training is appropriate. In this sense, the corporation has altered the ability to define the options available to the individual. This, as noted in the first chapter, is an outgrowth of technological rationality which has left the individual subject to and dependent upon an intricate web of social institutions not only for nurture, but equally for survival.

Herein lies the importance of Galbraith's emphasis upon social justice. Rather than campaigning for a broader opportunity structure, as such, Galbraith is intent upon promoting a more egalitarian social structure--a structure, that is, which facilitates not only equal opportunity but equitable result as well. He is quick to reject the apologies of the survival-of-the-fittest Social Darwinists. Although not insensitive to the plight of Sumner's "forgotten man," Galbraith is more concerned with the rights and dignities of those who, according to the conventional wisdom, are indolent and thus deserve to suffer the consequences of their choice.[10]

In a technologically sophisticated society, the notion of the rugged individual becomes an anachronism. Without access to organization, the individual becomes less and less able to improve his/her position. Denied "proper" training, the poor find that the opportunity structure, although allegedly non-discriminatory, is beyond their reach.[11] To rectify this situation, Galbraith has forged a pragmatic program which goes beyond "the subtly philosophical quandaries of meritocracy vs. equality."[12]

Property rights, according to Galbraith, rather
than a safeguard of individual liberty, are a major
cause of economic and political inequities. Social
change has effectively transformed the function of
property, equipping it with the power to confer un-
deserved gain, to broaden the gap between those at
the top and those at the bottom of the social structure, and to impose cumulative costs and discomforts
upon the community.[13] Given a complex social order
it becomes impossible to ignore the myriad inter-
dependencies which invalidate traditional claims to
prerogatives. Hence the need to assert human rights
over property rights.

Equally damaging to the orthodox philosophy
is the decline of competition within the economy.
Once it is recognized that the mature corporations
possess vast power in both the economic and political spheres, invocation of free enterprise ration-
alizations becomes less persuasive.[14] Application
of reason and foresight to the socioeconomic arena
begins to seem both beneficial and necessary. To
assert that the individual is not a passive recipient of his/her external environment is to open the
way for progressive change. It is also to admit that
technology has provided the opportunity for the e-
rection of a truly human community inhabited not only
by the comfortable three-fifths of the affluent
society, but by those currently outside of the mainstream as well.[15]

To advance these ends requires more responsive
governmental action, not less government intervention.
Due to the nature of the disparities outlined in
chapters four and five, remedial action to establish
a parity between the planning and market systems
must be a concerted national effort.[16] So long as
powerful corporations can assert their will upon
both the public and the state, future developments
will proceed according to their specifications. Only
by redefining goals and priorities and enacting
measures geared to strengthen the bargaining position
of the market-oriented firm can redistribution of
resources and income be accomplished.

Galbraith's analysis is informed by a further departure from the traditional view. Rather than direct
his energies toward scientific specialization, he has
sought to demonstrate the importance of a holistic

146

perspective. Inherent in specialization is the risk of losing touch with the larger context since each discipline, in an attempt to achieve a higher degree of sophistication, severs the connection between itself and other disciplines. Public policy prescriptions are, accordingly, often formulated with a limited understanding of how changes in other parts of the culture effect the workability of the various proposals.

The fundamental difference between the orthodox perspective and the Galbraithian vision seems to be an outgrowth of divergent definitions of the purpose of economic research. If the social scientist is primarily interested in behavioral propositions and highly sophisticated means of predicting responses under certain conditions, then it is quite justifiable to suspend reality in the name of science. Yet, to the humanist, such abstraction often culminates in what Dwight MacDonald has described as a "coefficient of comprehensibility that decreases in direct ratio to the mass and length of the study, with a standard deviation from the obvious, inversely related to the magnitude of the generalization."[17]

Thus, in keeping with a humanistic stance, the social scientist may choose to employ the discipline as a means of illuminating extant disparities and shaping responsive policies. If this be the aim, the analyst is forced to question the underlying purposes of human behavior, to study the human condition within the sociocultural context, and to propose alternatives to the status quo. Only by studying both the internal and external dynamics of the system can the social scientist transcend the restrictiveness of the equilibrium model and broaden the discipline in order to bring it into touch with current social problems.

III

Throughout this analysis of the Galbraithian vision, emphasis has been placed upon Galbraith's willingness to adjust his thinking in response to social and cultural changes. This willingness to change demonstrates not inconstancy, but the weight of changing situational imperatives. A revealing parallel occurred in the early days of the Johnson administration. Despite (or possibly because of) Galbraith's commitment to Kennedy, he never wavered in his decision to work for Johnson following Kennedy's death. Commenting on the situation somewhat later, Galbraith recalled:

> Arthur (Schlesinger) divided the community in
> Washington into two categories, the realists and
> loyalists. The loyalists would resign and try to
> find an alternative to Johnson. The realists, a
> group to which, alas, I was assigned, took the
> Democratic Party in earnest and would continue to
> give their best to it, however little that might
> be.[18]

He has assumed a similar stance in the face of socio-
economic change. Less intent upon being consistent
than on being "in touch," if you will, he has repeatedly discarded those ideas and proposals which no
longer seem to "fit" the external reality.

The lack of rigidity can be seen as an outgrowth
of his definition of the economists' role in society.
For Galbraith the terms "economic theory," "political
economics," and "economics" are all synonymous. Accordingly, he recognizes a dual role for economists:
they must be willing and able to describe the socio-
economic landscape in terms which are comprehensible
and useful to those outside the profession; they must
also be prepared to take a responsive stance, to reassess past presumptions and judgments.

The extent to which Galbraith has fulfilled these
roles becomes clear when one compares the proposals
advanced in _American Capitalism_ and those propounded
in _Economics and the Public Purpose_. Such a comparison bears out Heilbroner's observation:

> It is difficult to believe today that in _American
> Capitalism_, published in 1952, power—while al-
> ready identified as the crucial problem within
> capitalist economics—was on the whole treated
> kindly and regarded as essentially self-annulling
> through the "countervailing" competition among
> power-holders.[19]

The point is that at this stage in his career Galbraith was still firmly committed to Keynesian economics and invested much energy in gaining it respectability. Within the political climate of the 1950s—
a climate teeming with accusations and fear and hardly
responsive to unorthodox viewpoints—this was doubtless a sufficiently arduous task to make one question
whether complacency might not be a far more viable
(safer) stance.

Yet, as early as 1953, Galbraith became disenchanted with the Keynesian preoccupation with employ-

ment _qua_ employment and production _qua_ production.
Further, he suspected that the Keynesian revolution had
been absorbed by the mature corporations insofar as
government expenditures tended to be devoted disproportionately to military and industrial development.
The need, as he came to define it, was for a more realistic socioeconomic theory which would lay bare the
disparate tendencies affecting the performance of the
various economic sectors. Thus, instead of construct-
ing elaborate path analyses, Venn diagrams, or preference curves, he set out to formulate a theory based on
valid assumptions--a theory which, while lacking the
abstract minutia and technical sophistication of orthodoxy, would nevertheless provide a basis for more
accurate anticipation of corporate behavior. In this
sense, his work reflects what C. Wright Mills termed
a search for enlightenment rather than obscurantism.

In his search for the causes of poverty, he was
initially impressed by the intrinsic connection between
social services and economic welfare. The time had
come, he argued, to place less emphasis upon production
and more emphasis upon redistribution and public services. While Keynesians railed that without increased
production there could be no improving the plight of
the poor, Galbraith insisted that postponing decisions
to reallocate resources and restrain growth until
everyone had achieved a subsistence level of income
would merely intensify existing disparities and frustrate, perhaps permanently, attempts to achieve a more
egalitarian society. While the impact of this argument cannot be measured with precision, it is significant that since its publication, economists who would
trust an expansive Gross National Product to resolve
pressing social tensions have become an almost extinct
species.

Many of the insights which Galbraith propounded
in The Affluent Society continue to occupy a central
position in his vision. Manipulation of the consumer,
starvation of the public services and the somewhat irrational commitment to production have been the most
durable. The most significant shift which has informed
his work is to be found in his proposed reforms.

Neither price and wage control nor a guaranteed
income played a major role in his 1958 scheme; nor,
in retrospect, does it seem likely that either would
have won widespread political endorsement. In their

place, Galbraith offered his Cyclically Graduated Compensation scheme which would have provided a federal subsidy to state unemployment compensation. This payment would have varied directly with the level of unemployment at a given time. With three percent unemployment, for example, the worker would have received fifty percent of the difference between his previous wage and his state compensation; with six percent unemployment, on the other hand, the federal supplement might have been as high as eighty percent of the difference.

Subsequently, this proposal was laid to rest, perhaps in part because, in Galbraith's assessment, "it may well have been the only economic reform, good or bad, never to have enlisted a single advocate apart from its author."[20] Gone too in later books was his emphasis upon the desirability of implementing a more stringent sales tax in order to provide municipalities with the funds needed to redress social imbalances.

Conversely, his emphasis upon the need to humanize the workaday world has remained central to his vision. In The New Industrial State, he returned to a concern introduced toward the end of The Affluent Society, with employing our technological and material capabilities to increase the options available to the average worker. In his earlier work, his major concern seemed to be with promoting a "New Class"--a class of professionals who were engaged in employment which they found both satisfying and challenging. Through educational endowment (with the educational institution exercising paramount authority and/or discretion over its curriculum and its resources) it was Galbraith's hope that participation in this class would continue to grow. In his later work, he suggests a number of options which could be made available to the worker; each is modeled to a significant extent upon the options available to the academic. There is, of course, the possibility of sabbaticals or extended leaves of absence. But, beyond this, and probably more practicable, is the option to elect several months of paid vacation in return for a lower annual pay.

The significance of such proposals lies in the fact that they provide the individual with alternatives which can be chosen in accordance with personal needs rather than in compliance with the needs of the industrial system. This takes on special importance in his

more recent discussions of how to integrate women into
the work force. Legal support via affirmative action,
according to Galbraith, is only part of the answer.
There is additionally the need for increased educational opportunities and day care services.

But more important still is an extension of the
range of choices as to the length of the work week and
year for the individual. To make the transition easier
for the women who are attempting to alter their situation, but still have old responsibilities to meet, a
15 to 20 hour work week, for example, would be of immeasurable importance. Further, with an increasing
number of dual career families, flexibility becomes
even more imperative. Commitment to a standard work
week and year assumes, as Galbraith notes, that "all
workers have roughly the same preference as between income and what it buys and leisure and the enjoyments
it allows."[21] Such an assertion, Galbraith argues,
flies in the face of reason and reifies what is managerial convenience rather than an economic necessity.

Whether Galbraith will continue to propose remedies broadly similar to those discussed in chapter
six, remains to be seen. Yet, it is of some significance that his latest books, Money: Whence It Came,
Where It Went (1975) and The Age of Uncertainty (1977)
reveal a broad continuity between their proposals and
those of previous books. In Money, Galbraith identifies six imperatives, none of which is wholly unprecedented in his other books. They include: reduced
use of monetary policy; increased use of a dynamic
fiscal policy (one capable of restraining as well as
stimulating demand); equity in income distribution; a
national planning agency which can anticipate shortages and adjust supply and use to one another; and
international currency stabilization.[22]

IV

Galbraith's confidence in human rationality is perhaps the key to understanding his intellectual orientation. Although he often chides the consumer for
gullibility, rebukes the politician for lack of im-
magination and scolds the economist for obtuseness,
he speaks from deep within the democratic tradition.
His progressive orientation reveals itself in his
relentless campaign for leaders who are responsive
and willing to innovate. The alternative to a people's
government, Galbraith insists, is government by the
mature corporation.

Galbraith's peripatetic spiritual forefather,
Thorstein Veblen, saw a similar need to loosen the hold
of the predatory culture and its barbarian-pecuniary
values. Yet, he placed little faith in the efficacy
of reform, despite his occasional flirtations with the
notion of a soviet of engineers. While not misan-
thropic, Veblen scoffed at the efforts of the humani-
tarians--Dewey, Lloyd, Addams and others--who sought
to renovate petrified institutions; he distrusted their
fervor and held that only the painstaking process of
machine discipline could eventually break the hold of
conventional attitudes and prejudices. Veblen's
naturalism, no less than his contempt for the "cap-
tains of erudition," left him skeptical, bitter and
extremely pessimistic about the future. He was, therefore, unable (or unwilling) to propose positive remedies for the contradictions which he depicted.

Galbraith, on the other hand, believes that the
intellectual must be both a system builder and a
prophetic agitator, as it were. This requires both
criticism and policy prescriptions. There is always
the possibility that had Veblen been exposed to a less
pietistic academic and social milieu, he, too, might
have committed himself to social reform. His agnostic-
ism, as well as his idiosyncratic personality, ill-
equipped him for the temper of the time. Additionally,
as Breit and Ransom have indicated,

Veblen wrote in a period when the progressive
movement had made little headway against the
orthodoxy of the nineteenth century liberalism.
Few took his proposals seriously in the first
decade of this century. It is less clear that
the same could be said of Galbraith. Set in a
far more conducive atmosphere for recommen-
dations for government action, Galbraith's policy oriented observations have attracted wide
attention.[23]
Also of importance in understanding Galbraith's more
optimistic bent is the growing influence of intellectuals within the industrialized society. Specialization has increased the status commanded by education, just as it has made those in power dependent
upon specialists for technical assistance.[24]

Herein lies the explanation for Galbraith's
emphasis upon the power of education and the professional community. There is a perverse similarity
between Galbraith's view of the intellectual and that

expressed by Joseph Schumpeter. Both see the intellectual as a nay-sayer, who has the ability to transform the very manner in which people define the external reality. Where the two men part company is in their reaction to this development. For Schumpeter, the intellectual is a subverter using words as weapons to delude the masses and to engender an environment which is hostile to capitalism. For Galbraith, the intellectual is an emancipator using reason to break the hold of the mature corporation upon the public and the government.

Galbraith's faith in the ability of the intellectual is, it should be noted, reminiscent of Mannheim's belief that the free floating intelligentsia could transcend both ideology and utopia. In fact, Galbraith's insistence that his reforms are an outgrowth, not of ideology, but of historical necessity, merely reinforces this interpretation. Yet, given the support which orthodox thought accords to the status quo and, hence, to a perpetuation of corporate power, the need for critical examination of both the ideology and the operation of the existing system can hardly be denied. Galbraith merely offers an alternative way of looking at reality; the task of initiating reform remains with the public.

While his optimism may be somewhat exaggerated, it places him not among the utopians, but among the "possibilitists" who maintain that man is not a hapless creature, but a dynamic actor with the capacity to improve the human condition. His is a philosophy of social experimentalism within the context of a mixed economy. The "enemy" is not big government or big business, but unrestrained power and privilege. Only by eliminating these, albeit gradually, can the classless or open society be constructed.

His involvement with the New Deal is at least partially responsible for his faith in the efficacy of reform. As far as it went, Roosevelt's legislation did much to mitigate the economic insecurity of the worker and the instability of the market. Of cardinal importance is the fact that it broke the barrier between government and free enterprise and thus provided the necessary wedge with which to implement much more comprehensive reform. While the New Deal stopped short of transforming the basic power structure of society, as Sievers notes, the "economic responsibility of government has been established, and accordingly government must be looked to for future progress."[25]

The explanation for the shortcomings of the New Deal are many and are, finally, beyond the scope of this discussion. What is important to understand, however, is that the limitations were, at least in part, situationally determined. Formulated in response to crisis, the major goal was restoration rather than re-creation; the means were devised to cure particular problems rather than to alter the overall structure. The problem, as Galbraith came to define it, was that the old order (laissez faire capitalism) had been undermined, but the new order remained inchoate. Rather than averting his eyes or postponing decision, Galbraith sought to analyze what he saw as a conflict between the working values and espoused values and to propose a social reorganization which could come to terms with this dilemma.

Herein lies the major appeal of the Galbraithian viewpoint; it offers a vision which revolves around the democratic values of freedom (from the planning system), dignity (of all persons) and equality (of result rather than opportunity). The means which Galbraith proposes are, it is true, Hamiltonian insofar as they revolve around an enlarged state, but given the concrete presence of large, powerful corporations, espousal of a decentralized or unregulated socio-economic system is tantamount to sanctioning the status quo. The welfare of the people at large, according to Galbraith, can only be insured by a comprehensive program of reform.

Galbraith's early exposure to the tradition of the self sufficient farmer conjoined with his training in Calvinist doctrine might, in the absence of other influences, have led to his dogmatic defense of traditional values. Yet, as indicated in chapter two, he was schooled within an atmosphere keynoted by the rivalry of the Scotch Liberals and the English Tories. As in America, industrialization was galvanizing agrarian resentment. Galbraith's father's denunciations of the privileges accorded the townsmen, no less than the royal family, manifested a strong populist emphasis. This, rather than the harsh Calvinism, left a lasting imprint on Galbraith's vision. Galbraith, like his father, has refused to sit back and await change; he has insisted upon promoting it.

In the course of his career, he was exposed to the tension-riven atmosphere of the Depression, but also to the idealism of the Roosevelt administration. His own rapid advancement from Ontario to Berkeley and then to Harvard (which, to read his account, was in no way extraordinary), surely contributed to his optimistic outlook. His decision to direct his writing to a non-specialized audience reflected his confidence in the people's capacity for skepticism as well as his own dissatisfaction with traditional explanations and justifications for the imbalances within the economy and the inequity within the society. These concerns continue to impel his writing and will, in all likelihood, continue to do so as long as economic and social forces seem to remain in the service of the powerful rather than the populists.

V

Having come to the end of this study, we are left with one final question--what is Galbraith's contribution? If he has drawn upon the work of countless specialists in industrial organization, labor relations, and other areas, why should he, rather than they, be credited with originality? While these questions are valid ones, and while historians may well side with those who would reduce him to a footnote, yet in terms of the present, his significance seems undeniable.

The importance of his formulations as compared to those of his more orthodox colleagues lies in both the angle of his vision and his method of presentation. Galbraith is both a generalist and an iconoclast; he brings sociohistorical data to his study of the economy. Accordingly, he has been able to go beyond partial investigation and to propound a general theory of economic society which relates to the broader socio-economic pressures which shape the contemporary American experience. In so doing, he has been more able to see the interrelationships between the various findings of the specialists and to integrate these into a broader ranged theory.

Directly related to the significance of this synthesis of myriad specialized studies is the wide circulation which his ideas have received. Since the vast majority of even the college educated population has little contact with technical economics, save possibly one or two basic courses, there is little likelihood that they will be aware of specialized

studies of economic concentration, market power, corporate behavior or even welfare economics. While they
may sense that the system is not operating as it
should, they will have more difficulty understanding
why. In fact, even if the advanced studies of the
economy were made available, people might still have
trouble, since they would be unprepared to decipher
the charts, graphs, diagrams and equations.

Herein lies a large part of Galbraith's appeal.
Not only has he synthesized a vast body of material,
but even more important, he has presented it in such
a way as to make it comprehensible to a nonprofessional
audience. In so doing, he has injected into "the dismal science" a large dose of humanism. By rejecting
traditional economic measurements as unreliable indicators of the quality of life, he has championed
the causes of the farmer, the consumer, the artist, the
small businessman and the environment. Additionally,
his humor, while sometimes urbane and often caustic, is
seldom artless and does much to enhance his readability
and to enlarge his audience. Even his recent history
of money is filled with _good_ _humor_ and sparks with
life.

His unorthodox perspective, his responsiveness,
his progressive vision (no less than his iconoclasm,
his synthesizing and his comprehensiveness) when taken
together have earned him a place in the annals of the
twentieth century. Yet the critic's place in history
is, by definition, ambiguous for reasons suggested in
chapter one. Therefore, rather than attempting to
outguess the muses of history, it seems fitting to
take heed of Daniel Aaron's assessment of the earlier
progressives:

> America has never deified its iconoclasts. But
> the disturbers of the peace, although ordinarily
> unappreciated and ignored by the majority, are a
> complacent nation's most precious possession. A
> true evaluation of America's great men would in-
> clude not only the generals and statesmen and
> athletes, the builders of mousetraps and pipe
> lines, but our 'prophetic agitators,' excluded
> from the American pantheon, who devoted themselves
> to the unprofitable and thankless task of human
> betterment.[26]

Galbraith's alliance with those who would promote
change and bring America closer to the communitarian
ideal espoused throughout our history remains firm.

Regardless of whether his exact system of reforms is
accepted, few would deny that he has added an important
component to the on-going dialogue which will determine
America's priorities and goals and, by extension, America's future.

NOTES

1
INTRODUCTION: THE CRITICAL CHALLENGE

[1]Marvin Meyers, The Jacksonian Persuasion: Politics and Belief (Stanford, California: Stanford University Press, 1960), p. vii.

[2]Frederick G. Dutton, Changing Sources of Power
(New York: McGraw Hill Company, 1971), p. 12. See also
Andrew Hacker, The End of the American Era (New York:
Atheneum, 1971).

[3]John Kenneth Galbraith, Economics Peace and
Laughter (New York:New American Library, Signet edition, 1972), p. 24.

[4]Allen M. Sievers, Revolution, Evolution, and the
Economic Order (Englewood Cliffs, New Jersey: Prentice-
Hall, Inc., 1962), p. 2. Daniel Bell indicates: "The
key question remains one of political economy. On a
technical level, economic answers to the organization
of production, control of inflation, maintenance of
full employment, etc., are available. Political answers, in an interest-group society like ours, are not
so easy." Daniel Bell, The End of Ideology, revised
(New York: The Free Press, 1965), pp. 93-4.

[5]See Thomas Kuhn, The Structure of Scientific Revolution, second edition (Chicago: University of Chicago
Press, 1970).

[6]Robert L. Heilbroner, The Worldly Philosophers,
fourth edition (New York: Simon and Schuster, Touchstone edition, 1972), p. 319. Significantly, Robert
Lekachman observes that "Retreating from 'subjective'
value judgments to observed behavior and measurable
data, welfare theorists no longer believe that inter-
personal judgments and comparisons can be made, at
least by scientists. But if they cannot be made, then
there is no objective way to say, for example, that a
tax change which redistributes income from rich to
poor is more likely to improve welfare than a shift
which takes income from the poor and gives it to the
rich....the tendency is evident in conventional econ-

159

omics' reliance upon <u>neutral</u> <u>concepts</u> <u>which</u> <u>have</u> <u>the</u> <u>actual</u> <u>effect</u> <u>of</u> <u>reinforcing</u> <u>existing</u> <u>institutional</u> <u>arrangements</u> <u>or</u> <u>at</u> <u>the</u> <u>least</u> <u>softening</u> <u>the</u> <u>outlines</u> <u>of</u> <u>genuine</u> <u>real</u> <u>world</u> <u>problems</u>." (Emphasis added.) Robert Lekachman, "Special Introduction" in David Mermelstein (ed.), <u>Economics:Mainstream Readings</u> <u>and</u> <u>Radical</u> <u>Critiques</u> (New York: Random House, 1970), p. xii.

[7]For a more extended discussion of the need for change see Sievers, <u>op.</u> <u>cit.</u>, pp. 3-6. See also Gabriel Kolko, <u>Wealth</u> <u>and</u> <u>Power</u> <u>in</u> <u>America</u> (New York: Praeger Publishers, 1962). In the words of the late C. Wright Mills, "Fresh perception now involves the capacity continually   to unmask and to smash the stereotypes of vision and intellect with which modern communications swamp us....If the thinker does not relate himself to the value of truth in political struggle, he cannot responsively cope with the whole of live experience." C. Wright Mills, <u>Power,</u> <u>Politics</u> <u>and</u> <u>People</u> (New York: Ballantine Books, 1963), p. 299.

[8]See Allen Wheelis, <u>The</u> <u>Quest</u> <u>for</u> <u>Identity</u> (New York: W.W. Norton and Company, Inc., 1958). See also Peter Berger, <u>The</u> <u>Sacred</u> <u>Canopy</u> (Garden City, New York: Doubleday and Company, Inc., 1969) for an extended analysis of the processes of institutionalization and its subsequent impact upon belief.

[9]Thorstein Veblen, <u>The</u> <u>Theory</u> <u>of</u> <u>the</u> <u>Leisure</u> <u>Class</u> (Boston: Houghton Mifflin, 1973), p. 145. It is in this sense that Berger and Luckmann use the term "legitimization": "Legitimization 'explains' the institutional order by giving a normative dignity to its practical imperatives." Peter Berger and Thomas Luckmann, <u>The</u> <u>Social</u> <u>Construction</u> <u>of</u> <u>Reality</u> (Garden City, New York: Doubleday and Company, Inc., 1967), p. 93.

[10]Wheelis, for one, concludes that "Reality can be altered, particularly if it is closely observed. Indeed, the better one understands it and the more tools one has to deal with it, the more radically it can be changed." Wheelis, <u>op.</u> <u>cit.</u>, p. 75.

[11]Herbert Marcuse, <u>One-Dimensional</u> <u>Man</u> (Boston: Beacon Press, 1964), p. 79.

[12]Gibson Winter, <u>Being</u> <u>Free</u> (New York: The Macmillan Company, 1970), p. 69.

[13]See Allan G. Gruchy, Modern Economic Thought: The American Contribution (New York: Prentice-Hall, Inc., 1947), pp. 23-4. Of significance in this regard is Seligman's observation that there is a strange ad hoc quality about recent social science research--"the efforts of the economist seem unrelated to those of the sociologist; the investigations of the social psychologist appear completely distinct from the insights of the political scientist; the social worker refuses to listen to operations analysts; and none will pay heed to the philosopher or historian." Ben B. Seligman, Economics of Dissent (Chicago: Quadrangle Books, 1968), p. xi.

[14]Burkart Holzner, Reality Construction in Society, revised edition (Cambridge, Massachusetts: Schenkman Publishing Company, Inc., 1972), p. 87.

[15]Robert Fogel and Stanley Engerman, Time on the Cross: The Economics of Slavery in the Antebellum South (Boston, 1974).

[16]Marcuse, op. cit., pp. 107-8. More extensive examination of this phenomenon will be presented in chapter three.

[17]The terms are taken from Alvin W. Gouldner, The Coming Crisis of Western Sociology (New York: Avon Books, 1971). See also Burkart Holzner, op. cit.; Thomas Kuhn, op. cit.; Karl Mannheim, Ideology and Utopia (New York: Harcourt, Brace and World, Inc., 1936); and Kenneth E. Boulding, The Image (Ann Arbor: University of Michigan Press, 1968).

[18]Sievers, op. cit., p. 8.

[19]Paul and Percival Goodman, Communitas, revised (New York: Vintage Books, 1960). Following a critique of what has gone wrong with functional analysis, they propose a neo-functionalism. "We therefore, going back to Greek antiquity, propose a different line of interpretation altogether; form follows function, but let us subject the function itself to a formal critique. Is the function good? Bona fide? Is it worthwhile? Is it worthy of man to do that? What are the consequences? Is it compatible with other, basic human functions? Is it a forthright or at least ingenious part of life? Does it make sense?" (p. 19.)

161

[20]Edward Shils, The Intellectuals and the Powers and Other Essays (Chicago: University of Chicago Press, 1972), p. 154.

[21]John R. Commons, Myself (New York: The Macmillan Company, 1934), p. 110. See also pp. 124-5.

[22]Sidney Willhelm, "Elites, Scholars, and Sociologists," in Larry T. and Janice M. Reynolds (eds.), The Sociology of Sociology (New York: David McKay Company, Inc., 1970), p. 121. Kolko concurs: "Instead of assuming an attitude of criticism, contemporary social observers have become advocates of the equalitarian society they believe to exist. Conservative in their approach they neither draw implications for the future nor point to any shortcomings in the present. Instead, they hail the accomplishments of the status quo. In this way they avoid the need to subject their assertions to any rigorous scrutiny." Kolko, op. cit., p. 133. In regard to the inherent conservativism of marginal analysis in economics see Lekachman, "Special Introduction," op. cit., p. xi.

[23]Malcolm Cowley, "Who are the Intellectuals?" New Republic, February 25, 1957, p. 14.

[24]Daniel Bell, op. cit., p. 402.

[25]Ralph Waldo Emerson, "The American Scholar, " in Stephen E. Whicher (ed), Selections from Ralph Waldo Emerson (Boston: Houghton Mifflin Company, Riverside edition, 1957), p. 67. As Daniel Aaron notes: "The function of Emerson's scholar was to mold the plastic world and shake the 'cowed' and the 'trustless' out of their lethargy. The scholar was to create an intellectual revolution by gradually 'domesticating' the ideas of culture." Daniel Aaron, Men of Good Hope (New York: Oxford University Press, 1951), p. 12.

[26]Gouldner, op. cit., p. 16.

[27]Thomas Kuhn, op. cit., and James D. Watson, The Double Helix (New York: Signet Books, 1969), Both have demonstrated the significance of those individuals who resist the lure of mainstream thinking and choose to work outside of the given definitions, methods and theorems. Generally, they note, the accepted paradigm

162

acts to limit and channel research and block creative innovation. Only by stepping beyond these boundaries can one deal with longstanding anomalies.

[28]Cited in John Kenneth Galbraith, "Introduction," in Veblen, op. cit., p. xix.

[29]See Hugh S. Norton, The World of the Economist (Columbia, South Carolina: University of South Carolina Press, 1973), p. 68.

[30]Christopher Lasch, The New Radicalism in America (New York:Vintage Books, 1965), p.ix. In their distinction between the intellectual (or critic) and the man of knowledge (scholar), Berger and Luckmann indicate that "One historically important type of expert ...is the intellectual, whom we define as an expert whose expertise is not wanted by the society at large. This implies a redefinition of knowledge vis-a-vis the 'official lore,' that is, it implies more than just a somewhat deviant interpretation of the latter. The intellectual is thus, by definition, a marginal type ....He appears as the counter-expert in the business of defining reality. Like the'official' expert, he has a design for society at large. Berger and Luckmann, op. cit., pp. 125-6

[31]The term is borrowed from Daniel Aaron, op. cit.

[32]Daniel R. Fusfeld, The Age of the Economist (Glenview, Illinois: Scott, Foresman and Company, 1966), p. 94.

[33]Gruchy, op. cit., p. 1.

[34]Heilbroner, op. cit., p. 211

[35]Hacker, op. cit., pp. 200-1

[36]Willhelm, op. cit., p. 115. Additionally, it should be noted that the retreat of the postwar intellectuals was influenced by what they saw as a betrayal of socialism in the U.S.S.R. Witnessing increasing bureaucratization and war-orientation, compounded by the Moscow Trials, the murder of Trotsky, the forced labor camps and the Nazi-Soviet Pact, they retreated from the notions of progress and perfectability. The Jewish extermination, Stalinism and the Atom Bomb all forced a reassessment of their view of man and society.

[37] Shils, _op. cit._, pp. 171-2

[38] "End of Ideology" is taken from Daniel Bell, _op. cit._ and "civil politics" from Edward Shils, _op. cit._ The sociohistorical factors undergirding such arguments are suggested by Richard King, _The Party of Eros_ (New York: Dell, 1973), p. 12.

[39] See Winter, _op. cit._, pp. 23-30. See also Staffan Burenstam Linder, _The Harried Leisure Class_ (New York: Columbia University Press, 1970). As will become evident in subsequent chapters, this situation is part of the basis for Galbraith's dismissal of growth as _the_ answer. As he argued in response to Crosland's Fabian pamphlet, _A Social Democratic Britain_: "in the United States, as is now sadly evident, economic growth does little for those at the bottom of the economic pyramid. They lack the education, skill, work discipline, often the health that allows them to participate effectively in the economy and therewith in the increasing income that growth provides. Growth only helps those who have a foothold in the system and it helps those who have the most. Moreover...the impression on the liberal Left that economic growth would solve the problem of poverty was (and remains) an excuse for eliding the action--federal aid to education, civil equality, help for women who head families, health insurance, a guaranteed income, all supported by much more strongly redistributive taxation--that is a remedy." John Kenneth Galbraith, "Galbraith Answers Crosland," _New Statesman_, 81 (January 22, 1967), p. 101.

[40] Frederic Jameson, _Marxism and Form_ (Princeton, New Jersey: Princeton University Press, 1971), p. 110.

[41] Marcuse, _op. cit._, p. 11.

[42] Winter, _op. cit._, p. 38. A similar conclusion is put forth by Dutton who argues that as individual freedoms are diluted in a depersonalized and increasingly organized society, the "real revolt is against government, mass politics, pragmatism, gradualism, and long prevailing liberal methods as much as against the private organization world and its establishment." Dutton, _op. cit._, p. 49.

[43] Commons, _op. cit._, p. 129.

[44]Allan Gruchy, "Introduction," in David Hamilton, Evolutionary Economics (Albuquerque: University of New Mexico Press, 1970), p. xi.

[45]John Kenneth Galbraith, The Liberal Hour (New York: New American Library, Mentor, 1960), p. 32.

[46]Fusfeld, op. cit., introduction.

[47]See Berger, Sacred Canopy, op. cit.

[48]Thomas Berger, Brigitte Berger, Hansfried Kellner, The Homeless Mind (New York: Random House, 1973).

[49]Charles H. Hession, John Kenneth Galbraith and His Critics (New York: New American Library, 1972), p. 17.

2
EMINENCE AND EMERGENCE

[1]Thorstein Veblen, The Theory of the Leisure Class (Boston: Houghton Mifflin, 1973), p. 138.

[2]Robert L. Heilbroner, "Capitalism Without Tears," New York Review of Books, June 29, 1967, p. 16

[3]Myron Sharpe, John Kenneth Galbraith and the Lower Economics (White Plains, New York: International Arts and Sciences Press, Inc., 1973), p. 4. See also Ben B. Seligman (ed.), "Introduction, " Molders of Modern Thought (Chicago: Quadrangle Books, 1970). Elsewhere Seligman cites an effort "to indicate that the economic growth can be expressed mathematically by an equation in which Y, the national product, is set as a function of capital stock services, the rate of use of natural resources, applied knowledge, and the cultural milieu in which the economy operates. Stated verbally, the expression makes some sense. But when the mathematical equation sets forth the last element as U, implying that the cultural background can be subjected to the mathematical operations of differentiation and integration, then we have simply approached the boundaries of intellectual aridity." Ben B. Seligman, Economics of Dissent (Chicago:Quadrangle Books, 1968), p.8.

[4]Bernard Collier, "A Most Galbraithian Economist," New York Times Magazine, February 18, 1973, p. 58.

[5]Harold Demetz, "Where is the New Industrial

State?" _Economic Inquiry_, 12 (March 1974), p. 11.

[6]Colin Clark, "The Eminence of Professor Galbraith," _National Review_, 20 (March 12, 1968), p. 242. Similarly, Scott Gordon argues that Galbraith's ideas have become important elements in the contemporary popular culture of American social thought." Scott Gordon, "The Close of the Galbraithian System," _Journal of Political Economics_, 76 (July/August 1968), p. 636. See also Elmo Roper, "Whose Affluent Society?" _Saturday Review_, 42 (June 6, 1959), pp. 15, 39, for an interesting comparison of the reactions of economists and businessmen to _The Affluent Society_.

[7]Jean Boddewyn, "On Galbraith and Potatoes," _South Atlantic Quarterly_, 58 (Winter 1964), p. 31.

[8]Significantly Linder comments that the influence of _The Affluent Society_ "on contemporary thought is not in proportion to its fame. The economists, at least, seem to be entirely unaffected by Galbraith's theses. ...Among the professionals his work has come to be regarded as mere opinion in a saleable carton of attractive prose. The poverty of subsequent discussion on affluence emerges clearly in three articles where a well-known economist, Harry G. Johnson, has tried to deal with Galbraith's important book. After dissecting what should more appropriately be utilized as a stimulus for further thought, Johnson achieves the following winged words with their comforting conclusions in favor of the conventional wisdom:'The argument I have been presenting is concerned with the welfare problem raised by created wants, and leads to the comforting conclusion that the fact of want-creation does not invalidate the assumption that an increase in national income carries with it an increase in welfare.'" Staffan Burenstam Linder, _The Harried Leisure Class_ (New York: Columbia University Press, 1970), pp. 141-2.

[9]John Kenneth Galbraith, "How the Economy Hangs on Her Apron Strings," _MS._, May 1974, p. 75. The point which should be stressed is that Galbraith is not suggesting a "no-growth" economy. As indicated in note 39 in chapter one, he holds that it is a mistake to rely on growth as a solution to pressing social problems. As will become evident, he argues for a more balanced growth. The proper boundaries for production and growth as he sees it are "those that minimize the damage to environment--that provide for orderly and agreeable use

of space, prohibit the disposal of waste in the air or surrounding waters, outlaw damaging production agents and damaging consumer goods." John Kenneth Galbraith, Who Needs the Democrats and What It Takes to Be Needed (Garden City, New York: Doubleday and Company, Inc, 1970), pp. 81-2.

[10]Irving Kristol, "Professor Galbraith's 'New Industrial State'," Fortune, July 1967, p. 90. See also William Breit and Roger Ransom, The Academic Scribblers (New York: Holt, Rinehart and Winston, Inc., 1967) for a discussion of the connection of Galbraith's style and his reputation.

[11]At least one exception should be noted--Herbert Stein, Chairman of the Council of Economic Advisors. As Collier reports in his own less than laudatory article on Galbraith--Stein's comments "were sincerely nasty," Collier, op. cit., p. 58.

[12]Robert Lekachman, "Introduction," in Charles Hession, John Kenneth Galbraith and His Critics (New York: New American Library, 1972), p. x.

[13]Paul Samuelson, "On Galbraith," Newsweek, July 3, 1967, p. 68.

[14]Both Harris and Schlesinger's assessments are taken from "The Great Mogul," Time, February 16, 1968, p. 26. See also Breit and Ransom, op. cit., p. 160.

[15]William Barber, "The Economics of Affluence," The South Atlantic Quarterly, 55 (Summer 1961), p. 251. For a comparison of Galbraith and John Dewey see John S. Gambs, John Kenneth Galbraith (New York: St. Martin's Press, 1975), p. 113.

[16]"The Great Mogul," op. cit., p. 24; "The Galbraithian Dimension," Newsweek, October 2, 1967, pp. 24, 29.

[17]"The Great Mogul," op. cit., p. 26.

[18]Richard Hefner and Esther Kramer, "A Man for All Pursuits," Saturday Review, 51 (April 20, 1968), p. 35.

[19]John Kenneth Galbraith, "Will Managed Capitalism Pull Us Through?" Commentary, 12 (August 1951), p. 127.

[20] Anthony Burgess, "Fable of Foreign Relations," _Saturday Review_, 51 (April 20, 1968), p. 34.

[21] Although at least two sources attribute a fictionalized history--_A History of the Modern Age_--to Galbraith, he denies any connection. In personal correspondence he replied, in true Galbraithian style, that he "didn't think it was terribly good." He was quick to add, "Of course it might not have been any better had I written it."

[22] Collier, _op. cit._, p. 12.

[23] Hession, _op. cit._, p. 17. Previously reported in "Playboy Interview: John Kenneth Galbraith," _Playboy_, June 1968, p. 64.

[24] Quoted in Robert L. Heilbroner, _The Worldly Philosophers_ (New York: Simon and Schuster, Touchstone edition, 1972), pp. 277-8.

[25] Sievers observes that Galbraith's career has "somehow been representative of his generation." Allen M. Sievers, _Revolution, Evolution and the Economic Order_ (Englewood Cliffs, New Jersey: Prentice-Hall, Inc., 1963), p. 59. This assessment is borne out by the fact that of the major posts readily available to economists, Galbraith has paid dues to academia, government and politics. Although he has never been employed by a large firm, he has served on the editorial board at _Fortune_. For a discussion of the major sources of employment now open to the economist see Hugh S. Norton, _The World of the Economist_ (Columbia, South Carolina: University of South Carolina Press, 1973).

[26] Samuelson, _op. cit._, p. 68.

[27] Colin Clark, _op. cit._, p. 242.

[28] John Kenneth Galbraith, _Economics Peace and Laughter_ (New York: New American Library, Signet edition, 1972), p. 43.

[29] David Halberstam, "The Importance of Being Galbraith," _Harpers_, November 1967, p. 47.

[30] John Kenneth Galbraith, _The Scotch_ (Boston: Houghton Mifflin, 1964), p. 130.

[31] Ibid., p. 51.

[32] Halberstam, op. cit., p. 50.

[33] John Kenneth Galbraith, "Royalty on the Farm," The Reporter, 21 (October 15, 1959), p. 37.

[34] Galbraith, "Introduction," in Veblen, op. cit., p. xxi.

[35] Galbraith, The Scotch, op. cit., p. 73.

[36] Ibid., pp. 53-4.

[37] Ibid., p. 75.

[38] Ibid., p. 75.

[39] Veblen, op. cit., pp. 90-1.

[40] Galbraith, The Scotch, op. cit., p. 94.

[41] Ibid., p. 94.

[42] Ibid., p. 95.

[43] Ibid., p. 96.

[44] Ibid., p. 105.

[45] Ibid., pp. 24-5.

[46] Ibid., p. 26.

[47] Ibid., p. 87.

[48] Ibid., p. 132.

[49] Ibid., p. 133.

[50] Although Galbraith entered high school at the age of ten, ill health forced him to drop out of high school for a year, "the ill health evidently being related to the strain from starting a bit too young." He spent another year at home after high school. His graduation was postponed one more year since the college program consisted of five years, one of which was equivalent to a fifth year of high school.

[51]Galbraith, _Economics Peace and Laughter_, _op. cit._, p. 261.

[52]"The Other Side of Affluence," _Business Week_, April 18, 1964, pp. 190-6.

[53]Galbraith, _Economics Peace and Laughter_, _op. cit._, p. 259.

[54]_Ibid._, p. 259.

[55]_Ibid._, p. 261.

[56]_Ibid._, p. 261.

[57]_Ibid._, p. 264.

[58]_Ibid._, p. 264.

[59]_Ibid._, p. 264.

[60]_Ibid._, p. 269.

[61]_Ibid._, p. 270.

[62]_Ibid._, p. 49. See also John Kenneth Galbraith, _Money: Whence It Came, Where It Went_ (Boston: Houghton Mifflin, 1975), pp. 226-7.

[63]Galbraith, "Managed Capitalism," _op. cit._, p.130.

[64]Breit and Ransom, _op. cit._, p. 87.

[65]Galbraith, _Economics Peace and Laughter_, _op. cit._, p. 50. See also _Money_, _op. cit._, pp. 230-4.

[66]John Kenneth Galbraith, _Age of Uncertainty_ (Boston: Houghton Mifflin, 1977), pp. 218, 220. See also _Money_, _op. cit._, p. 232.

[67]John Kenneth Galbraith, "Professor Gordon on 'The Close of the Galbraithian System,'" _Journal of Political Economics_, 77 (July/August 1969), p. 496n.

[68]"Looking Back at the Great Crash," _Business Week_, April 23, 1955, p. 98.

[69]See John Kenneth Galbraith, "The Businessman as Philosopher," _Perspectives U.S.A._, 13 (Autumn 1955),

p. 65 and John S. Gambs, op. cit., pp. 39-40.

[70]See, for example, his "Monopoly Power and Price Rigidities," Quarterly Journal of Economics, 50 (May 1936), pp. 456-475. Also of interest is his "The Selection and Timing of Inflation Controls," Review of Economics and Statistics, 23 (May 1941), pp. 82-5, which deals with war time stabilization policy. In this article he emphasizes the fact that the real limits are "the institutional and technical resistances to the reorganization that will permit the employment of the employable labor force." (p. 83.) In view of this fact he urges the need to anticipate resistances to reorganization of resources, develop specific price controls in those industries displaying such resistances, reduce investment for specific classes of consumer goods and capital goods and, as a final resort, an overall reduction of spending. Following the war, he published three additional articles dealing with his experiences as a price controller: "Reflections on Price Control," Quarterly Journal of Economics, 60 (August 1946), pp. 475-89; "The Disequilibrium System," American Economic Review, 37 (June 1947), pp. 287-302; and "The Strategy of Direct Control in Economic Mobilization," Review of Economics and Statistics, 33 (February 1951), pp. 12-17.

[71]Galbraith, Age of Uncertainty, op. cit., p. 221.

[72]John Kenneth Galbraith, A Theory of Price Control (Cambridge, Massachusetts: Harvard University Press, 1952), p. 7.

[73]Halberstam, op. cit., p. 5.

[74]Ibid., p. 52.

[75]Ibid., p. 52.

[76]Collier, op. cit., p. 59.

[77]Sharpe, op. cit., p. ix.

[78]Victor S. Navasky, "Galbraith on Galbraith," New York Times Book Review, June 25, 1967, p. 3.

[79]Galbraith, Theory of Price Control, op. cit., p. 75.

[80] John Kenneth Galbraith, "Power and the Useful Economist," The American Economic Review, 63 (March 1973), p. 2.

[81] Halberstam, op. cit., p. 52.

[82] John Kenneth Galbraith, "Dissent in a Free Society," Atlantic, February 1962, p. 45.

[83] For a comprehensive review of the reactions which Galbraith's books have received see Charles Hession, op. cit. Hession not only catalogues Galbraith's views up through The New Industrial State, but also gives Galbraith's critics a chance to be heard. The book is, finally, a very balanced treatment of the on-going dialogue. The National Review has been particularly harsh in its critiques of Galbraith's work. See, for example, Ferdinand Mount, "The Spoiled Minister's Sermon," National Review, 25 (December 21, 1973), pp. 1415-17; Colin Clark, "The Horrible Proposals of Mr. Galbraith," National Review, 6 (October 11, 1958), pp. 237-9, 255. For the left's reaction, see inter alia Robert Fitch, "A Galbraith Reappraisal," Ramparts, May 1968, pp. 73-84; Frank Ackerman and Arthur MacEwan, "Galbraith and the Liberal Purpose," The Nation, January 19, 1974, pp. 85-88. To Ralph Milibrand, Galbraith's analysis reveals "the confusion and bafflement of the latter-day liberalism which Professor Galbraith represents, in regard to an 'industrial system' which it approaches with a mixture of admiration and distaste, and whose basic irrationalities, some aspects which it perceives, it is either unable or unwilling to locate and transcend." Ralph Milibrand, "Professor Galbraith and American Capitalism," in David Mermelstein (ed.), Economics: Mainstream Readings and Radical Critiques (New York: Random House, 1970), pp. 531-2.

3
PERSPECTIVES AND PREDECESSORS

[1] See chapter one pages 5-7.

[2] Thomas Kuhn, The Structure of Scientific Revolution, second edition (Chicago: University of Chicago Press, 1970), p. 5. For Galbraith's comments on the difficulty of inducing change within the economics profession see John Kenneth Galbraith, "Market Structure and Stabilization Policy," Review of Economics

and Statistics, 39 (May 1957), p. 133.

[3]From Alain C. Enthoven, "Economic Analysis in the Department of Defense," cited in Robert H. Haveman and Kenyon A. Knopf, The Market System, second edition (New York: John Wiley and Sons, Inc., 1970), p. xi.

[4]John Kenneth Galbraith, Economics Peace and Laughter (New York: New American Library, Signet edition, 1972), p. 41.

[5]Kuhn's observation in regard to normal scientific activity is significant in this regard: "No part of the aim of normal science is to call forth new sorts of phenomena; indeed, those that will not fit the box are often not seen at all....Instead, normal science research is directed to articulation of those phenomena and theories that the paradigm already supplies." Kuhn, op. cit., p. 24.

[6]Assar Lindbeck, The Political Economy of the New Left (New York: Harper and Row, 1971), p. 22.

[7]Hughel B. Wilkins and Charles B. Friday (eds.), The Economics of the New Frontier (New York: Random House, 1963), p. 5. The advantages of following such a course are suggested by Robert Theobald: "If neoclassical assumptions were accepted as true, economics became a "pure" science. Economists appeared to have effectively eliminated from their discipline the complexity of man as well as the economic, social, and political issues raised by power. The elimination of complexity and power created a theoretical world in which it was possible to draw firm conclusions to develop increasingly detailed theories." Robert Theobald, The Economics of Abundance (New York: Pitman Publishing Corporation, 1970), p. 19.

[8]Galbraith, Economics Peace and Laughter, op. cit., p. 42. See also Jacob Oser and William C. Blanchfield, The Evolution of Economic Thought, third edition (New York: Harcourt Brace Jovanovich, Inc., 1975) pp. 366-7. The significance of this mechanistic orientation will be taken up again toward the end of this chapter.

[9]Ben B. Seligman (ed), Molders of Modern Thought (Chicago: Quadrangle Books, 1970), p. 32. Similarly,

adherence to Say's Law which posited a direct relationship between supply and demand and thus predicted economic equilibrium at a level of full employment, "until
late in the '30's no candidate for a Ph.D. at a major
American university who spoke seriously of a shortage
of purchasing power as a cause of depression could be
passed. He was a man who saw only the surface of
things, was unworthy of the company of scholars. Say's
Law stands as the most distinguished example of stability of economic ideas, including when they are wrong."
John Kenneth Galbraith, Money: Whence It Came, Where It
Went (Boston: Houghton Mifflin Company, 1975), p. 219.

[10]Richard T. Gill, Evolution of Modern Economics
(Englewood Cliffs, New Jersey: Prentice-Hall, Inc.,
1967), p. 81.

[11]Harry G. Johnson, "The Economic Approach to Soc-
ial Questions," in David Mermelstein (ed), Economics:
Mainstream Readings and Radical Critiques (New York:
Random House, 1970), p. 16.

[12]See Kenyon and Knopf, op. cit., chapter 1. See
also John Kenneth Galbraith, The Affluent Society
(New York: New American Library, Mentor edition, 1958),
especially chapters 1-4.

[13]Galbraith, Money, op. cit., p. 275.

[14]Obviously these charges overstate the poverty
of economic orthodoxy but, as Marris has argued in his
review of The New Industrial State: "It has been replied that there has been a continuous study of oligopolistic pricing since Hall and Hitch, and that Galbraith presents a caricature of contemporary micro-
theory taught only in elementary courses or on back-
woods campuses. But, if I may say so, under the American system, "Econ 1" is the only economics most cit-
izens ever get, and one suspects their considerable
number forms a significant element in Galbraith's best-
seller readership. It also appears that the mathematical and scientific convenience of the so-called competitive model, whose rediscovery coincided with a
period of increased demand for intellectual rational-
izations of western capitalism, and the subsequent
success of the classical revival, has made the pressure
for 'approved contradiction' more intense, rather than
less, as compared with, say, fifteen years ago." Robin
Marris, "Economic Systems: Planning and Reform: Cooperation," American Economic Review, 58 (March 1968),
p. 241.

[15]Lindbeck, op. cit., pp. 9-27.

[16]Ibid., p. 22.

[17]Allan G. Gruchy, "Foreward," in David Hamilton,
Evolutionary Economics (Albuquerque: University of New
Mexico, 1970), pp. vii-viii. Significantly, Lekachman
observes that marginal analysis "deliberately abstracts
from history and institutional specifications and centers its gaze upon the mechanics of choice....peopling
the economic landscape with large figures, corporate,
union, and governmental, which have neither history or
explanation attached to them." Lekachman in Mermelstein, op. cit., p. xi. See also Fritz Machlup,
"Theories of the Firm: Marginalist, Behavioral, Managerial," in Edwin Mansfield (ed), Microeconomics (New
York: W.W. Norton and Company, Inc., 1971), p. 102.

[18]Hugh S. Norton, The World of the Economist
(Columbia, South Carolina: University of South Carolina
Press, 1973), p. 19. Confirmation comes from Lekachman:
"Young men and women who enjoy intellectual puzzles,
welcome the opportunity to earn rapid reputations by
solving the puzzles, and respect the tidiness and cer-
tainties of the 'hard' natural sciences, have in significant numbers flocked to economics and promptly
worked to reinforce the characteristics of the subject
which initially attracted them." Lekachman in Mermelstein, op. cit., p. viii.

[19]Kenyon and Knopf, op. cit., p. 265.

[20]Noting that the 1920's invalidated the efficacy
of monetary policy as the Great Depression and World
War II proved fiscal policy incapable of restraining
inflation, Galbraith concludes that "The learning was,
in all cases, imperfect. The hope that monetary policy
would work, the faith in the magic of men managing
the modern economy from around a polished table, would
survive in economic pedagogy and have disastrous resurgence in practical policy a quarter century on.
Nostalgia combines regularly with manifest respectability to give precedence to old error as opposed to
new truth." Galbraith, Money, op. cit., p. 236.

[21]Galbraith, Affluent Society, op. cit., p. 17.
In Money, he dubs this tendency to choose comfortable
and accepted ideas the Belmont Syndrome. (p. 118.)

[22]Taken from his Yale Commencement remarks, June 11, 1962. Quoted in Bernard Nossiter, The Mythmakers (Boston: Houghton Mifflin, 1964), p. 1.

[23]John Kenneth Galbraith, American Capitalism, revised (Boston: Houghton Mifflin, Sentry, 1956), p. xi.

[24]Galbraith, Money, op. cit., p. 276.

[25]Michael Harrington, "Mr. Nixon's Reactionary Revolution," Commentary, November 26, 1971, p. 200.

[26]See chapter six for an analysis of Galbraith's proposed system of reform.

[27]Galbraith, American Capitalism, op. cit., p. x.

[28]Ibid., p. xi.

[29]John Kenneth Galbraith, "Introduction," in Thorstein Veblen, The Theory of the Leisure Class (Boston: Houghton Mifflin, 1973), p. xxi.

[30]John Kenneth Galbraith, "Royalty on the Farm," The Reporter, 21 (October 15, 1959), p. 35.

[31]"In the economics profession there is a well-defined order of precedence. At the top are the economic theorists, and their professional eminence in the pecking order is shared by those who do teaching and research on banking and money. At the bottom of this hierarchy are agricultural economists and home economists." Galbraith, Money, op. cit., p. 211.

[32]Gill, op. cit., p. 89.

[33]Norton, op. cit., p. 32.

[34]See Galbraith, "Introduction" in Veblen, op. cit.

[35]Wilkins and Friday, op. cit., p. 18.

[36]John Kenneth Galbraith with J.D. Black, "The Quantitative Position of Marketing in the United States," Quarterly Journal of Economics, 49 (May 1935), p. 396.

[37]See Ibid., pp. 412-13.

[38]Holism is the term prefered by Allan Gruchy for those heterodox economists who advanced an evolutionary version of economics. The term was originated by Jan Christiaan Smuts who derived it from the Greek word holos meaning whole. Smuts applied it to the work of Charles Darwin, Antoine Henri Becquerel and Albert Einstein. What unites the holists is an evolutionary perspective and an emphasis upon the interrelation of the various parts of the whole. See Allan G. Gruchy, Modern Economic Thought (New York: Prentice-Hall, Inc., 1947), pp. 3-5.

[39]It was the work of Edward Chamberlin and Joan Robinson in England and the research of Adolph Berle and Gardiner Means in the United States which forced imperfect competition rather than assuming that an industry was characterized either by competition or monopoly. Recognition of increasing concentration, price rigidities among oligopolies and the growing power of managers "appeared to toll the knell on competitive capitalism as it seemed, in somewhat roseate retrospect to have been. Unlike the 1897-1904 episode, new industrial changes now seemed to lead only to syndicalism and the Organic State rather than to sheer efficiency....In any event, the shock of recognition of the real world cast a pall of apprehension among economists. And the subject has not yet shed the atmosphere of crisis, prophetic--occasionally theological--dispute, and hyperbole." William G. Shepherd, Market Power and Economic Welfare (New York:Random House, 1970), p. 15.

[40]Although initial concern regarding oligopoly and concentration was marked, Shepherd indicates that "pessimism did not last long. Empirical denials of the fact and relevancy of the administred price hypothesis appeared as early as 1937....The onset of World War II finished off what was already a dwindling public concern. After massive study, the Temporary National Economic Committee, inaugurated by President Roosevelt in 1938, issued an insipid final report in 1942 to an uninterested public. Indeed, the War and the new Keynesian analysis helped to restore confidence that the economy would function efficiently if macroeconomic policy were properly managed." Ibid., pp. 15-16.

[41]John Kenneth Galbraith, "Monopoly Power and Price Rigidities," Quarterly Journal of Economics, 50 (May 1936), p. 468.

[42]"Monopoly power," following Galbraith, is here used broadly to refer to the power of the seller to exercise control over both supply and price. See _Ibid_.

[43]_Ibid_., p. 474.

[44]Although more extensive treatment will be given to this point in later chapters, it might be observed that in **American Capitalism** Galbraith suggests that the government adopt policies which facilitate the development of countervailing power. In subsequent works, with a clearer understanding of the inequities operating within the economic system and adversely effecting the small firms, he deals with the possibilities of exemption of small business from antitrust, government regulation of prices and production in the **market system** and government support for development in underdeveloped industries. See _Economics and the Public Purpose_ (Boston: Houghton Mifflin, 1973), pp. 256-60.

[45]Kuhn, _op. cit._, p. 6.

[46]Donald R. Fusfeld, _The Age of the Economist_ (Glenview, Illinois: Scott, Foresman and Company, 1966), p. 95.

[47]Galbraith, _Money, op. cit._, pp. 220-1.

[48]John Kenneth Galbraith, **A Theory of Price Control** (Cambridge, Massachusetts: Harvard University Press, 1952), p. 61. Recently he has expanded this explanation. See Galbraith, _Money, op. cit._, p. 309n.

[49]Galbraith, _Theory of Price Control, op. cit._, p. 2. Wilkins and Friday observe ironically that "Only during World War II was a high growth rate coupled with relatively   stable prices and full employment. But it was done then by using price and wage controls and a War Production Board to allocate strategic resources. In other words, it was done by abandoning the market system." Wilkins and Friday, _op. cit._, p. 9.

[50]In **A Theory of Price Control** Galbraith explains that in the imperfect market or the monopolistically competitive market, "It is possible for the sellers (or vice-versa the buyers) to allocate scarce supplies to specific customers....In such markets, in other words, price fixing is accomplished, _pari passu_, by

allocation or rationing." Similarly, he notes that insofar as much pricing is done out of habit or convenience, profit maximization, one of the main justifications for the competitive market, is not longer
operative.(pp. 11, 18.)

[51]Allen M. Sievers, Revolution, Evolution and the
Economic Order (Englewood Cliffs, New Jersey: Prentice-
Hall, Inc., 1962), p. 93. Even earlier C.E. Ayres
expressed the opinion that he could think of no one
who "has been more candid in his recognition of the
essentially theological character of the classical doctrine of competition." Further, he argued that Galbraith restored economic theory "to an objective science with neither gods nor devils lurking in the shad-
ows of the market." C.E. Ayres, "The Grown-Up Boss,
Saturday Review, 35 (April 12, 1952), p. 33.

[52]Seligman, Molders of Modern Thought, op. cit.,
p. 32.

[53]Significantly, Robin Marris has observed that
"For the professional analytical economist, it is
essential to accept from the outset that Galbraith is
dealing in loose but not necessarily unreal concepts,
of whose descriptive value he seeks to convince by a
mixture of literature and some logic, based on causal
observation, induction, and selected evidence. Thus,
his "Technostructure" is an organism of large autonomous cells, interacting, but not colluding, in a manner that justifies sometimes treating the whole as if
it were a unified elite. His objectives are also wider
than that of traditional 'political economists.' He
is concerned not only to influence public attitudes on
strictly economic questions, but to suggest the broader
social implications of his total picture; in other
words, he aspires to contribute as much in the field
of political science as in what is now regarded as the
proper field of economic science." Marris, op. cit.,
p. 240.

[54]Kuhn, op. cit., p.37.

[55]Robert Solow, "The New Industrial State or Sons
of Affluence," The Public Interest, Fall 1967, p.100ff.

[56]In so doing, the holistic economists were, as
noted below, led to question and repudiate many of the

179

mechanistic assumptions of economic orthodoxy. The significance of such a development is suggested by Berger and Luckmann: "The appearance of an alternative symbolic universe poses a threat because its very existence demonstrates empirically that one's own universe is less than inevitable." Peter Berger and Thomas Luckmann, The Social Construction of Reality (Garden City, New York: Doubleday and Company, Inc., 1967), p. 108. In this sense orthodoxy's rejection of the heretics must be seen as related to its own vested interests. To acknowledge the plausibility of the critics' charges would be to weaken one's own case for scientific validity.

[57] The holistic economists are often called institutionalists. The term was coined by Walter Hamilton in 1919 to refer to the commonalities of his own work and that of Veblen and Robert Hoxie. It was later applied to the writing of Mitchell, Commons, and Tugwell. Like holism, it may be defined as a "study of the disposal of scarce means within the framework of our developing system." Allan G. Gruchy, "Discussion," following Kenneth Boulding's "A New Look at Institutionalism," America Economic Review, 57 (May 1957), p. 13. Since "institutionalism" is often applied strictly to Veblen's work and since many of the holistic economists do not speak of themselves as institutionalists, I will continue to use the term holism to refer to their work.

[58] Gruchy, Modern Economic Thought, op. cit., p.21.

[59] Alvin Gouldner, "Anti-Minotour: The Myth of Value Free Sociology," in Irving Louis Horowitz (ed.), The New Sociology (New York: Oxford University Press, 1964) p. 210.

[60] Robin Marris, "Galbraith, Solow, and the Truth About Corporations," in Mermelstein, op. cit., p. 517.

[61] E. J. Misham, "The Myth of Consumers' Sovereignty," in Mermelstein, op. cit., p. 544. Additional discussion of this issue will be included in chapter 5.

[62] Hamilton, op. cit., pp. 121-2.

[63] See footnote 17 Supra.

[64] Shepherd, op. cit., p. 16.

[65] Marris, "Economic Systems: Planning and Reform; Cooperation," op. cit., p. 242.

[66] Herbert A. Simon, "Theories of Decision-Making in Economics and Behavioral Science," in Mansfield, op. cit., p. 88.

[67] T.E. Hulme, "Romanticism and Classicism," in his Speculations (New York: Harcourt, Brace and Company, 1924), p. 116. For a more extensive discussion of the limitations of the formalist or orthodox view of human nature, see Hamilton, op. cit., chapter 3.

[68] Gruchy in Hamilton, op. cit., p. vii.

[69] Lekachman, "Special Introduction," op. cit., p. xi. See also Nossiter, op. cit., p. 45.

[70] John Kenneth Galbraith, "The Emerging Public Corporation, " Business and Society Review, 1 (Spring 1972), p. 55.

[71] Karl Marx and Frederick Engles, "Concerning the Production of Consciousness," in James E. Curtis and John Petras (eds.), The Sociology of Knowledge (New York: Praeger Press, 1970), p. 102.

[72] Of particular importance is his discussion of change as it relates to economic organization in The New Industrial State, revised edition (New York: New American Library, Mentor edition, 1971), chapters 1-3. See also Economics and the Public Purpose, op. cit., especially chapter nine.

[73] For an interesting discussion of Galbraith and determinism see Gambs, op. cit., pp. 30 ff.

[74] Technological advancement, according to Galbraith, induces increasing specialization which, in turn, requires the development of a complex organization to unify the various specialists. Increasingly, more time and resources must be invested in any one production item and, due to the specialized nature of both the physical and human capital, this investment becomes inelastic. This being the case, it follows that the large corporation cannot afford the risk and uncertainty of the market; instead, it must preempt the market by gaining control of costs and prices. Furhter, the "initiative in deciding what is to be produced

comes not from the sovereign consumer who, through the market, issues the instructions that bend the productive mechanism to his ultimate will. Rather it comes from the great producing organization which reaches forward to control the markets that it is presumed to serve and, beyond, to bend the consumer to its needs." Galbraith, New Industrial State, op. cit., p. 26.

[75]Typical in this regard are William Appleton Williams, The Great Evasion (Chicago: Quadrangle Books, 1968); Gabriel Kolko, The Triumph of Conservatism (New York: Free Press, 1963); Simon Lazarus, "Halfway Up From Liberalism, Regulation and Corporate Power," in Ralph Nader and Mark J. Green (eds.) Corporate Power in America (New York: Grossman Publishers, 1973), pp. 215-234.

[76]See chapter six for a discussion of Galbraith's specific proposals.

[77]It is for this reason, I would argue, that Galbraith pays little attention to the theories of bilateral monopoly in American Capitalism. Whether what he is describing often resembles bilateral monopoly, is not his concern. What is important is the process of adaptation which produces this revised structure.

[78]In large measure, Galbraith argues, the two groups have adopted a conciliatory policy "not because labor leaders and vice presidents in charge of labor relations have entered upon an era of pacific enlightenment, the operative agent being the rise of industrial statesmanship and the somewhat delayed triumph of Judeo-Christian ethics and the golden rule. It has come about because interests that were once radically opposed are now much more nearly in harmony. Behavior is not better, it is merely that interests are concordant." Galbraith, New Industrial State, op. cit., p. 258. We will have occasion to return to this issue in chapter six. There is reason to believe that Galbraith's emphasis upon the cleavage which separates the large and small firms has led him to ignore very real cleavages operating within the mature corporation as between managers and workers.

[79]C.E. Ayres, "The Nature and Significance of Institutionalism" Antioch Review, 26 (Spring 1966), pp. 82-3.

[80]Gruchy, _Modern Economic Thought, op. cit._, pp. 18-19. Instead, the holistic economists, as Hamilton explains, contend that "behavior cannot be explained on an 'individual' basis. There is no such thing as individual behavior. All behavior is cultural. Culture is subject to a process of cumulative development and change, and human behavior is therefore subject to this same process." Hamilton, _op. cit._, p. 54.

[81]See Norton, _op. cit._, pp. 31-2

[82]Sievers, _op. cit._, p. 94. See also David Mermelstein, _op. cit._, preface. In essence, what Mermelstein is calling for and what Galbraith is attempting is "neo-functional" analysis as set forth in the introduction.

[83]Linder, _op. cit._, p. 139. Again the point is that statistical studies pay inadequate attention to non-quantifiable factors such as quality of education, environmental preservation, urban development and community services. See also in this regard Charles Hession and Hyman Sardy, _Ascent to Affluence_ (Boston: Allyn and Bacon, Inc., 1969), p. 539 ff. It is of some significance that since Galbraith began his campaign against the conventional wisdom, a growing number of textbooks have been according at least one or two chapters for the discussion of the diseconomies which Galbraith has charged them with overlooking. Whether this is a reflection of the influence of Galbraith and other heterodox thinkers or a response to an altered climate of opinion would be difficult to determine. In all likelihood, both have had an influence.

[84]Veblen, _op. cit._, p. 133.

[85]Galbraith, _Affluent Society, op. cit._, p. 21.

[86]_Ibid._, p. 257. A similar conclusion propels Gibson Winter to conclude that the "control exercised by the techno-society depends upon unquestioning commitment to the goodness of increasing growth." Winter, like Galbraith, seems to see signs of hope in recent resistances by the public to environmental destruction and the growing power of the military establishment. He also shares Galbraith's hope that the "organized contradictions" will induce the people to actively work to build a new social order. See Gibson Winter, _Being Free_ (New York: Macmillan Company, 1970), p. 76 ff.

[1]Myron Sharpe, John Kenneth Galbraith and the Lower Economics (White Plains, New York: International Arts and Science Press, Inc., 1973), p. 8. Similarly, Heilbroner has observed that "American Capitalism was traditional in its picture of the economy as a self-regulating entity, but it struck out on its own decribing the regulative force as no longer that of the competitive market." Robert Heilbroner, Between Capitalism and Socialism (New York: Random House, 1970), p. 227.

[2]John Kenneth Galbraith, Ambassador's Journal (Boston: Houghton Mifflin, 1969), p. 394.

[3]John Kenneth Galbraith, Money: Whence It Came, Where It Went (Boston: Houghton Mifflin, 1975), p. 312.

[4]Galbraith, Ambassador's Journal, op. cit., p. 26.

[5]John Kenneth Galbraith, "Dissent in a Free Society," Atlantic, February 1962, p. 45.

[6]See his introduction to The Affluent Society, second edition (Boston: Houghton Mifflin, 1969).

[7]William G. Shepherd, Market Power and Economic Welfare (New York: Random House, 1970), p. 21.

[8]See, for example, Freidrich A. von Hayek, The Road to Serfdom (London: George Routledge and Sons, 1944). This book was widely read and particularly influential among von Hayek's colleagues at the University of Chicago.

[9]That Galbraith shared this view is indicated from the nature of much of the writing he produced in the early and middle fifties. One of the stated aims of American Capitalism, for example, was to suggest those policies which he deemed necessary to induce "high and reasonably stable production, employment, and prices." In a somewhat later article, following a review of possible expenditures and taxation policies, Galbraith indicated that "The real enemy of a balanced budget in the United States...is insufficient production. The measures here proposed are for the purpose of bringing the economy back to full production." John Kenneth Galbraith, "Economics for 1955," The Reporter, 12 (Feb-

ruary 24, 1955), p. 21. See also Charles H. Hession, John Kenneth Galbraith and His Critics (New York: New York: New American Library, 1972), pp. 60-61.

[10]John Kenneth Galbraith, Economics and the Public Purpose (Boston: Houghton Mifflin, 1973), p. 183.

[11]A more extended analysis of individual liberty in an industrial society will be presented in chapter five which deals with Galbraith's perception of the place of the individual in modern society.

[12]John Kenneth Galbraith, "Causes of Economic Growth," Queen's Quarterly, 45 (Summer 1958), p. 181. See also The Affluent Society, op. cit.

[13]Galbraith, Affluent Society, op. cit., p. xxii.

[14]Galbraith, Money, op. cit., p. 268.

[15]Ibid., p. 273. For a somewhat different slant on this issue see Bernard Nossiter, The Mythmakers (Boston: Houghton Mifflin, 1964), chapter one.

[16]For an extensive discussion of the import of these policies see Nossiter, op. cit., chapter two.

[17]Robert Lekachman, The Age of Keynes (New York: Random House, 1966), p. 285.

[18]The problem as Galbraith indicated was that "money from tax reduction goes into the pockets of those who need it least; lower taxes will become a ceiling on spending." Galbraith, Ambassador's Journal, op. cit., p. 387.

[19]John Kenneth Galbraith, Economics and the Public Purpose (Boston: Houghton Mifflin, 1973), p. x. It is a similar interpretation which has led Gibson Winter to observe: "We have created a participatory network through our technological triumph; we now need a new social morality and institutions to give communal expression to that participatory reality." Gibson Winter, Being Free (New York: Macmillan Company, 1970, p. 37. It should be observed that some orthodox economists have tried to come to terms with market power and to measure its effect. See, for example, Shepherd, op. cit., p. 4; Edwin Mansfield, Microeconomics (New York: W.W. Norton and Company, 1971), p. 114. Galbraith, however, interprets market power in a somewhat different manner than do those involved with industrial org-

anization. For Galbraith, the central concern is the impact of power disparities on overall economic performance and the consequent inequalities and injustices of production and income distribution. The more orthodox economist, on the other hand, tends to focus largely upon the performance of specific industries in an attempt to predict the strictly economic implications of market power. Rates of innovation, growth and productivity under variable degrees of concentration within a specific industry, rather than the camparative performance of several industries is, thus, primary.

[20]Arnold M. Rose, The Power Structure (New York: Oxford University Press, 1967), p. 33.

[21]For an excellent discussion and analysis of this development and an explication of the various ideologies espoused by these organizations, see R. Joseph Monsen and Mark W. Cannon, The Makers of Public Policy (New York: McGraw Hill, 1965).

[22]As Nossiter has indicated, "the existence of private power centers disturbs the soothing national belief in a pluralistic society. It is more agreeable to picture a world in which power is diffused, where one-man, one-vote expresses more than a formal political arrangement and reflects an underlying reality. Most of all, it is upsetting to acknowledge the existence of private power without public accountability." Nossiter, op. cit., p. 45.

[23]Ralph Nader and Mark J. Green (eds.) Corporate Power in America (New York: Grossman Publishers, 1973), pp. vii-viii.

[24]Andrew Hacker, The End of the American Era (New York: Athenium Press, 1971), p. 38.

[25]See his "The Decline of American Power," Esquire March 1972, p. 84.

[26]Galbraith, Ambassador's Journal, op. cit., p. 212. The impact of this development seems to be due in part to the State Department's persistent efforts to "assist" Galbraith with his job. These efforts led him to write in the journal that "Everyone in Washington wants to send us a team and be on it himself. And if anyone is uncertain what to do, he proposes a team to find out what team should be sent." (525)

[27]This point was raised by Demetz in his critique of The New Industrial State. "It is not quite clear whether Galbraith attributes this power to control important market dimensions to the sheer size of firms or to the structure of the industry. When discussing the sales maximization policy, he seems to stress the absolute size of the firm and its advertising expenditures, but when discussing the attainment of stability, Galbraith seems to emphasize the structure of the industry...and advertising intensity." Harold Demetz, "Where is the New Industrial State?" Economic Inquiry, 12 (March 1974), p. 11.

[28]Bruce R. Scott, "The Industrial State: Old Myths and New Realities," Harvard Business Review, 51 (March/April 1973), p. 142.

[29]Walter Adams, "The Antitrust Alternative," in Nader and Green, op. cit., pp. 134-5. See also Shepherd, op. cit., p. 37.

[30]In response to the charge that medium firms rather than the giants are responsible for most innovation, Galbraith has commented: "I am willing to concede every one of those dreary studies is right...including some I haven't read." But, argues Galbraith, this is largely beside the point: "Bigness is upon us, whether it is necessary or good is irrelevant." Thus, "the crucial question...is what society ought to do about the massive corporate power in its midst. If antitrust is going to alter the structure of the corporate world, it must begin all-out dissolution proceedings against General Motors, Ford, the oil majors, U.S. Steel, General Electric, IBM, Western Electric, DuPont, Swift, Bethlehem, International Harvester, North American Aviation, Goodyear, Boeing, National Dairy Products, Procter and Gamble, Eastman Kodak, and all of comparable size and scope." "Too big for antiturst to handle?" Business Week, July 8, 1967, p. 72.

[31]Significantly, Robert T. Averitt suggests that by expanding "they blend into the economy which contains them. So long as the general economy prospers, they prosper. So long as the economy grows, they grow," Robert T. Averitt, The Dual Economy (New York: W.W. Norton and Company, 1968), p. 18. It is also important to note that Averitt reached virtually the same conclusions regarding the general structure of the economy as Galbraith reached in The New Industrial State which appeared the year before Averitt's book. What sets Gal-

braith's work apart is that Galbraith always has one eye upon the social and cultural implications of the developments which he is describing; thus, while devoid of some of the detail and "economic sophistication" of others, Galbraith's books reach beyond them and hence provide a sounder basis for assessing the costs of uneven development.

[32]Since the largest corporation, for example General Motors, can undercut price reductions offered by other coprorations in a given field, it would prove disingenious to disregard the will of the leader. In 1969, for instance, Anheuser Busch, the largest of the breweries, was attempting to increase prices to build profits. Meanwhile the second largest corporation, Joseph Schlitz, attempted to increase its share of the market by discounting its prices. As a result, Anheuser did not boost prices, The conflict came to a head late in 1972 when Anheuser slashed prices "with a vengeance" while expanding capacity. Not only did this effectively neutralize Schlitz' price cutting, but also left them sorely in need of a price increase. See Robert Metz, "The Big Five in Beer," The New York Times, June 15, 1975, section 3.

[33]The extent to which this engenders a community of interest between labor and management is difficult to determine precisely. While labor-management relations are obviously more pacific than was thought possible in the pre-New Deal era, a strong case can be made for an ongoing political cleavage between the two groups. This will be discussed in more detail in chapter six.

[34]Nossiter, op. cit., p. 52.

[35]John Kenneth Galbraith, The New Industrial State, revised (New York: New American Library, Mentor edition, 1971), p. 200.

[36]Ibid., p. 89.

[37]Sharpe, op. cit., p. 12.

[38]This position is ably presented by Shepherd who argues that "In symmetrical oligopoly, all leading firms are under pressure to innovate as a means (defensive and offensive) of nonprice competition. Innovation would also destabilize efforts at collusion by causing cost and motivational differences among the

firms. Under assymmetry, the smaller leaders must innovate to offset the input-price and other advantages of
the dominant firm, while the dominant firm may adopt a
passive role, imitating rather than inventing or inno-
vating." Shepherd, op. cit., p. 58. Later he notes that
in oil, steel, tin, cans, chemicals, and the like it
has been secondary firms which were the key innovators.
"There are many specific instances of a major innovation being forced upon the industry leader; stainless
steel razor blades, synchronous satellites, and the ox-
ygen steelmaking process are recent examples." (208)

[39]This assessment of Galbraith's stance is advanced by Colin Clark, "The Horrible Proposals of Mr.
Galbraith," National Review, 6 (October 11, 1958), p.
237.

[40]This accusation is voiced by Ferdinand Mount,
"The Spoiled Minister's Sermon," National Review, 25
(December 21, 1973), p. 1417.

[41]Robert Fitch, "A Galbraith Reappraisal: The
Ideologue as Gadfly," Ramparts, May 1968, p. 82.

[42]If, by business industry, as Gruchy has argued,
Veblen meant the demise of laissez faire capitalism,
Galbraith would surely concede the point. See Allen G.
Gruchy, "Theory of Economic Growth," in Douglass F.
Dowd (ed.), Thorstein Veblen: A Critical Reappraisal
(Ithica, New York: Cornell University Press, 1958), pp.
168-9.

[43]See Supra notes 37 and 39.

[44]See, for example, Sharpe, op. cit., pp. 14-15.

[45]"Conversations with an Inconvenient Economist,"
Challenge, September/October 1973, p. 29. Elsewhere he
has commented: "Were it not for the government and the
farm equipment and chemical firms, agriculture would be
technologically stagnant." Economics and the Public
Purpose, op. cit., p. 19.

[46]Galbraith, Economics and the Public Purpose, op.
cit., p. 49.

[47]Ibid., p. 276. Significantly, Averitt identifies
the availability of funds (internal and external) and
the quality of management as the two most important
long-run assets. Both are disproportionately available

to the mature corporation; hence its ability to diversify, decentralize, integrate vertically and horizontally and utilize new technologies. But, contends Averitt, "Inherent financial limitations and inappropriate managerial structure effectively prohibit periphery firms from utilizing these essentials of long-run survival and prosperity." Averitt, op. cit., p. 101.

[48]Murray L. Weidenbaum, "How Galbraith Would Reform the Economy," Business Week, September 22, 1973, p. 10.

[49]Third World imperialism, for Galbraith, "is an extension of the relationship between the planning and the market system in the advanced country. As with the market system in the advanced country, abundant supply, slight or no control over prices, a labor supply that lends itself to exploitation all mean intrinsically adverse terms of trade. The result is the same tendency of income inequality between developed and under developed countries as exists within the industrial country between the planning and market system." Economics and the Public Purpose, op. cit., p. 125.

[50]It was for this reason that Galbraith emphasized the importance of power in his address to the American Economics Association in 1973. See John Kenneth Galbraith, "Power and the Useful Economist," The American Economic Review, 63 (March 1973).

[51]John Kenneth Galbraith, "Market Structure and Stabilization Policy," Review of Economics and Statistics, 39 (May 1957), p. 133. For a more recent illustration of the discriminatory impact see Robert A. Mundell, Man and Economics (New York: McGraw-Hill Book Company, 1968), p. 130.

[52]The extent to which ownership and effective control have been separated has, of late, been subject to much dispute. Several recent studies have identified various means available to the upper class for influencing the policies and performance of the American society. See for example: G. William Domhoff, The Higher Circles (New York: Vintage Books, 1971); Maurice Zeitlin, "Corporate Ownership and Control: The Large Corporation and the Capitalist Class," American Journal of Sociology, 79 (March 1974), pp. 1073-1119; Ralph Milibrand, "Professor Galbraith and American Capitalism," in Mermelstein, op. cit., pp. 531-42; Robert Sheehan, "Properties in the World of Big Business,"

Fortune, June 15, 1967, pp. 179-83, 242.

[53]See H.H. Gerth and C. Wright Mills (eds.), From Max Weber (New York: Oxford University Press, 1958), pp. 221 ff. and Reinhard Bendix, Max Weber (New York: Anchor Books, 1962), pp. 429 ff.

[54]Charles Hession and Hyman Sardy, Ascent to Affluence (Boston: Allyn and Bacon, Inc., 1969), p. 544. See also Averitt, op. cit., p. 108.

[55]Galbraith, Ambassador's Journal, op. cit., p.28.

[56]Ibid., p. 94.

[57]Significantly, Robin Marris observes that the "functional essence of management lays in the provision of organization. Organization involves not only making decisions, but also co-ordinating decisions and generally seeing that they are made swiftly, consistently, and apparently in accordance with policy....In other words, in this society, a man's ability and hence his status within the group may well be judged primarily by his ability as an organizer." Marris, Economic Theory of 'Managerial' Capitalism, op. cit., p. 57.

[58]Colin Clark, "The Eminence of Professor Galbraith," National Review, 20 (March 12, 1968), p. 243.

[59]Galbraith, New Industrial State, op. cit., p.82.

[60]Frank Ackerman and Arthur MacEwan, "Galbraith and the Liberal Purpose," The Nation, January 19, 1974, p. 85. See also Milibrand, op. cit., pp. 535-6.

[61]Heilbroner, op. cit., p. 233.

[62]"Conversations with an Inconvenient Economist," op. cit., p. 31.

[63]Galbraith, Economics and the Public Purpose, op. cit., pp. 95-6.

[64]Robin Marris, though in general agreement with Galbraith, suggests a crucial limitation to Galbraith's explanation. He begins by concurring that "the real-world system almost certainly behaves very differently from the way implied in the conventional theory; the conventional theory would imply that corporations would grow considerably more slowly and reward stockholders

significantly better." Yet, argues Marris, Galbraith is unclear as to how this difference can occur because he (Galbraith) is too quick to dismiss the need for profit despite profits' relation to growth. Marris then posits a functionalist model by which management's target growth rate determines their optimal profit rate. He concludes, however, in a manner very similar to Galbraith; he insists that "it is inevitable that the safe minimum level of the price of a corporations' stock will be significantly lower, and the safe maximum growth rate correspondingly higher, than the values which would be chosen by a management that really did care only for the welfare of the stockholder." Marris, "Galbraith, Solow and the Truth about Corporations," op. cit., pp. 519-21.

[65]Galbraith, New Industrial State, op. cit., p. 174. The significance of this shift is suggested by Daniel Bell: "Perhaps the most important fact, sociologically, about the American business community today is the insecurity of the managerial class....The new class of managers, recruited from the general grab bag of middle class life, lacks the assured sense of justification which the older class-rooted system provided....Hence, the growing need for achievement as a sign of success." Daniel Bell, The End of Ideology (New York: Free Press, 1965), pp. 89-90.

[66]Galbraith is aware of the limitations of this model of the technostructure's preference schedule. But, he argues, "Beyond some hierarchy of things maximized--growth, security, technological virtuosity and earnings--I have seen no way of expressing the matter which does not involve sacrifice of what is intuitively plausible for what would be theoretically more elegant." John Kenneth Galbraith, "Professor Gordon on 'The Close of the Galbraithian System,'" Journal of Political Economics, 77 (July/August 1969), p. 496.

[67]Galbraith, New Industrial State, op. cit., p. 378.

[68]For an interesting analysis of these various schools of thought see Heilbroner, op. cit., pp. 3-31.

[69]See Monsen and Cannon, op. cit., for a competent analysis of the various ideologies which have come to characterize the major institutional groups. See also Nossiter, op. cit., p. 105 ff.

[70]See his discussion in "Market Structure and

stabilization Policy," op. cit. At this point in his career he contends that "the price policy which leaves these firms with unliquidated monopoly gains is inherent in the different process of adaptation and in part in inescapable differences between long- and short-run maximization. The preferred position of the oligopolistic firms is the product of circumstance, not decision. So accordingly is the discrimination." (132n.)

[71]UPI Release, "Who Speaks for Consumer," Quad City Times, September 21, 1975, p. 4D.

[72]Nossiter, op. cit., p. 122. See also Hacker, op. cit., p. 68 and Shepherd, op. cit., pp. 83-8.

[73]See for example Gabriel Kolko, The Triumph of American Conservatism (New York: Free Press, 1963) and Railroads and Regulation (Princeton: Princeton University Press, 1965). For a general overview of the issue see Simon Lazarus, "Halfway Up from Liberalism," in Nader and Green, op. cit., pp. 215-34. With this kind of record it is difficult to see the basis for ex-Secretary of the Treasury William Simon's claim that the financial distress of railroads, airlines and utilities stems from over-zealous regulation. He uses this as a basis for the opinion that "It's time we loosened the shackles and removed the many impediments which government itself has placed in the path of economic progress--the impediments that hurt service, raise costs and spur inflation." John Minachan, "Is 'Free Market' a Dirty Word?: An Interview with the Secretary of the Treasury," Saturday Review, July 12, 1975, p. 18. See, in the same issue, Simon's "A Strategy for Prosperity," pp. 10-16, 20.

[74]The recent revelations regarding the interlocking directorate shared by Northrop and the Air Force should be taken as symptomatic; optimistically, it may signal a new awareness of a much larger problem.

[75]Galbraith, New Industrial State, op. cit., p. 305.

[76]Ibid., p. 230. In his study of the transportation industry, Samuel Huntington (using the term "clientalism") reached the conclusion that the agency and industry "tend to fuse into one smooth harmonious whole with a common purpose and a common outlook." He added: "If there is any complaint about the activities of the client-group the cliental agency can always be pointed

to in defense as proof that the matter is actually in proper hands." Cited in Nossiter, op. cit., p. 124.

[77]See his Ambassador's Journal, op. cit., pp. 87, 133, passim.

[78]John Kenneth Galbraith, "A Decade of Disasters in Foreign Policy," The Progressive, 35 (February 1971), p. 37.

[79]Anthony Lewis, "The World Through Galbraith's Eyes," reprinted in Ben B. Seligman (ed.), Molders of Modern Thought (Chicago: Quadrangle Books, 1970), p. 279. As will become clear in chapter six, Galbraith believes that it is possible to shake the hold which the planning system maintains over the government and hence make it responsive to the popular will.

[80]John Kenneth Galbraith, "The Emerging Public Corporation," Business and Society Review, 1 (Spring 1972), p. 56.

[81]The very priorities and measurements by which we judge ourselves--increased and more efficient production and consumption of goods and a rising standard of living effectively serve industrial goals. These plus a "powerful preference for goods over leisure, an unqualified commitment to technological change, autonomy for the technostructure, an adequate supply of trained and educated manpower," as Galbraith observes, "have become coordinate with social virtue and human enlightenment." New Industrial State, op. cit., p. 331.

[82]Galbraith, Economics and the Public Purpose, op. cit., p. 200.

5
THE RIDDLE OF PROGRESS

[1]John Kenneth Galbraith, The Liberal Hour (New York: New American Library, Mentor, 1960), p. 39.

[2]Playboy Interview: "John Kenneth Galbraith," Playboy, June 1968, p. 138.

[3]Irving Kristol, "Corporate Capitalism in America," The Public Interest, 41 (Fall 1975), p. 134.

[4]"Conversation with an Inconvenient Economist," Challenge, September/October 1973, p. 28.

[5]John Kenneth Galbraith, Economics and the Public Purpose (Boston: Houghton Mifflin, 1973), p. 277.

[6]Referring to the reception of The New Industrial State, Galbraith observes that "It is my impression that the adult reader was always more skeptical than the economists of the neo-Keynesian nirvana. Economic life was not meant to be that easy. And perhaps some sensed what I here urge, that what was called success was less what served the individual than what served the goals of great industrial and military bureaucracies which had come, the economic myth notwithstanding, to comprise so large a part of the economic system." Galbraith, The New Industrial State (New York: New American Library, Mentor, 1971), p. xi.

[7]Richard D. Heffner and Esther H. Kramer, "A Man for All Pursuits," Saturday Review, April 20, 1968, p. 35.

[8]It will be recalled that Kuhn has indicated that scientific revolutions--paradigm shifts--are generally initiated by those who are young and not yet initiated fully into the dominant way of thinking. Thomas S. Kuhn, The Structure of Scientific Revolution (Chicago: University of Chicago Press, 1970), p. 90. Significantly, Collier observes that among young economists "Mr. Galbraith is regarded as an aging rebel who earned their respect in graduate school because he published effective ridicule against the orthodox faith." Bernard Collier, "A Most Galbraithian Economist," New York Times Magazine, February 18, 1973, p. 58.

[9]John G. Cawelti, Apostles of the Self-Made Man (Chicago: University of Chicago Press, 1965), p. 44.

[10]Galbraith, "The Businessman as Philosopher," Perspectives U.S.A., 13 (Autumn 1955), p. 59.

[11]Arthur M. Johnson, The American Economy (New York: Free Press, 1974), p. 158.

[12]John Kenneth Galbraith, American Capitalism (Boston: Houghton Mifflin, Sentry, 1956), p. 27. Speaking of the impact of the economic pedagogy, Galbraith has indicated that it "makes the modern corporation the nearly powerless automaton of the market and thus largely excludes from view, and therewith from discussion, the exercises of authority that it enjoys."

John Kenneth Galbraith, "What Comes After General Motors," New Republic, 171 (November 2, 1974), p. 14.

[13]"It's No Sin to be Rich," Business Week, February 23, 1952, p. 124.

[14]In American Capitalism, for example, Galbraith articulated the fear that "The definition of competition was gradually accomodated to the requirements of a modern economic society; it became not the definition that described reality but the one that produced ideal results. The preoccupation ceased to be with interpreting reality and came to be with building a model economic society." (p. 16.)

[15]Galbraith, Economics and the Public Purpose, op. cit., p. 232.

[16]Galbraith comments: "I do not write...to provoke, I am concerned to persuade. The economic and social system is worth understanding, and in the form in which it exists." Galbraith, New Industrial State, op. cit., p. xii.

[17]Michael Harrington, The Other America (Baltimore, Maryland: Penguin Books, 1971), p. 31.

[18]Robert L. Heilbroner, The Worldly Philosophers, fourth edition (New York: Touchstone Books, 1972), p. 319.

[19]Galbraith, Economics and the Public Purpose, op. cit., p. 73.

[20]For an extended discussion of this issue, see Gabriel Kolko, Wealth and Power in America (New York: Vintage Books, 1971).

[21]See for example Kingsley Davis and W.E. Moore, "Some Principles of Stratification," American Sociological Review, 10 (April 1945), pp. 242-249.

[22]Galbraith,"What Comes After General Motors," op. cit., p. 15.

[23]Herbert Gans, "The Positive Functions of Poverty," American Journal of Sociology, 78 (September 1972) p. 228.

[24]John Kenneth Galbraith, The Affluent Society

(New York: New American Library, Mentor, 1958), p. 83.

[25] Leon Keyserling, "Eggheads and Politics," New Republic, 139 (October 27, 1958), p. 15.

[26] Galbraith, Affluent Society, op. cit., p. 94.

[27] This has led Galbraith to conclude that "there is no way within the Keynesian modalities to reconcile adequately high employment with reasonably stable prices. It is possible to combine a politically unacceptable level of unemployment with a socially damaging rate of inflation." "The Left in Britain and the U.S.," New Statesman, 80 (December 4, 1970), p. 748. For a more detailed, non-technical discussion of the Phillips curve see William Breit and Roger L. Ransom, The Academic Scribblers (New York: Holt, Rinehart and Winston, 1967), pp. 129-31.

[28] Staffan Burenstam Linder, The Harried Leisure Class (New York: Columbia University Press, 1970), p. 141.

[29] Commission of Population Growth and American Future, "The Quality of American Life," in Johnson, op. cit., p. 42.

[30] Galbraith, Affluent Society, op. cit., p. 220.

[31] "Playboy Interview," op. cit., p. 70. See also his "Left in Britain and the US," op. cit., p. 749.

[32] John Kenneth Galbraith, "Let Us Begin," Harpers, March 1964, p. 18.

[33] John Maynard Keynes, Essays in Persuasion (Cambridge, England: Macmillan, 1972), pp. 325-6.

[34] Heilbroner, op. cit., p. 284.

[35] Breit and Ransom, op. cit., p. 10.

[36] Galbraith, New Industrial State, op. cit., p. 215.

[37] James M. Roche, "American Business is Plainly in Trouble," in Johnson, op. cit., p. 208.

[38] Galbraith, Affluent Society, op. cit., p. 117.

[39]Keynes, op. cit., p. 326.

[40]Ibid., p. 326.

[41]Breit and Ransom, op. cit., p. 11.

[42]Galbraith, Affluent Society, op. cit., p. 109.

[43]Ibid., p. 126. To avoid confusion, it should be indicated that, as always, Galbraith posits a two-directional flow of influence. Thus he would concede that individual values serve to stimulate production just as production serves to reinforce individual values.

[44]Ibid., p. 153.

[45]Significantly, Linder observes that "Since 1945, the Printer's Ink advertising index has risen by 400 per cent. During the corresponding 20 year period, Gross National Product and private consumption in the United States only doubled." He also points out that the average individual is exposed to 1600 advertisements daily and 10,000 yearly. In his estimation, this reflects by and large the growing need for surrogate information in order to make a growing number of consumption decisions each day. Linder, op. cit., p. 72.

[46]Galbraith, New Industrial State, op. cit., p. 203.

[47]Galbraith, Affluent Society, op. cit., p. 128.

[48]In response to Scott Gordon's complaint that wants are equally contrived in poor societies because "Every gothic spire in Europe, every temple in India, certifies the power of dominant social institutions in achieving major manipulation of income allocation," Galbraith responds: "But does this alter the personal consumption situation of the poor in these societies? Would anyone deny that income can be squeezed from the poor by spiritual or temporal authority, or, indeed, that this is (or was) other than a reason why they are poor? Because Shah Jahan, the greatest of builders could indulge his fancy with the Pearl Mosque or the Taj Mahal (or its adjacent places of worship if Professor Gordon wants to reamin strictly with religion), this does not mean that the Hindu villager could do likewise, or could influence that choice or had any options, assuming he wanted to remain alive, but to concentrate his consumption on bread grains." Scott

Gordon, "The Close of the Galbraithian System," <u>Journal</u>
<u>of</u> <u>Political</u> <u>Economics</u>, 76 (July/August 1968), p. 641;
John Kenneth Galbraith, "Professor Gordon on 'the Close
of the Galbraithian System'," <u>Journal</u> <u>of</u> <u>Political</u>
<u>Economics</u>, 77 (July/August 1969), p. 498.

[49]Robin Marris, <u>The</u> <u>Economic</u> <u>Theory</u> <u>of</u> 'Managerial' <u>Capitalism</u> (New York: Free Press, 1964), p. 60.

[50]Galbraith, <u>New</u> <u>Industrial</u> <u>State</u>, <u>op</u>. <u>cit</u>., p.
348.

[51]<u>Ibid</u>., p. 209.

[52]"The Price of Affluence," <u>Economist</u>, 188 (September 20, 1958), p. 928.

[53]David Potter, <u>People</u> <u>of</u> <u>Plenty</u> (Chicago: University of Chicago Press, 1964), p. 171.

[54]George C. Allen, <u>Economic</u> <u>Fact</u> <u>and</u> <u>Fantasy</u> (London: Institute on Economic Affairs, 1969), p. 23.

[55]See Linder, <u>op</u>. <u>cit</u>., pp. 70 ff.

[56]Cited in Breit and Ransom, <u>op</u>. <u>cit</u>., p. 105.

[57]See <u>Ibid</u>., pp. 186 ff. See also Galbraith,
"Economics and the Quality of Life," <u>Science</u>, 145
(July 10, 1964).

[58]Myron Sharpe, <u>John</u> <u>Kenneth</u> <u>Galbraith</u> <u>and</u> <u>the</u>
<u>Lower</u> <u>Economics</u> (White Plains, New York: International
Arts and Science Press, Inc., 1973), pp. 29-32.

[59]Jean Boddewyn, "On Galbraith and Potatoes,"
<u>South</u> <u>Atlantic</u> <u>Quarterly</u>, 58 (Winter 1964), p. 347.

[60]F.A. Hayek, "The Non Sequitur of the Dependence
Effect," <u>The</u> <u>Southern</u> <u>Economics</u> <u>Journal</u>, 27 (April
1961), p. 347.

[61]John Kenneth Galbraith, "A Review of a Review,"
<u>The</u> <u>Public</u> <u>Interest</u>, 9 (Fall 1967), p. 114.

[62]Kolko, <u>op</u>. <u>cit</u>., p. 105.

[63]Galbraith, <u>Affluent</u> <u>Society</u>, <u>op</u>. <u>cit</u>., p. 160.

[64]Commission of Population Growth, <u>op</u>. <u>cit</u>., p.43.

[65] Galbraith, "Economics and the Quality of Life," op. cit., p. 120.

[66] Galbraith, Economics and the Public Purpose, op. cit., p. 192.

[67] William G. Shepherd, Market Power and Economic Welfare (New York: Random House, 1970), pp. 76-7.

[68] Galbraith, New Industrial State, op. cit., p. 333.

[69] Office of Management and Budget, The United States Budget in Brief, 1976 (Washington, D.C.: Government Printing Office, 1975), pp. 20-32.

[70] Galbraith, Economics and the Public Purpose, op. cit., p. 294.

[71] For a more extended discussion of this point, see Galbraith, "Let Us Begin, op. cit., pp. 17-26.

[72] For a discussion of the means employed by the automobile companies see Fred R. Harris, "The Politics of Corporate Power," in Ralph Nader and Mark Green (eds.) Corporte Power in America (New York: Grossman Publishers, 1973), pp. 27-9.

[73] Galbraith, "Left in Britain and the US," op. cit., p. 749.

[74] Galbraith, Economics and the Public Purpose, op. cit., p. 30.

[75] Ibid., p. 154.

[76] Ibid., p. 145.

[77] Galbraith, Affluent Society, op. cit., p. 201.

[78] Ibid., pp. 203-4.

[79] John Kenneth Galbraith, "How Much Should a Country Consume?" in Harry Jarrett (ed.) Perspectives on Conservation (Baltimore, Maryland: Johns Hopkins Press, 1958), p. 95.

[80] Galbraith, Economics and the Public Purpose, op. cit., p. 146.

[81]*Economic Priorities Report*, volume 2 (September/October 1971), p. 19.

[82]Galbraith, *New Industrial State*, *op. cit.*, p. 337.

[83]Significantly, Gibson Winter has reached a similar conclusion and contends that "So long as those common means and resources in which we all participate and upon which all of us now depend operate independent of the common good and common will, we shall fall further into disorder and decay." Winter, *Being Free* (New York: Macmillan Company, 1970), p. 32.

[84]Galbraith, *Affluent Society*, *op. cit.*, p. 203.

[85]Galbraith, "Economics and the Quality of Life," *op. cit.*, p. 118.

6
GALBRAITH'S AMERICAN DREAM

[1]Bernard Collier, "A Most Galbraithian Economist," *New York Times Magazine*, February 18, 1973, p. 58.

[2]Edward T. Chase, "Technology's Brave New World," *Commonweal*, 99 (December 14, 1973), p. 298. Also of interest is Lekachman's assessment: "A prophet not quite without honor in his adopted country, Galbraith won reluctant converts in 1971 in the Nixon administration." Robert Lekachman, "A Synopsis of John Kenneth Galbraith's Economics," *New York Times Magazine*, February 18, 1973, p. 12. Of interest is the shift in Lekachman's evaluation since 1956 when he argued that by directing his books at a general audience, Galbraith was being quite unfair in by-passing his economic brethren who had answered him "in learned journals, particularly in the far from lively pages of the *American Economic Review*, whose publication is surely smaller than that of *Women's Wear Daily*....Mr. Galbraith's critics have the better of the argument, but the rights and wrongs of the controversy are less important than that it has occurred at all and that Mr. Galbraith's audience, being innocent of its existence, accepts for want of an accessible alternative his side of the issue." Lekachman, "Economics for Everybody?" *Commentary*, 21 (January 1956), p. 79.

[3]As he has argued, he is discussing "historical

imperatives. This means that they are not matters of
ideological preference as is commonly imagined. To
see economic policy as a problem of choice between
rival ideologies is the greatest error of our time.
Only rarely, and usually on matters of secondary importance, do circumstances vouchsafe this luxury." John
Kenneth Galbraith, Money: Whence It Came, Where It
Went (Boston:Houghton Mifflin, 1975), p. 305. For a
discussion of the ambiguity of Galbraith's use of
"circumstances" as a prime-mover, see John S. Gambs,
John Kenneth Galbraith (New York: St. Martin's Press,
1975), p. 100.

[4]Lekachman, op. cit., p. 12. In a similar vein
Edmund J. Sheehey has commented that although "his
righteousness and lack of empirical analysis do not
make his contentions any easier to accept, his concern
with the realities of power has begun to give new direction to the study of economic policy." Edmund J.
Sheehey, "Economics and the Public Purpose," America,
March 23, 1974, p. 226.

[5]John Kenneth Galbraith, Economics and the Public
Purpose (Boston: Houghton Mifflin, 1973), p. 7.

[6]"Playboy Interview: John Kenneth Galbraith,"
Playboy, June 1968, p. 138.

[7]John Kenneth Galbraith, Who Needs the Democrats
and What It Takes to Be Needed (Garden City, New York:
Doubleday and Company, Inc., 1970), p. 81. It is a
similar assessment which has led Michael Harrington to
the conclusion that "Our technology could indeed be the
instrument of enslavement; or it couls for the first
time ever, provide the material base for a genuine human community that would democratize economic and social as well as political power." Michael Harrington,
Socialism (New York: Saturday Review Press, 1970), pp.
4-5.

[8]Galbraith, Economics and the Public Purpose, op.
cit., p. 221. Until belief is emancipated, he argues,
the technostructure and the planning system "will continue to pursue its purposes under the protection of
the belief that its goals are those that best serve
the public. The unequal development, unequal income,
unequal and bizarre distribution of public expenditures, environmental damage, discriminatory and ineffective stabilization policies will continue, for it

will continue to be imagined that they reflect accidental or sui generis error. It not being believed that
any systemic conflict between public purpose and that
of the planning system is involved, no continuing effort will be made on behalf of the public." (p. 221.)

[9]Ibid., p. 230.

[10]Ibid., p. 232.

[11]Ibid., p. 163.

[12]Harris' stance is suggested by his contention
that "if we are to deal effectively with corporate power we must get the issues out into the open, where the
public interest can--and does--win. We must insist that
every man and woman who runs for President, Senate or
Congress face up to the question of corporate power in
our country." Fred R. Harris, "The Politics of Corporate Power," in Ralph Nader and Mark Green (eds.),
Corporate Power in America (New York: Grossman Publishers, 1973), p. 41.

[13]As Galbraith has observed recently, "Once we
spoke of economics as something that described reality.
Now we refer to neoclassical economics (orthodox or
accepted economics) as something which serves the purposes of the textbooks, which occupies students and
professors but which is not imagined greatly to illum-
inate life as it is. So there is an indication of
change even here." "Conversations with an Inconvenient
Economist," Challenge, September/October 1973, p. 33.

[14]Gibson Winter, Being Free (New York: Macmillan
Company, 1970), p. 33.

[15]See Galbraith's discussion in Money, op. cit.,
p. 189. Significantly, Harrington has chronicled the
development of Roosevelt's positions as they related
to the worker and concluded that "It was only when the
NRA was declared unconstitutional that FDR began a belated campaign for the Wagner Act. Thus even if Roosevelt's first term had been indecisive, it ended with
his moving toward the organized workers." Harrington,
op. cit., p. 259. See pages 83-84 for Keynes' impact
upon economic thinking.

[16]Richard Polenberg, Radicalism and Reform in the
New Deal (Reading, Massachusetts: Addison-Wesley Pub-

lishing Company, 1972), p. 5. See also Ben B. Seligman, _Economics of Dissent_ (Chicago: Quadrangle Books, 1968), p. 19.

[17]It was this phenomenon which led Galbraith to the conclusion expressed in 1955 that "None of the great questions of economic policy which provided such a rich fuel for political controversy in the 1930's and 40's now retains its old standing as a subject of disagreement." John Kenneth Galbraith, _Economics and the Art of Controversy_ (New Brunswick, New Jersey: Rutgers University Press, 1955), p. 95. Thus, for example, with the recognition of the CIO by US Steel in 1937 and the subsequent acceptance of collective bargaining, labor was loosed from its position of peonage and labor relationships assumed a previously unthinkable calm. So, too, with the debate over farm supports, government involvement in the economy and the need for social legislation. Debate now centers not on the large issues, but on particular applications. Of special significance was Richard Nixon's belated and reluctant conversion first to Keynesian economics and then to wage and price controls to restrain corporate giants.

[18]Galbraith, _Economics and the Public Purpose, op. cit._, p. 221.

[19]It is this same tendency which has led a number of the other heterodox thinkers to repudiate the "stock of well known remedies" for economic deprivation, unemployment and uneven development which ignore vast structural changes within the economy. For a wide sampling of opinion on this issue see Nader and Green, _op. cit._, See also Andrew Hacker, _The End of the American Era_ (New York: Atheneum, 1971) and Bernard D. Nossiter, _The Mythmakers_ (Boston: Houghton Mifflin Company, 1964), pp. 164 ff.

[20]John Kenneth Galbraith, _American Capitalism_ (Boston: Houghton Mifflin, Sentry, 1956), pp. 143-4.

[21]UPI Release, "GM Sets Out to Grab Market," _Quad City Times_, September 21, 1975, p. 3C. Significantly, William Shepherd has observed that "the main lines of antitrust policy in what was widely thought to mark a distinct step forward, came to rely increasingly on horizontal market structure (particularly market shares) in defining market power. Market shares and trends in industrial concentration increasingly took

center stage in antitrust evaluations and decisions, and they seemed to provide a simple, direct and concrete approach to defining and attacking market power. ...Yet there have been almost no direct efforts during the last 15 years to reduce concentration, only to restrain its rise through merger. This double standard toward mergers and existing concentration has had the effect of acquiescing in the position of the established leading firms in highly concentrated industries." William G. Shepherd, Market Power and Economic Welfare (New York: Random House, 1970), p. 20. Also of importance is his observation that "After some early antitrust victories in 1911, the burden of proof that market power was harmful was, in effect, placed upon the antitrust agencies. Roughly speaking, the holders of market power came to be assumed to be innocent unless they could be shown to have gained their market power in an abusive way, or to have exercised that power unreasonably." (p. 14)

[22] Nossiter, op. cit., pp. 49-50.

[23] For an extensive discussion of ITT's practices see Willard F. Mueller, "Corporate Secrecy vs. Corporate Disclosure," in Nader and Green, op. cit., especially pp. 114-20.

[24] For an analysis of techniques available to the large corporation to overturn judiciary decisions, see Fred R. Harris, op. cit., especially pp. 30-1. See also, Simon Lazarus, "Halfway Up From Liberalism: Regulation and Corporate Power," in Nader and Green, op. cit., p. 229.

[25] In large measure, as Michael Harrington has observed, in accordance with economic orthodoxy, "national enterprises are to be confined to the sectors that capitalism has so fouled up that they are no longer profitable....social property is then hobbled with restrictions that do not apply to the private sector." Harrington, op. cit., p. 301.

[26] John Kenneth Galbraith, The New Industrial State, revised (New York: New American Library, Mentor, 1971), p. 188. In a similar vein, during the 1967 joust between Galbraith and his critics (Assistant Attorney General Donald F. Turner, chief of the Justice Department Antitrust Division; Willard F. Mueller, chief Federal Trade economist; and Walter Adams, economics pro-

fessor at Michigan State), Galbraith expressed his
position as follows: "'If a firm is already large, it
is substantially immune under the antitrust laws...it
will not be demerged.' But if two medium sized companies
unite to deal more effectively with the giants, Galbraith added, the law will 'be on them like a tiger.'
This is because it is far more difficult under the
antitrust laws to attack dominant, existing corporations than to challenge mergers of smaller competitors." "Too big for antitrust to handle?" Business
Week, July 8, 1967, p. 71.

[27] Galbraith, Economics and the Public Purpose,
op. cit., p. 216. See also Shepherd, op. cit., pp.
20-21.

[28] Colin Clark, "The Eminence of Professor Galbraith," National Review, 20 (March 12, 1968), p. 244.

[29] Ralph Nader, "The Case for Federal Chartering,"
in Nader and Green, op. cit., especially pp. 67-79. In
a similar vein Galbraith has argued that the fundamental problem with taking antitrust laws seriously
"is that economists will neglect the real questions of
how to deal effectively with the modern corporate
world. At the very least...antitrust should be allowed
to 'quietly atrophy'." "Too big for antitrust?" op.
cit., p. 72. This view receives further support from
Shepherd's conclusion that "since about 1952, antitrust has largely abandoned attempts to make changes
in established structure, even where structural monopoly would appear to warrant it." He continues, "antitrust policy has now largely acquiesced in, and therefore ratified, existing market structure." Shepherd,
op. cit., p. 166.

[30] Ironically, historical evidence points to a
rather convoluted relationship between antitrust legislation and concentration of economic power. The first
onslaught of mergers occurred the decade following the
enactment of the Sherman Act (1890); the second wave
followed in the wake of the Clayton Act (1914); the
third overlapped with the passage of the Celler-Ke-
fauver Amendment (1950). See Nossiter, op. cit., pp.
72 ff.

[31] Galbraith, American Capitalism, op. cit., p.178.

[32] Galbraith, Economics and the Public Purpose, op.
cit., p. 310.

[33] _Ibid._, p. 310.

[34] Ralph Winter, "Trend Bucker? He's Paying for Recession Now," reprinted from _Wall Street Journal_ in _Quad City Times_, October 12, 1975, p. 2A.

[35] See _Economics and the Public Purpose, op. cit._, pp. 304-5.

[36] _Ibid._, p. 304.

[37] While I am not accusing Galbraith of bad faith, his sudden interest in the position of women and his lack of discussion of poverty invite comment. Apparently circumstances, as Galbraith might say, have forced him to refocus his attention. He is, in this sense, both a trend setter and a trend follower.

[38] See _Economics and the Public Purpose, op. cit._, pp. 275-7.

[39] See Harrington, _op. cit._, especially chapter 8.

[40] It is this aspect of Galbraith's thought which most clearly places him within the democratic tradition. This allegiance, discussed briefly in chapter five, will be pursued at greater length in chapter seven.

[41] As he has argued, one of the inflationary spurs in the modern economy is increased claims for goods which press upon capacity. Speaking of the late sixties he remarked: "Increasingly, in all countries these accepted and prescriptive limits on income and consumption were under strain. Everywhere the less privileged were asserting more strongly their claim to some part of the consumption that previously had been thought the natural right only of the privileged." Galbraith, _Money, op. cit._, p. 293.

[42] For Galbraith's reaction to Reich's _The Greening of America_ (New York: Random House, 1970), see his "Who's Minding the Store?" in Philip Nobile (ed.), _The Con III Controversy_ (New York: Pocket Books, 1971), pp. 18-20.

[43] Galbraith, _Economics and the Public Purpose, op. cit._, p. 277.

[44]Such an interpretation is suggested by Seymour
Martin Lipset's discussion of political parties in
America in which he discusses proclivities of politicians to reduce the salience of the class issue in
order to appeal to a wider constituency. Lipset, Political Man (New York: Anchor Books, 1963), pp. 226,331.

[45]Abram Mileikovsky, "Crisis of Bourgeois Economic Theory and Galbraith's 'New Ideas'," New Times
(Moscow), 28 (July 1972), p. 20.

[46]Galbraith, Economics and the Public Purpose,
op. cit., p. 161.

[47]See among others Ely Chinoy, Automobile Workers
and the American Dream (Boston: Beacon Press, 1955);
Stanley Weir, "U.S.A.: The Labor Revolt," in Maurice
Zeitlin, American Society, Inc., (Chicago: Markham
Publishing Company, 1970), pp. 446-501. See also
Studs Terkel, Working (New York: Avon Books, 1972).

[48]Chinoy, op. cit., p. 4.

[49]Ibid., especially chapters five through seven.

[50]Sidney M. Peck, "The Rank-and-File Union
Leader's Consciousness," in M. Zeitlin, op. cit., p.
462.

[51]Irving M. Zeitlin, Marxism: A Re-Examination
(New York: Van Nostrand Reinhold Company, 1967), pp.
108-115. The impact of automation on the workplace also
receives attention from Ben B. Seligman, "Man, Work,
and the Automated Feast," in his Economics of Dissent,
op. cit., pp. 48-65.

[52]This possibility is discussed by Weir toward the
end of his examination. It is also the subject of Robert Avakian's "Worker-Student Alliance?" in M. Zeitlin,
op. cit., pp. 502-5.

[53]See Robert Fitch, "A Galbraith Reappraisal: the
Ideologue as Gadfly," Ramparts, May 1968, pp. 80-2.

[54]Weir, op. cit., p. 500.

[55]Ibid., p. 492.

[56]R. Joseph Monsen and Mark W. Cannon, The Makers

of Public Policy (New York: McGraw Hill Book Company, 1965), p. 75.

[57]See Harrington, op. cit., pp. 264 ff.

[58]Robert L. Heilbroner, "Galbraith's Progress," Dissent, 21 (Winter 1974), p. 107.

[59]Significantly, Kemp observed that Galbraith "refused to make a full qualitative assessment of American society. He avoids a deep analysis of power relations....If he plumbed these depths he would be bound to make an analysis in terms of the class division in American society and the real social relations which impede the full and harmonious development of the production forces in the richest country in the world." Tom Kemp, "Galbraith as Prophet of American Neo-Capitalism," Science and Society, 29 (Fall 1965), p. 396.

[60]Galbraith, Who Needs the Democrats, op. cit., pp. 1-2.

[61]Ibid., p. 3.

[62]Harrington, op. cit., pp. 255 ff.

[63]Robert L. Heilbroner, The Worldly Philosophers, (New York: Touchstone Books, 1972), p. 320.

[64]Galbraith, Who Needs the Democrats, op. cit., p. 47.

[65]Ibid., pp. 49-50.

[66]Galbraith, Economics and the Public Purpose, op. cit., p. 249.

[67]Of interest in this regard is Polenberg's observation that "Roosevelt also believed that an extension of the liberal program required reform of the Democratic Party. Accordingly, the President proposed a broad-gauged plan of government reorganization, and in the Fall of 1938 attempted to defeat several conservative Democrats most of them Southerners, who had blocked his program in Congress. But Roosevelt met with no more success in these endeavors than in the Court fight." Polenberg, op. cit., p. 6.

[68]See Who Needs the Democrats, op. cit., p. 54.

[69]Significantly, during the height of the Vietnam

protests, Galbraith and other veteran McCarthy sup-
porters organized a group called "Referendum '70" which
sought to frustrate the reelection of legislators who
had endorsed the Administration's Vietnam policy. "The
Galbraith Purge," as the movement was dubbed by Kenneth
Crawford, sought to oust such notables as Henry Jackson
(Washington), Gale McGee (Wyoming), Hubert Humphrey
(Minnessota), John Rooney (New York) and Philip Philbin
(Massachusetts). Of these, only Philbin failed to win
reelection. See Kenneth Crawford, "The Galbraith
Purge," Newsweek, February 9, 1970, p. 29. and Crawford,
"The Other Purge," Newsweek, November 23, 1970, p. 39.
Admittedly, this campaign, which revolved around a sin-
gle issue, is not strictly comparable to an effort to
oust those whose basic orientation is in some ways
antithetical to the change-oriented commitments of the
Democratic Party. There remains doubt, however, that
even the more comprehensive "purge" would be effective.

[70]Frederick G. Dutton, Changing Sources of Power
(New York: McGraw-Hill Company, 1971), p. 93.

[71]Naomi Bluen, "For Better, Not for Worse," New
Yorker, December 31, 1973, p. 58.

[72]Galbraith, Economics and the Public Purpose, op.
cit., p. 258.

[73]Shepherd, op. cit., p. 77.

[74]Galbraith, Economics and the Public Purpose, op.
cit., p. 258.

[75]Ibid., p. 262.

[76]G. Winter, op. cit., p. 35.

[77]Galbraith, Economics and the Public Purpose, op.
cit., p. 280.

[78]For the importance of such loopholes see Gabriel
Kolko, Welath and Power in America (New York: Praeger
Publishers, 1962), especially chapters one and two.

[79]See John Kenneth Galbraith, A Theory of Price
Control (Cambridge: Harvard University Press, 1952);
and Galbraith, Money, op. cit., pp. 245 ff.

[80]Curiously, Galbraith first describes socializing the mature corporation and then in his discussion

of the "socialist imperative" refers only to the defense and armament industries.

[81]See Supra note 23.

[82]Galbraith, Economics and the Public Purpose, op.
cit., p. 318.

[83]Significantly, Senators Jacob Javits and Hubert
Humphrey, encouraged by the Initiative Committee for
National Economic Planning, concluded in early 1975
that the failures of the private economy made necessary
a Federal agency for economic planning.

[84]As Nossiter explains, in both Europe and Japan,
"A group of government economists tentatively select a
plausible rate of growth for their nation's economy.
This rate, perhaps five percent a year, is based on two
central elements: population forecasts of the probable
growth in the labor force and the likely pace at which
productivity of these workers will increase at full employment. Then, combining past experience and possible
future policies, the technicians draw up a model or
projection of the economy's broad outlines four or five
years in the future." This is then reviewed by industry,
labor, farmers, and consumers (or their representatives)
as well as by government. Differences are reconciled,
bottlenecks spotted and inconsistencies eliminated. The
revised projections then serve as a guide to decisions
of all relevant groups. Nossiter, op. cit., pp. 195 ff.

[85]John Kenneth Galbraith, "The Emerging Public
Corporation," Business and Society Review, 1 (Spring
1972), p. 56.

[86]Harrington, op. cit., p. 300.

[87]Gambs, op. cit., p. 110.

[88]Although this issue is nowhere specifically
addressed in Economics and the Public Purpose, Galbraith has elsewhere expressed a strong desire to dis-
establish the Washington bureaucracy. Only by doing so,
he has argued, can foreign policy be loosed from bureaucratic control and be made responsive to political
control. Thus he argued: "None will doubt the extent
of the exercise of Presidential and other political
authority that will be needed. It is not easy to associate the prospect with the passive tendencies of President Nixon. The proper policy toward the Third World
requires not only new doctrines but also elimination of

the need for a large part of the military, intelligence
and civilian bureaucracy that conditions the present
policy. The survival of that bureaucracy depends upon
making policy on the wrong assumptions. It would be
naive to imagine that these organizations will acqui-
esce easily in the change, however effectively they are
proven in error and however ghastly the resulting experience. Not wickedness but the dynamic of big organization is involved." John Kenneth Galbraith, "A Decade
of Disaster in Foreign Policy," The Progressive, 35
(February 1971), p. 38.

[89]Heilbroner, "Galbraith's Progress," op. cit.,
p. 107.

[90]Galbraith, Economics and the Public Purpose, op.
cit., p. 284.

[91]Shepherd, op. cit., p. 165.

7
A MAN OF GOOD HOPE: THE VISION REVIEWED

[1]Rexford G. Tugwell, "America Takes Hold of Its
Destiny," in Richard Polenberg (ed.) Radicalism and
Reform in the New Deal (Reading, Massachusetts: Addison
Wesley Publishing Company, 1972), p. 44.

[2]John Gambs, John Kenneth Galbraith (New York: St.
Martin's Press, 1975), p. 116.

[3]Naomi Bluen, "For Better, Not for Worse," New
Yorker, December 31, 1973, p. 57.

[4]Another related point of distinction is suggested
by William Breit and Roger Ransom: "The appearance of
The New Industrial State prompted the Senate Subcom-
mittee on Monopoly to hold hearings and gather testimony on the implications of the Galbraithian system.
Few other economists have seen such rapid response to
their work." William Breit and Roger L. Ransom, The
Academic Scribblers (New York: Holt, Rinehart and Winston, Inc., 1967), p. 162.

[5]As far back as 1831 de Tocqueville stressed the
value which Americans placed upon practical activity,
independence, freedom, and individuality. More important for present purposes was his observation that the
"American republics of the present day are like companies of adventure, formed to explore in common the
wasteland of the New World and busied in a flourishing

212

trade. The passions that agitate the Americans most deeply are not their political but their commercial passions; or, rather, they introduce the habits of business into their political life." Alexis de Tocqueville, Democracy in America, volume 1 (New York: Vintage Books, 1945), p. 308. The emphasis was upon free enterprise and individual competition. As both David Potter and John Cawelti have demonstrated, the myths of equality and the belief in individual success have had a major impact upon virtually all American history. See David Potter, People of Plenty (Chicago: University of Chicago Press, 1954) and John Cawelti, Apostles of the Self-Made Man (Chicago: University of Chicago Press, 1965). See also Ely Chinoy, Automobile Workers and the American Dream (Boston: Beacon Press, 1955).

[6]William E. Simon, "A Strategy for Prosperity," Saturday Review, 2 (July 12, 1975), p. 11.

[7]Ibid., p. 20.

[8]Significantly, George C. Lodge has recently advanced an analysis of a "new American ideology" which bears striking resemblance to the Galbraithian vision as it is here presented. Since Lodge's book appeared as this work was drawing to a conclusion, I have not attempted to integrate it into this discussion. Like Galbraith, Lodge is responding to what appears to him to be an "ideological schizophrenia" deeply rooted in the American mind--a manner of thinking which frustrates responsive solutions to contemporary problems. See George C. Lodge, The New American Ideology (New York: Alfred A. Knopf, Inc., 1975).

[9]Because power resides in large economic organizations, argue Monsen and Cannon, "today in America, membership in a major power group provides common purposes and shared emotional meanings as well as relatively defined roles and status." R. Joseph Monsen and Mark W. Cannon, The Makers of Public Policy (New York: McGraw-Hill Book Company, 1965), p. 329, passim.

[10]Milton Friedman is perhaps the most well known proponent of this view. Although couched in economic concepts such as risk aversion, his position betrays his Spencerian, laissez fairre allegiances. C.E. Ayres has paraphrased Friedman's view as follows: "In short Harlem is populated in part by people who (though penniless) took the appalling risk of migrating from Alabama or Puerto Rico but failed to find Utopia, and also by people who, though thoroughly dissatisfied with a

ghetto existence, stubbornly refuse to get out and organize a corporate conglomerate, being in this respect as timid as the wealthy dowagers who crouch in their penthouse apartments and never venture out except to visit their banks or clip the coupons on their municipal bonds (on which they pay no income tax)." C. E. Ayres, "Foreward," to Ben B. Seligman, _Economics of Dissent_ (Chicago: Quadrangle Books, 1968), p. viii.

[11]For example, racial equality, according to Galbraith, "means continuing and doing better the things on which equality depends--in providing full access to political life, education, employment, income, union membership, housing and protection of law." John Kenneth Galbraith, _Who Needs the Democrats and What it Takes to Be Needed_ (Garden City, New York: Doubleday and Company, Inc., 1970), pp. 70-1.

[12]Edward F. Chase, "Technology's Brave New World," _Commonweal_, 59 (December 14, 1973), p. 298.

[13]Thus, according to Galbraith, "Automobile use in the central city, aircraft travel adjacent to populated areas, supersonic travel, random residential use of land are all cases where the advantage of the particular consumer is outweighed by the adverse effect on the community as a whole. In the past presumption has favored individual convenience even in the face of larger social cost, and this has reflected the purposes of the planning system. The rational legislative decision requires the exclusion from consumption of products, services and technology where the social cost and discomfort are deemed to outweigh the individual advantages." John Kenneth Galbraith, _Economics and the Public Purpose_ (Boston: Houghton Mifflin, 1973), pp. 290-1.

[14]As Galbraith has argued in regard to the status of economics as a discipline and the primacy of economic goals: "To enhance the well-being of the individual has, in the past seemed a sound social purpose. To assist the individual in his subordination to General Motors will not be so regarded. The sanctity of economic purpose will also be questioned if well-being as conventionally measured continues to improve and leaves unsolved problems associated with collective need--those of the cities and their ghettoes and the by-passed rural areas--or if this progress involves an unacceptable commitment to the technology of war." John Kenneth Galbraith, "A Review of a Review," _The Public_

Interest, 9 (Fall 1967), pp. 117-18.

[15]Thus among the required planks of a sound urban policy Galbraith urges public land ownership and the recognition that private enterprise cannot (or will not) provide the services needed by the city dweller. "This is true especially of housing construction, housing repair, rehabilitation, maintenance and management, and the provision of local commuter and interurban transportation....The answer is to take these tasks proudly--as the Dutch housing authorities build houses, as the Swiss run trains, as Toronto, London and Moscow run their mass transit and we have long operated that fine old manifestation of domestic bolshevism, the TVA. The city is an intensely social institution, it should surprise no one that it can only be served on important matters by social action." Galbraith, Who Needs the Democrats op. cit., pp. 72-3.

[16]The central problem as Galbraith defines it is equalizing the power available to the planning and the market systems (the large corporations and the small corporations). In his view, governmental action "--agricultural price-fixing, other supplements to small businessmen, support to collective bargaining, minimum wage legislation, the proposed provision of a guaranteed minimum income, international commodities arrangements, even some protective tariffs--is an intensely logical response to the bargaining weakness of the market system. We have not moved too rapidly and incautiously with such legislation, as the accepted economics strongly holds. It is not a response to special circumstances or special hardship or politics which is the normal explanation or justification. Given the structure of the modern economy--given the two systems--such action is the logical response to need. We suffer because we have moved too slowly and too cautiously and with too great a sense of guilt with measures to equalize the power wielded by the two systems." Galbraith, Economics and the Public Purpose, op. cit., p. 253.

[17]Cited in Ayres, op. cit., p. xiv.

[18]John Kenneth Galbraith, Ambassador's Journal (Boston: Houghton Mifflin, 1969), p. 593.

[19]Robert L. Heilbroner, "Galbraith's Progress," Dissent, 21 (Winter 1974), p. 105.

[20]John Kenneth Galbraith, The Affluent Society,

second edition (Boston: Houghton Mifflin Company,
1969), p. xxxi. For a sampling of the objections which
this plan evoked see Allen M. Sievers, Revolution,
Evolution and the Economic Order (Englewood Cliffs,
New Jersey: Prentice-Hall, Inc., 1962), p. 79.

[21]Galbraith, Economics and the Public Purpose,
op. cit., p. 236

[22]Galbraith, Money: Whence It Came, Where It Went
(Boston: Houghton Mifflin, 1975), pp. 305-11.

[23]William Breit and Roger L. Ransom, The Academic
Scribblers (New York: Holt, Rinehart and Winston, Inc.,
1967), p. 181.

[24]R. Joseph Monsen and Mark W. Cannon, The Makers
of Public Policy (New York: McGraw-Hill Book Company,
1965), for example, devote an entire chapter to the '
power which specialization has afforded the intellectual. They observe that intellectuals, as advisors,
consultants, writers and managers, have gained access
to important seats of power. It is not that they control the power so much as it is that they can influence
each of the other power groups. (pp. 218 ff.)

[25]Sievers, op. cit., p. 162.

[26]Daniel Aaron, Men of Good Hope (New York: Oxford University Press, 1961), p. 308.

BIBLIOGRAPHY

BOOKS BY JOHN KENNETH GALBRAITH

The Affluent Society. New York: New American Library,
     Mentor edition, 1958.
     Boston: Houghton Mifflin Company, revised, 1969.
The Age of Uncertainty. Boston: Houghton Mifflin Com-
     pany, 1977.
Ambassador's Journal: A Personal Account of the Kennedy
     Years. Boston: Houghton Mifflin Company, 1969.
America and Western Europe. New York: Public Affairs
     Commission, Inc., 1950.
American Capitalism: The Theory of Countervailing Pow-
     er. Revised edition. Boston: Houghton Mifflin
     Company, Sentry edition, 1956.
Beyond the Marshall Plan. Washington D.C.: National
     Planning Association International Committee,
     1949
A China Passage. Boston: Houghton Mifflin Company,
     1973.
Economics and the Art of Controversy. New Brunswick,
     New Jersey: Rutgers University Press, 1955.
Economics and the Public Purpose. Boston: Houghton
     Mifflin Company, 1973.
Economic Development in Perspective. Cambridge, Massa-
     chusetts: Harvard University Press, 1962.
Economics Peace and Laughter. New York: New American
     Library, Signet edition, 1972.
The Great Crash: 1929. Boston: Houghton Mifflin Com-
     pany, Sentry edition, 1972.
How to Control the Military. Garden City, New York:
     Doubleday and Company, Inc., 1968.
How to Get Out of Vietnam. New York: New American
     Library, Signet edition, 1967.
Indian Paintings. With Mohinder Singh Randhawa.
     Boston: Houghton Mifflin Company, 1968.
Journey to Poland and Yugoslavia. Cambridge, Massa-
     chusetts: Harvard University Press, 1958.
The Liberal Hour. New York: New American Library,
     Mentor edition, 1960.
The McLandress Dimension. Pseudonym Mark Epernay.
     Boston: Houghton Mifflin Company, 1962.
Marketing Efficiency in Puerto Rico. With Richard H.
     Holton. Cambridge, Massachusetts: Harvard Uni-
     versity Press, 1955.
Modern Competition and Business Policy. With H.S.
     Dennison. New York: Oxford University Press, 1938.
Money: Whence It Came, Where It Went. Boston: Houghton
     Mifflin Company, 1975.

217

The New Industrial State. Second edition, revised. New
    York: New American Library, Mentor edition, 1971.
Recovery in Europe. Washington D.C.: National Planning
    Association, 1946.
The Scotch. Boston: Houghton Mifflin Company, 1964.
A Theory of Price Control. Cambridge, Massachusetts:
    Harvard University Press, 1952.
The Triumph: A Novel of Modern Diplomacy. Boston:
    Houghton Mifflin Company, 1968.
Who Needs the Democrats and What It Takes to Be Needed.
    Garden City, New York: Doubleday and Company,
    Inc., 1970.

ARTICLES BY JOHN KENNETH GALBRAITH

"An Agenda for American Liberals." Commentary, 41
    (June 1966), pp. 29-34.
"Are Living Costs Out of Control?" Atlantic Monthly,
    February 1957, pp. 37-41.
"Art, Diplomacy and Vice Versa." Esquire, March 1967,
    pp. 113-19, 130-35.
"The Businessman as Philosopher." Perspectives U.S.A.,
    13 (Autumn 1955), pp. 57-69.
"The Case for George McGovern." Saturday Review, 55
    (July 1, 1972), pp. 23-27.
"Causes of Economic Growth: The Canadian Case." Queens
    Quarterly, 45 (Summer 1958), pp. 169-82.
"Comment on Solomon." Review of Economics and Statis-
    tics, 40 (May 1958), p. 168.
"A Communication." Washington Post, November 25, 1963.
    Reprinted in his Ambassador's Journal, pp. 629-32.
"Conventional Signs." The Spectator, July 29, 1960,
    pp. 174-5.
"Countervailing Power." American Economic Review, 44
    (May 1954), pp. 1-6.
"A Decade of Disasters in Foreign Policy." The Pro-
    gressive, 35 (February 1971), pp. 33-8.
"The Disequilibrium System." American Economic Review,
    37 (June 1947), pp. 287-302.
"The Decline of American Power." Esquire, March 1972,
    pp. 79-84.
"Dissent in a Free Society." Atlantic Monthly, Feb-
    ruary 1962, pp. 44-8.
"Economics and the Quality of Life." Science, 145
    (July 10, 1964), pp. 117-23.
"Economics as a System of Belief." American Economic
    Review, 60 (May 1970), pp. 469-78.
"The Economics of the American Housewife." Atlantic
    Monthly, August 1973, pp. 78-83.
"Economics for 1955: Hardheaded Bemusement." Reporter,
    12 (February 24, 1955), pp. 19-22.

"Economist as an Innovator." Twentieth Century, 159
    (April 1956), pp. 344-49.
"The Emerging Public Corporation." Business and Society
    Review, 1 (Spring 1972), pp. 54-6.
"Fabianism Revisited." Review of Economics and Statis-
    tics, 35 (August 1953), pp. 206-8.
"Foreign Policy: The Stuck Whistle." Atlantic Monthly,
    February 1965, pp. 64-8.
"Galbraith answers Crosland." New Statesman, 81 (Jan-
    uary 22, 1971), p. 101.
"Galbraith Has Seen China's Future--and it works." New
    York Times Magazine, November 26, 1972, pp. 38-9,
    88-101.
"Germany Was Badly Run." Fortune, December 1945, pp.
    173-179, 196-200.
"Heresy Revisited: An Economist's Notebook in Warsaw
    and Belgrade." Encounter, 12 (January 1959), pp.
    pp. 45-53.
"Hindsight." New Republic, August 24, 1974, p. 8.
"How the Economy Hangs on Her Apron Strings." Ms.,
    May 1974, pp. 74-77, 112.
"An Inflation Catechism: A Not Quite Straight 'Liberal'
    View." Current, November 1974, pp. 3-10.
"Inflation, Recession or Controls." New York Times
    Magazine, June 7, 1970.
"James Mill's India." Encounter, 30 (March 1968),
    pp. 40-4.
"A Layman's Guide to Monetary Crisis." Playboy,
    January 1971, pp. 90-94, 248-50.
"Left in Britain and the US." New Statesman, 80
    (December 4, 1970), pp. 748-50.
"Let Us Begin: An Invitation to Action on Poverty."
    Harpers, March 1964, pp. 16-26.
"Let Us Now Praise (Faintly) Famous Economists."
    Esquire, May 1977, pp. 70-1, 158.
"The Maintenance of Agricultural Production During De-
    pression: The Explanations Reviewed." With J.D.
    Black. Journal of Political Economics, 46 (June
    1938), pp. 305-23.
"Making 'Point 4' Work." Commentary, 10 (September
    1950), pp. 229-33.
"Market Structure and Stabilization Policy." Review
    of Economics and Statistics, 39 (May 1957),
    pp. 124-133.
"Mr. Hunter on Countervailing Power: A Comment." Econ-
    omic Journal, 69 (March 1959), pp. 168-70.
"Monopoly Power and Price Rigidities." Quarterly
    Journal of Economics, 50 (May 1936), pp. 456-75.

"Neurosis of the Rich." <u>Playboy</u>, February 1974, pp. 129, 163-4.
"On Freedom Again--and Never Too Often." <u>Reporter</u>, 12 (June 2, 1955), pp. 42-3.
"The Perfect Place: New Fame Inn, Vermont." <u>Esquire</u>, April 1968, pp. 106, 148-52.
"The Pleasures and Uses of Bankruptcy." <u>Reporter</u>, 21 (August 20, 1959), pp. 21-3.
"The Poverty of Nations." <u>Atlantic Monthly</u>, October 1962, pp. 47-53.
"Power and the Useful Economist." <u>American Economic Review</u>, 63 (March 1973), pp. 1-11.
"The Production Credit System of 1933." With J.D. Black. <u>American Economic Review</u>, 26 (June 1936), pp. 235-47.
"Professor Gordon on 'The Close of the Galbraithian System'." <u>Journal of Political Economics</u>, 77 (July/August 1969), pp. 494-503.
"The Quantitative Position of Marketing in the United States." With J.D. Black. <u>Quarterly Journal of Economics</u>, 49 (May 1935), pp. 394-413.
"Rational and Irrational Consumer Preferences." <u>Economic Journal</u>, 48 (June 1938), pp. 336-42.
"Reflections on the Asian Scene." <u>Journal of Asian Studies</u>, 23 (August 1964), pp. 501-4.
"Reflections on Price Control." <u>Quarterly Journal of Economics</u>, 60 (August 1946), pp. 475-89.
"The Reith Lectures." <u>The Listener</u>, November 17, 1966, pp. 711-714; November 24, 1966, pp. 755-758; December 1, 1966, pp. 793-5, 812; December 8, 1966, pp. 841-3, 853; December 15, 1966, 881-884; December 22, 1966, pp. 915-918.
"A Review of a Review." <u>Public Interest</u>, 9 (Fall 1967), pp. 109-118.
"The Self-Winding Industry of Switzerland." <u>Holiday</u>, February 1971, pp. 12-14.
"The Strategy of Direct Control in Economic Mobilization." <u>Review of Economics and Statistics</u>, 33(February 1951), pp. 12-17.
"Royalty on the Farm." <u>Reporter</u>, 21 (October 15, 1959), pp. 35-7.
"Selection and Timing of Inflation Controls." <u>Review of Economics and Statistics</u>, 23 (May 1941), pp. 82-5.
"The Unbelievable Happens in Bengal." <u>New York Times Magazine</u>, October 31, 1971, pp. 13, 93-101.
"The Unseemly Economics of Opulence." <u>Harpers</u>, January 1952, pp. 58-63.

"U.S. Agriculture: Problem and Choices." Social Order,
    8 (October 1958), pp. 376-382.
"What Comes After General Motors?" New Republic,
    November 2, 1974, pp. 13-17.
"What the FBI Has on Me." Esquire, December 1971,
    pp. 136, 224.
"Will Managed Capitalism Pull us Through?" Commentary,
    12 (August 1951), pp. 126-31.

BOOKS ABOUT GALBRAITH (one or more chapters)

Allen, George C. Economic Fact and Fantasy: A Rejoinder
    to Galbraith's Reith Lectures. London: Institute
    of Economic Affairs, 1969.
Breit, William and Roger L. Ransom. The Academic Scrib-
    blers. New York: Holt, Rinehart and Winston, Inc.,
    1967.
Downs, Robert B. Books that Changed America. London:
    Macmillan Company, 1970.
Gambs, John S. John Kenneth Galbraith. New York: St.
    Martin's Press, 1975.
Hession, Charles H. John Kenneth Galbraith and His
    Critics. New York: New American Library, 1972.
Oser, Jacob and William C. Blanchfield. The Evolution
    of Economic Thought. Third edition, revised. New
    York: Harcourt Brace Jovanovich, Inc., 1975.
Seligman, Ben B. Molders of Modern Thought. Chicago:
    Quadrangle Books, 1970
Sharpe, Myron. John Kenneth Galbraith and the Lower
    Economics. White Plains, New York: International
    Arts and Sciences Press, Inc., 1973.
Sievers, Allen M. Revolution, Evolution and the Econ-
    omic Order. Englewood Cliffs, New Jersey: Prentice
    Hall, Inc., 1962.

RELATED BOOKS

Aaron, Daniel, Men of Good Hope. New York: Oxford
    University Press, 1951.
Averitt, Robert T. The Dual Economy: The Dynamics of
    Industry Structure. New York: W.W. Norton and
    Company, Inc., 1968
Bell, Daniel. The End of Ideology: On the Exhaustion
    of Political Ideas in the Fifties. New York:
    Free Press, 1965.
Bendix, Reinhard. Max Weber: An Intellectual Portrait.
    Garden City: Anchor Books, 1962.
Berger, Peter L. The Sacred Canopy: Elements of a
    Sociological Theory of Religion. Garden City, New
    York: Doubleday and Company, Inc., 1969.

With Thomas Luckmann. The Social Construction of
Reality: A Treatise in the Sociology of Knowledge.
Garden City, New York: Doubleday and Company,
Inc., 1967.

With Brigitte Berger and Hansfried Kellner. The
Homeless Mind: Modernization and Consciousness.
New York: Vintage Books, 1974.

Boulding, Kenneth E. The Image: Knowledge in Life and
Society. Ann Arbor, Michigan: University of
Michigan Press, 1968.

Cawelti, John. Apostles of the Self-Made Man: Changing
Concepts of Success in America. Chicago: University of Chicago Press, 1965.

Chinoy, Ely. Automobile Workers and the American Dream.
Boston: Beacon Press, 1955.

Commons, John R. Myself. New York: Macmillan Company,
1934.

Curtis, James and John Petras (eds.) The Sociology of
Knowledge: A Reader. New York: Praeger Press,
1970.

de Tocqueville, Alexis. Democracy in America. Two volumes. New York: Vintage Books, 1945.

Dobbs, Zygmund. Keynes at Harvard: Economic Deception
as a Political Credo. West Sayville, New York:
Probe Research, Inc., 1969.

Domhoff, G. William. The Higher Circles: Governing
Class in America. New York: Vintage Books, 1971.

Dowd, Douglas F. (ed.) Thorstein Veblen: A Critical
Reappraisal. Ithaca, New York: Cornell University
Press, 1958.

Dutton, Frederick G. Changing Sources of Power. New
York: McGraw-Hill Company, 1971.

Fusfeld, Daniel R. The Age of the Economist. Glenview,
Illinois: Scott, Foresman and Company, 1966.

Gerth, H.H. and C. Wright Mills (eds.). From Max
Weber: Essays in Sociology. New York: Oxford
University Press, 1958.

Gill, Richard T. Evolution of Modern Economics.
Englewood Cliffs, New Jersey: Prentice;Hall, Inc.,
1967.

Goodman, Paul and Percival Goodman, Communitas: Means
of Livelihood and Ways of Life. New York: Vintage
Books, 1960.

Gouldner, Alvin W. The Coming Crisis of Western Sociology. New York: Avon Books, 1971.

Gruchy, Allan G. Modern Economic Thought: The American
Contribution. New York: Prentice-Hall, Inc., 1947.

Hacker, Andrew. The End of the American Era. New York:
    Atheneum, 1971.
Hamilton, David. Evolutionary Economics: A Study of
    Change in Economic Thought. Albuquerque: Univer-
    sity of New Mexico Press, 1970.
Harrington, Michael. The Other America: Poverty in the
    United States. Revised edition. Baltimore, Mary-
    land: Penguin Books, 1971.

    Socialism. New York: Saturday Review Press, 1970.
Haveman, Robert H. and Kenyon A. Knopf. The Market Sys-
    tem. Second edition. New York: John Wiley and
    Sons, Inc., 1970.
Heilbroner, Robert L. Between Capitalism and Socialism:
    Essays in Political Economics. New York: Random
    House, 1970.

    The Worldly Philosophers: The lives and times and
    ideas of the great economic thinkers. Fourth
    edition. New York: Touchstone Books, 1972.
Hession, Charles and Hyman Sardy. Ascent to Affluence
    Boston: Allyn and Bacon, Inc., 1969.
Holzner, Burkart. Reality Construction in Society.
    Revised edition. Cambridge, Massachusetts:
    Schenkman Publishing Company, Inc., 1972.
Horowitz, Irving Lewis. The New Sociology. New York:
    Oxford University Press, 1964.
Hulme, T.E. Speculations. New York: Harcourt, Brace
    and Company, 1924.
Jameson, Fredric. Marxism and Form: Twentieth Century
    Dialectical Theories of Literature. Princeton,
    New Jersey: Princeton University Press, 1971.
Jarett, Henry (ed.). Perspectives on Conservation.
    Baltimore, Maryland: Johns Hopkins Press, 1958.
Johnson, Arthur M. The American Economy: An Historical
    Introduction to the Problems of the 1970's. New
    York: Free Press, 1974.
Keynes, John Maynard. Essays in Persuasion. Cambridge,
    England: Macmillan Press LTD, 1972.
King, Richard. The Party of Eros: Radical Thought and
    the Realm of Freedom. New York: Dell Books, 1973.
Kolko, Gabriel. The Triumph of Conservatism. New York:
    Free Press, 1963.

    Wealth and Power in America: An Analysis of Social
    Class and Income Distribution. New York: Praeger
    Publishers, 1962.
Kuhn, Thomas. The Structure of Scientific Revolutions.
    Second edition, revised. Chicago: University of
    Chicago Press, 1970.

Lasch, Christopher. The New Radicalism in America.
New York: Vintage Books, 1965.

Lekachman, Robert. The Age of Keynes. New York: Random
House, 1966.

Lindbeck, Assar. The Political Economy of the New Left:
An Outsider's View. New York: Harper and Row,
1971.

Linder, Staffan Burenstam. The Harried Leisure Class.
New York: Columbia University Press, 1970.

Lipset, Seymour Martin. Political Man: The Social Bases
of Politics. Garden City, New York: Anchor Books,
1963.

Mannheim, Karl. Ideology and Utopia. New York: Harcourt, Brace and World, Inc., 1936.

Mansfield, Edwin. Microeconomics: Selected Readings.
New York: W.W. Norton and Company, Inc., 1971.

Marcuse, Herbert. One-Dimensional Man: Studies in the
Ideology of Advanced Industrial Society. Boston:
Beacon Press, 1964.

Marris, Robin. The Economic Theory of 'Managerial'
Capitalism. New York: Free Press, 1964.

Mermelstein, David (ed.). Economics: Mainstream Readings and Radical Critiques. New York: Random
House, 1970.

Mills, C. Wright. Power, Politics and People. New York:
Ballantine Books, 1963.

Monsen, R. Joseph and Mark W. Cannon. The Makers of
Public Policy: American Power Groups and their
Ideologies. New York: McGraw-Hill Book Company,
1965.

Mundell, Robert A. Man and Economics. New York: McGraw-
Hill Book Company, 1968.

Nader, Ralph and Mark J. Green (eds.). Corporate Power
in America: Ralph Nader's Conference on Corporate
Accountability. New York: Grossman Publishers,
1973.

Nobile, Philip (ed.). The Con III Controversy: The
Critics Look at The Greening of America. New
York: Pocket Books, 1971.

Norton, Hugh S. The World of the Economist. Columbia,
South Carolina: University of South Carolina
Press, 1973.

Nossiter, Bernard D. The Mythmakers: An Essay on Power
and Wealth. Boston: Houghton Mifflin Company,
1964.

Polenberg, Richard (ed.). Radicalism and Reform in the
New Deal. Reading, Massachusetts: Addison-Wesley
Publishing Company, 1972.

Potter, David. People of Plenty: Economic Abundance and American Character. Chicago: University of Chicago Press, 1954.

Reynolds, Larry T. and Janice M. Reynolds (eds). The Sociology of Sociology. New York: David McKay Company, Inc., 1970.

Riesman, David. Thorstein Veblen: A Critical Interpretation. New York: Charles Scribner's Sons, 1953.

Rose, Arnold M. The Power Structure: Political Process in American Society. New York: Oxford University Press, 1967.

Seligman, Ben B. Economics of Dissent. Chicago: Quadrangle Books, 1968.

Shepherd, William G. Market Power and Economic Welfare. New York: Random House, 1970.

Shils, Edward. The Intellectuals and the Powers and Other Essays. Chicago: University of Chicago Press, 1972.

Stonequist, Everett V. The Marginal Man: A Study in Personality and Culture Conflicts. New York: Charles Scribner's Sons, 1937.

Taylor, O.H. Economics and Liberalism. Cambridge, Massachusetts: Harvard University Press, 1955.

Theobald, Robert. The Economics of Abundance: A Non-Inflationary Future. New York: Pitman Publishing Corporation, 1970.

Veblen, Thorstein. The Theory of the Leisure Class. Boston: Houghton Mifflin Company, 1973.

Bon Hayek, Freidrich A. The Road to Serfdom. London: George Routledge and Sons, 1944.

Watson, James D. The Double Helix. New York: Signet Books, 1968.

Wheelis, Allen. The Quest for Identity. New York: W. W. Norton and Company, Inc., 1958.

Wiebe, Robert H. The Search for Order: 1877-1920. New York: Hill and Wang, 1967.

Wilkins, B. Hughel and Charles B. Friday (eds.). The Economists of the New Frontier: An Anthology. New York: Random House, 1963.

Williams, William Appleman. The Great Evasion. Chicago: Quadrangle Books, 1968.

Winter, Gibson. Being Free: Reflections on America's Cultural Revolution. New York: Macmillan Company, 1970

Zeitlin, Irving M. Marxism: A Re-Examination. New York: Van Nostrand Reinhold Company, 1967.

Zeitlin, Maurice (ed.). American Society, Inc. Chicago: Markham Publishing Company, 1970.

ARTICLES

Ackerman, Frank and Arthur MacEwan. "Galbraith and the Liberal Purpose." The Nation, January 19, 1974 pp. 85-88.

Ayres, C. E. "The Grown-up Boss." Saturday Review, 35 (April 12, 1952), p. 33.

     "The Nature and Significance of Institutionalism." Antioch Review, 26 (Spring 1966), pp. 70-90.

Barber, William J. "The Economics of Affluence," The South Atlantic Quarterly, 55 (Summer 1961), pp. 249-61.

Barnet, Richard J. "Galbraith's General Theory of Reform." New York Times Book Review, September 16, 1973, pp. 1, 33-4.

Bell, Daniel. "The End of Scarcity?" Saturday Review, 1 (May 1973), pp. 49-52.

Berle, Adolph A. "American Capitalism." Review of Economics and Statistics, 35 (February 1953), pp. 81-4.

Bluen, Naomi. "For Better, Not for Worse." New Yorker, December 31, 1973, pp. 57-9.

Boddewyn, Jean. "On Galbraith and Potatoes." South Atlantic Quarterly, 58 (Winter 1964), pp. 25-31.

Boulding, Kenneth. "Institutional Economics: A New Look at Institutionalism." American Economic Review, 47 (May 1957), pp. 1-27.

     "Review of The Affluent Society." Review of Economics and Statistics, 41 (February 1959), p. 81.

Buckley, William F., Jr. "A Fine Irish Hand." National Review, 19 (November 28, 1967), pp. 1309-10.

     "Galbraith and Inflation." National Review, 26 (September 13, 1974), p. 1061.

     "The New Religion." National Review, 24 (August 4, 1972), pp. 866-7.

Burgess, Anthony. "Fable of Foreign Relations." Saturday Review, 51 (April 20, 1968), pp. 34, 80.

"Burying Free Enterprise." Time, January 6, 1967, p. 92.

Chase, Edward T. "Technology's Brave New World." Commonweal, 99 (December 14, 1973), pp. 296-8.

Chase, Stuart. "Capitalism Without Tears." Reporter, 6 (March 4, 1952), pp. 33-5.

     "The Economic Embarrassment of America's Riches." Reporter, 18 (June 26, 1958), pp. 34-6.

Christenson, C. L. "American Capitalism." Journal of
    Political Economics, 60 (June 1952), pp. 275-6.
Clark, Colin. "The Eminence of Professor Galbraith."
    National Review, 20 (March 12, 1968), pp. 242-5.

    "The Horrible Proposals of Mr. Galbraith." Nation-
    al Review, 6 (October 11, 1958), 237-9, 255.
"Clobbering Theory." Business Week, January 9, 1954,
    pp. 92-9.
Collier, Bernard. "A Most Galbraithian Economist." New
    York Times Magazine, February 18, 1973, pp. 12-
    13, 57-62.
"The Convention that Went Galbraithian." Business Week,
    January 1, 1972, pp. 16-17.
"Conversations with an Inconvenient Economist." Chal-
    lenge, September/October 1973, pp. 28-37.
Cooper, Arthur. "The Public Interest." Newsweek, Octo-
    ber 1, 1973, p. 94.
"Could There be a case for Nixon?" New Statesman, 80
    (October 16, 1970), pp. 476-7.
Cowley, Malcolm. "Who are the Intellectuals?" New
    Republic, February 25, 1957, p. 14.
Crawford, Kenneth. "The Galbraith Purge." Newsweek,
    February 9, 1970, p. 29.

    "The Other Purge." Newsweek, November 23, 1970,
    p. 39.

    "The Non-Debate." Newsweek, April 17, 1967, p. 46.
Crosland, C. A. R. "Production in the Age of Afflu-
    ence." The Listener, September 28, 1958, pp. 447-
    449.
Davis, Kingsley and W. E. Moore, "Some Principles of
    Stratification." American Sociological Review, 10
    (April 1945), pp. 242-9.
Demetz, Harold. "Where is the New Industrial State?"
    Economic Inquiry, 12 (March 1974), pp. 1-12.
Doerner, William R. "Crypto Servants and Socialism."
    Time, October 8, 1973, p. 109.
Douglas, Mary. "Puppet Consumers." New Statesman, 87
    (June 7, 1974), pp. 805-6.
Emerson, Ralph Waldo. "The American Scholar." In
    Stephen Whicher (ed.). Selections from Ralph
    Waldo Emerson. Boston: Houghton Mifflin Company,
    Riverside edition, 1957, pp. 63-80.
Fitch, Robert. "A Galbraith Reappraisal: The Ideologue
    as Gadfly." Ramparts, May 1968, pp. 73-84.
"Galbraith and His Critics." Business and Society Re-
    view, 8 (Winter 1973), pp. 12-16.

227

"The Galbraith Dimension." Newsweek, October 2, 1967,
    pp. 24, 29.
"Galbraith Gives Nixon an A-minus." Business Week,
    October 1973, pp. 3-6.
"The Galbraithian Revolution." Challenge, September/
    October 1973, pp. 3-6.
"Galbraith Meets China." National Review, 24 (December
    22, 1972), p. 1391.
Gans, Herbert J. "The Positive Functions of Poverty."
    American Journal of Sociology, 78 (September
    1972), pp. 275-89.
Gordon, Scott. "The Close of the Galbraithian System."
    Journal of Political Economy, 76 (July/August
    1968), pp. 635-44.

    "The Galbraithian System--Rejoinder." Journal of
    Political Economy, 77 (November/December 1969),
    pp. 953-56.
"The Great Mogul." Time, February 16, 1968, pp. 24-8.
Hazlitt, Henry. "The New Orthodoxy." Newsweek, June
    21, 1965, p. 82.
Halberstam, David. "The Importance of Being Galbraith."
    Harpers, November 1967, pp. 47-54.
Harrington, Michael. "Mr. Nixon's Reactionary Revo-
    lution." Commonweal, 95 (November 26, 1971), pp.
    199-202.
Hayek, F.A. "The Non Sequitur of the Dependence Ef-
    fect." The Southern Economics Journal, 27 (April
    1961), pp. 346-48.
Hefner, Richard and Esther H. Kramer. "A Man for All
    Pursuits." Saturday Review, 51 (April 20, 1968),
    pp. 35-6.
Heilbroner, Robert L. "Capitalism without Tears." New
    York Review of Books, June 29, 1967, p. 16.

    "Galbraith's Progress." Dissent, 21 (Winter 1974),
    pp. 105-8.
"Hoaxes: The Midnight Penman Returns." Time, September
    6, 1971, p. 20.
"It's No Sin to be Rich." Business Week, February 23,
    1952, pp. 120-7.
Kemp, Tom. "Galbraith as Prophet of American 'Neo-
    Capitalism.'" Science and Society, 29 (Fall 1965),
    pp. 385-400.
Keyserling, Leon. "Eggheads and Politics." New Repub-
    lic, October 27, 1958, pp. 13-17.
Kristol, Irving. "Corporate Capitalism in America."
    Public Interest, 41 (Fall 1975), pp. 124-41.

    "Professor Galbraith's 'New Industrial State'."
    Fortune, July 1967, pp. 90-2, 194-5.

Lekachman, Robert. "Economics for Everybody?" Commentary, 21 (January 1956), pp. 76-9.

"Galbraith's New Economics." New Republic, June 9, 1958, pp. 17-18.

"A Symposium of John Kenneth Galbraith's Economics." New York Times Magazine, February 18, 1973, p. 12.

"Looking Back at the Great Crash." Business Week, April 23, 1955, pp. 92-98.

MacDonald, H. Ian. "The American Economy of Abundance." Canadian Journal of Economics and Political Science, 25 (August 1959), pp. 352-7.

McDowell, Edwin. "Galbraith Was Wrong Again." National Review, 22 (October 20, 1970), p. 1108

Mann, Fritz Karl. "Institutionalism and American Economic Theory: A Case of Interpretation." Kyklos, 13 (1960), pp. 307-24.

Marris, Robin. "Economic Systems, Planning and Reform; Cooperation." American Economic Review, 58 (March 1968), pp. 240-7.

Meade, J.E. "Is the 'New Industrial State' Inevitable?" Economic Journal, 78 (June 1968), pp. 372-92.

Meltzer, Allan. "A Comment on Market Structure and Stabilization Policy." Review of Economics and Statistics, 40 (November 1958), pp. 413-15.

Metz, Robert. "The Big Five in Beer." New York Times, June 15, 1975, section 3.

Mileikovsky, Abram. "Crisis of Bourgeois Economic Theory and Galbraith's 'New Ideas'." New Times (Moscow), 28 (July 1972), pp. 18-21.

Miller, Vincent. "Workmanlike Job in New Delhi." National Review, 22 (January 13, 1970), pp. 39-40.

Minachan, John. "Is 'Free Market' a Dirty Word?: An Interview with the Secretary of the Treasury." Saturday Review, 2 (July 12, 1975), p. 18.

Mount, Ferdinant. "The Spoiled Minister's Sermon." National Review, 25 (December 21, 1973), pp. 1415-17.

Navasky, Victor S. "Galbraith on Galbraith." New York Times Book Review, June 25, 1967, pp. 2-3, 38-9.

Office of Management and Budget. The United States Budget in Brief, 1976. Washington D.C.: Government Printing Office, 1975.

"Playboy Interview: John Kenneth Galbraith." Playboy June 1968, pp. 63-78, 138, 164-74.

Potter, David. "Between Two Worlds." Saturday Review, 40 (June 7, 1958), pp. 31-2.

"The Price of Affluence." Economist, September 20, 1958, pp. 928-9.

Robinson, Joan. "American Capitalism." Economic Journal, 62 (December 1952), pp. 925-8.

_____. "Joan Robinson on Galbraith, women and economic sense." Spectator, March 30, 1974, pp. 392-3.

Roper, Elmo. "Whose Affluent Society?" Saturday Review, 42 (June 6, 1959), pp. 15, 39.

Ruby, Michael. "Galbraith Strikes Again." Newsweek, September 8, 1975, pp. 61-3.

Samuelson, Paul A. "On Galbraith." Newsweek, July 3, 1967, p. 68.

Saulnier, Raymond J. "The Shape of Things." New York Book Review, June 25, 1967, pp. 2-3, 36-7.

Scott, Bruce R. "The Industrial State: Old Myths and New Realities." Harvard Business Review, 51 (March/April 1973), pp. 133-48.

Sheehan, Robert. "Properties in the World of Big Business." Fortune, June 15, 1967, pp. 179-83.

Sheehy, Edmund J. "Economics and the Public Purpose." America, 130 (March 23, 1974), pp. 225-6.

Silk, Leonard. "The Money Muddle." Saturday Review, 2 (September 6, 1975), pp. 26-7.

Simon, William E. "A Strategy for Prosperity." Saturday Review, 2 (July 12, 1975), pp. 10-16, 20.

Solomon, Robert. "Galbraith on Market Structure and Stabilization Policy." Review of Economics and Statistics, 40 (May 1958), pp. 164-7.

Solow, Robert. "The New Industrial State or Son of Affluence." The Public Interest, 9 (Fall 1967), pp. 100-108. "A Rejoinder." pp. 118-119.

Sosnick, Stephen. "On Galbraith's 'Affluent' Society." American Journal of Economics and Sociology, 19 (April 1960), pp. 323-9.

Stigler, George G. "The Economist Plays with Blocks." American Economic Review, 44 (May 1954), pp. 7-14.

Strachey, John. "Unconventional Wisdom." Encounter, 11 (October 1958), pp. 73-80.

"Too big for antitrust to handle?" Business Week, July 8, 1967, pp. 70-2.

Ulmer, Melville. "Against the Economics Grain." New Republic, May 8, 1971, pp. 28-33.

_____. "The Heterodox Economists." New Republic, February 3, 1973, pp. 28-30.

_____. "Money." New Republic, September 13, 1975, pp. 27-29.

(UPI) "GM Sets Out to Grab Market." Quad City Times,
    September 21, 1975, p. 3C.
(UPI) "Who Speaks for the Consumer?" Quad City Times,
    September 21, 1975, p. 4D.
Van Doren, Mark. "Fundamentalism in Finance." Reporter,
    12 (May 5, 1955), pp. 38-41.
Vining, Rutledge. "The Affluent Society." American
    Economic Review, 49 (March 1959), pp. 112-19.
Weidenbaum, Murray L. "How Galbraith Would Reform the
    Economy." Business Week, September 22, 1973.
Wijesinghe, F. D. C. "Galbraith in Ceylon." Con-
    temporary Review, 199 (February 1961), pp. 65-67.
Winter, Ralph. "Trend Bucker?" from Wall Street Journal
    in Quad City Times, October 12, 1975, p. 2A.
Zeitlin, Maurice. "Corporate Ownership and Control:
    The Large Corporation and the Capitalist Class."
    American Journal of Sociology, 79 (March 1974),
    1073-1119.

235